THE

CATHOLIC

STORY

THE CATHOLIC STORY

*To Rose Marie & Peter
Blessings for 2
Beautiful People.
Your Cousin Vinnie
Cacau
3/11/16*

VIC CIPRIANO

TATE PUBLISHING
AND ENTERPRISES, LLC

The Catholic Story
Copyright © 2015 by Vic Cipriano. All rights reserved.

No part of this publication may be reproduced, stored in a retrieval system or transmitted in any way by any means, electronic, mechanical, photocopy, recording or otherwise without the prior permission of the author except as provided by USA copyright law.

Scripture quotations marked (ESV) are from *The Holy Bible, English Standard Version*®, copyright © 2001 by Crossway Bibles, a publishing ministry of Good News Publishers. Used by permission. All rights reserved.

Scripture quotations marked (KJV) are taken from the *Holy Bible, King James Version*, Cambridge, 1769. Used by permission. All rights reserved.

Scripture quotations marked (NASB) are taken from the *New American Standard Bible*®, Copyright © 1960, 1962, 1963, 1968, 1971, 1972, 1973, 1975, 1977, 1995 by The Lockman Foundation. Used by permission.

Scripture quotations marked (NIV) are taken from the *Holy Bible, New International Version*®, NIV®. Copyright © 1973, 1978, 1984 by Biblica, Inc.™ Used by permission of Zondervan. All rights reserved worldwide. www.zondervan.com

The opinions expressed by the author are not necessarily those of Tate Publishing, LLC.

This book is designed to provide accurate and authoritative information with regard to the subject matter covered. This information is given with the understanding that neither the author nor Tate Publishing, LLC is engaged in rendering legal, professional advice. Since the details of your situation are fact dependent, you should additionally seek the services of a competent professional.

Published by Tate Publishing & Enterprises, LLC
127 E. Trade Center Terrace | Mustang, Oklahoma 73064 USA
1.888.361.9473 | www.tatepublishing.com

Tate Publishing is committed to excellence in the publishing industry. The company reflects the philosophy established by the founders, based on Psalm 68:11,
"The Lord gave the word and great was the company of those who published it."

Book design copyright © 2015 by Tate Publishing, LLC. All rights reserved.
Cover design by Nikolai Purpura
Interior design by Jake Muelle

Published in the United States of America

ISBN: 978-1-63449-034-4
1. Religion / Christianity / Catholic
2. Religion / Comparative Religion
15.04.24

To Mary, our blessed Mother,
who first bore the good news in her womb.
To Theresa, my wife, whose patience,
understanding, and encouragement
made this book possible.

Acknowledgments

To Janellen Carignan, for her masterful editing and reformatting of the manuscript for publication.

To Joe Petrullo, an excellent teacher of church history, who shared his well-organized notes with his students. They were very helpful.

To Coralie and John Stolz, Andy Vissicchio, and Tony Mangini, for critiquing chapters

To my sons, Don and Ricky, and my daughter, Cindy MacDonald, for invaluable assistance.

Contents

Introduction 11

What Is Truth? 21

Knowing God Exists by Reason Alone 27

What Do the Christians and Jews Believe About God? 43

Judeo-Christian Connections 57

Jesus' Church: The First 400 Years 75

Jesus' Church: 400–800 AD 113

Jesus' Church: 800–1200 AD 149

Jesus' Church: 1200–1600 AD 177

Jesus' Church: 1600–2000 AD 215

Conclusions: What Is the Truth That Will Set Us Free? . . . 259

References 265

Index 269

Introduction

After sixty-six years, I finally understand what my college professor meant! It happened in my sophomore year at Boston University. One of my courses was an elective on great American novels of the nineteenth century—the greatest was *Moby Dick*, written by Herman Melville. The professor told our class that there were three ways you could look at this book. First, it was a great adventure story. Second, it described aspects of the whaling industry in great detail that had nothing to do with the plot. And third, Captain Ahab's unrelenting search for Moby Dick, the great white whale, could be looked at as an allegory about the search for truth.

I remember at the time being puzzled as to what the professor meant by "the search for truth." It seemed so general. I was aware of what it meant to tell the truth or not to tell the truth, but what did the search for truth mean? Other important things were happening in my life. My "search for truth" puzzlement was soon forgotten.

As I prepared to write *The Catholic Story*, I recalled that *Moby Dick* moment so many years earlier and realized how ironic it is that I am now writing a book answering the very question that had puzzled me back then.

My Religious Background

I entered this world in Waltham, Massachusetts, on August 28, 1925. My parents, Maria and Antonio, were first generation Italian immigrants who "came over on the boat." I was the second of five kids. Mary and Tony (their Americanized names) were both Catholic, so I received the four automatic sacraments—baptism in three weeks, confession and first communion at eight years, and confirmation at fourteen. At fifteen, there was one year of Bible history study. That is when I first heard names like Abraham, Isaac, Jacob, and Moses. That was my last year of formal Catholic education.

Sacred Heart, my parish, was referred to as the "Italian church" because it served the many Italian immigrants in the city. Mass was in Latin. Most sermons were in Italian. Graduating from high school, my religious background was not strong. Knowledgewise, it was weak.

In the family, we had a Bible, but nobody read it. The only time I remember seeing my father in church was on my wedding day. In fairness to him, he was very busy. In 1927, he had started Tony's Spa, which was a convenience store with a soda fountain. It was open sixteen hours a day, seven days a week, except for the Sundays. He was a one-man operation and just didn't have the time.

St. Mary's, the largest Catholic church in the city, was close by so that the after-Mass Sunday crowds made it the best business day of the week. After the crowd from the last Mass had been handled, my father would close the store for four hours so that he could eat with his family and get some rest. This was a special day for our family because that's the only time of the week that my father was with us for a meal.

My maternal grandparents, two uncles, and aunt, were all Italian immigrants, living in the same neighborhood. My mother, uncles, and aunt went to church, but religion was never discussed in the house, and we never prayed together. My grandmother (we called her mama-non), who didn't go to church, seemed the most "religious." She was house-ridden because of severe asthma but would pace back and forth in her long kitchen all day, reciting the rosary or reading from a well-worn prayer booklet. A red vigil light was always burning in her bedroom. She spoke no English, so any knowledge of the faith or wisdom she might have shared was lost.

The greatest faith influence for me was the tall, chubby, stern nun who had prepared us for first communion when I was eight. She warned us that one unconfessed mortal sin could keep us out of heaven and that missing Mass on Sunday was a mortal sin. That stuck! It programmed the way I practiced my faith, which was not to miss Mass on Sunday and get to confession on the first Saturday after I sinned. This was my idea of being a good Catholic. Keep a spotless soul. It was so simple that I didn't have to think.

At Forty-One, Things Were About to Change

I now had four children and was a member of St. Julia's parish in Weston, Massachusetts. The pastor, Msgr. Rossiter, took me aside one day and said, "I'd like you to teach in our high school CCD program." (CCD provided religious instructions for public school children.)

I replied, "I'm not qualified. I've never read the Bible."

He said, "You can learn." With four children in the program, I couldn't say no, so I accepted. Where would I begin?

I had been born into a faith that I wasn't knowledgeable about, practicing it in a routine way. Now I would be facing high school kids who, most likely, knew more than I and could ask challenging questions. My business background was sales. In sales, we needed to know our product and what benefits it would provide to a potential customer. Also, we needed to know our competitor's product. With this knowledge, you could make a sales presentation with confidence. This was my beginning dilemma. I didn't know my faith beliefs or the faith beliefs of other religions.

It was a wake-up call! I began asking myself questions like, "Can we know by reason alone that God exists?" There were a lot of other religions out there. What were they about? How did their beliefs compare with the one I was born into? Was there one faith that had the fullness of truth? If so, was I in the right one? It suddenly dawned on me that this could be a risky search for me. What if one of the others was the true faith? The Catholic faith had for centuries been the faith of my parents' families.

This was a challenge that would turn me into a Captain Ahab with an unrelenting search for truth on the big questions of life and faith. It would be a relentless search to follow the travel of truth wherever it would lead.

Fortunately, at that time, a master teacher program was being inaugurated in the Boston diocese. Its purpose was to develop a few master teachers at higher grade levels in each parish, who could be a source of help to other teachers at those levels. My pastor selected me and a woman to be trained to be master teachers for our parish.

The training program was four hours, one night a week for a semester and was held at a seminary in a nearby town. The course was specially designed to train master teachers. My responsibility would be for ninth- and tenth-grade teachers. This course was a big help because I had so many questions, and the priests teaching the course had the answers.

In my work world, I was successful in many self-initiated projects because I would always look at the big picture. Now I would be applying those business skills to see the big picture of my spiritual life.

I knew that reading my Bible's seventeen hundred pages would have to be a major part of my learning process. Reading the Bible and gathering this information would take time. I knew I could do it because I had learned a powerful study secret during my work career. It was called the power of one.

The Power of One

Back in 1953, I had been promoted from salesman to the field by the Schlitz Brewery. My title was assistant district manager. My job was to work with a Schlitz wholesaler's beer salesmen as they made retail calls, helping them to improve their selling and merchandising techniques. One day, I was working the Brockton, Massachusetts, trade area. The wholesaler's general manager was Jerry Belliveau, who had been my French teacher at Waltham High School. I had worked with one of his men the previous day and was reviewing my observations and suggestions for improvement with him.

Jerry said, "Vic, these men just don't understand the 'power of one' principle." I asked him what he meant. Jerry replied, "Just think, if a salesman opened up only one new account a day, that would be *five* a week, twenty a month, two hundred and forty a year, just by adding one a day." He had other examples that impressed me. I applied the principle and credit it as a major help in my life.

Let me share a few examples of how it works.

For several years, I was doing laps in my condo pool six days a week, swimming a half mile a day. A half mile a day is three miles a week, 150 miles a year. It would take me about twenty-two minutes. Thus, disciplining myself to twenty-two minutes a day in one year, I could cover the distance between Boston and Albany, New York. In ten years, 1,500 miles (the distance from Boston to Boca Raton, Florida), and in twenty years, 3,000 miles (the distance between Boston and Los Angeles)—all on a focused twenty-two minutes a day.

Another example is the *One Year Bible*, which is divided into daily readings. For each day, there is a portion of the Old Testament, the New Testament, Psalms, and Proverbs. These four separate daily readings are grouped on three or four consecutive pages. By reading each day's grouping, a person would finish the entire Bible in one year. It takes less than twenty minutes a day. That's the "power of one" principle at work. Thus I committed to twenty minutes *minimum* every day until I finished reading the Bible. This principle became a powerful help in my search for truth.

I once read the *One Year Bible* three years in a row. The second and third years, I added another wrinkle. William Barclay, a Scotsman, had a highly recommended series of seventeen books with commentaries on each of the New Testament books. I bought the set. Each day, I used his commentaries on the New Testament daily readings for that day. For the most part, the commentaries averaged less than half an hour. But there was a great richness of thought and understanding added to what I was reading. At the end of each of those last two years, not only had the entire Bible been read but also all of Barclay's seventeen books. That's the "power of one" principle in action.

I set three specific areas of research:

1. *The Bible.* There were the Old and New Testaments. Were they in any way connected? If so, how? How long ago did men in the Old Testament, like Abraham and Moses, live? Questions like these were answered at the seminary.

   My approach would be to read the Bible from cover to cover, which would give me a rough overview of characters and events. This took a year. The weakness of this approach was that it took too long to get to the New Testament stories of Jesus.

   Today, thanks to Jeff Cavins and Ascension Press, there is a much quicker way for a beginner to get the big picture of the Bible. By reading just fourteen selected books in the Bible (twelve Old Testament and two New Testament) a beginner will have that big picture in three months. The ten Old Testament books are: Genesis, Exodus, Numbers, Joshua, Judges, 1 Samuel, 2 Samuel, 1 Kings, 2 Kings, Ezra, Nehemiah, and 1 Maccabees. The two New Testament books are Luke and the book of Acts. These fourteen books will provide the storyline on how the Old and New Testaments work together as one. To accomplish this, you have to faithfully read four chapters per day. Remember the power of one. Bible chapters are short. When the three months are over, reading the rest of the books will make a lot more sense because they reinforce the storyline.

2. *God.* Could I convince myself of the existence of God by using reason alone? If I could, then I was confident I could convince any student who might challenge me with that question. Reason alone did convince me of the existence of God. Faith is not necessary to believe that. Chapter two will show why.

3. *Different faiths.* I knew there was a variety of religious faiths; the Catholic church was just one of many. I felt they must all have some connection to God. What were their stories? What did each of them believe? When did they begin? I checked the major Judeo-Christian religions:

- *Judaism* was founded by Abraham about 4000 years ago.
- *Christianity* was established by Jesus Christ in 33 AD.
- *Eastern Orthodox* churches split from Rome in 1054.
- *The Lutheran church* was started by Martin Luther, an ex-monk in the Catholic church, in 1521.
- *The Anglican church* began in England in 1534 when Pope Clement VII refused to give an annulment to King Henry VIII.
- *The Presbyterian church* was founded when John Knox brought the teachings of John Calvin to Scotland in the year 1560.
- *Baptists* owe their religious beliefs to John Smyth, who launched the Baptist church in Amsterdam in 1607.

- *The Episcopalian* religion was brought over from England to the American colonies. It became the American branch of the Anglican church in 1789.
- *Mormonism* was started by Joseph Smith in Palmyra, New York, in 1830.
- *The Jehovah Witnesses* were founded by Charles Taze Russell in Pennsylvania in 1874.
- *Pentecostals* began in the United States in 1901.

Jews and Christians, are linked in that they consider Abraham as their founder. Judaism is a fifteen-hundred-year historically revealed faith from Abraham four thousand years ago to the last Jewish prophet Malachi two thousand five hundred years ago. Christianity uses the Old Testament as the necessary foundation of its faith. In addition to these belief groups, there are atheists, who do not believe in God. If they don't believe in God, it follows that they don't believe in revelations from a God who, in their mind, doesn't exist.

The subject matters listed below illustrate the thought process I used to discover the truth that set me free:

What is truth? (chapter one);

We can know the existence of God by reason alone (faith is not needed) (chapter two);

Three questions for the Jewish and Christian religions: What is your story? What is your belief about God? What is your belief about an after-life? (chapter three);

The Judeo-Christian story (Adam to Jesus) (chapter four);

Jesus' church story (Jesus to us) (chapters five through nine);

Conclusions: What is the truth that will set us free? (chapter 10).

The fourth chapter will detail the Judeo-Christian connection. Christianity could not exist without Judaism, while the prophecies of Judaism would be incomplete without Christianity. This chapter will connect the dots from Adam to Jesus.

Christianity has many divisions: Catholics, the Eastern Orthodox churches, Protestants, Mormons, Jehovah Witnesses, etc.

Chapters five through nine will describe chronologically the history of key events and people of Christianity from Jesus to us today. This two-thousand-year history will be covered in increments of four hundred years.

The tenth and final chapter will be examining all the research of the first nine chapters, pinpointing with certainty the truth that will set us free.

What Is Truth?

Some years ago, my friend Jack Crowley and his son, Tim, were visiting the Boca Raton, Florida, area, where I live. Both were golfers, so I invited them to play a round of golf at my club. The twelfth hole was a par three, 190 yards with traps on the left and right side of the green. I hit a 5-wood. The ball headed toward the left trap. As we watched, Tim said, "It went into the trap."

I replied, "No, it didn't. It stopped before it got there."

Tim insisted, "No, no, it went into the trap."

I then commented, "This will be an excellent insight on truth. You really believe my ball continued and went into the trap. I really believe the ball stopped short. Truth is where the ball actually lies, and we'll find that out when we get there."

When we drove up to the trap, I happened to be right. But the important thing was the insight on truth. Truth stands alone. Truth trumps sincerity and enthusiasm. And by the same token, indifference does not make something untruthful. Truth is still there even if we choose to ignore it.

Webster defines truth as agreement with the facts.[1] Finding the truth about the golf ball was easy. A short ride in the golf cart and we had the answer. But how about "big truth" questions that really matter to every human? Here are five examples:

1. Does God exist? God exists, or he doesn't. One of these is an absolute truth.
2. If God exists, has he revealed to humans things we need to know?

3. If so, to whom? Is there an undeniable path of truth, connecting all the dots that answers all the big questions of life and death with the fullness of truth?

4. Does life have a meaning and purpose?

5. Is there an afterlife with reward or punishment for the way we live?

This is exactly what my *Moby Dick* professor meant so many years ago. The search for truth is to find answers to the big questions of life, which affect us individually and eternally. Captain Ahab is every person. All people should search for truth. Nobody's exempt. Whether we like it or not, we're all in the game of life. We were born. We have to make the life journey, and we have to die. Our search for truth will begin by taking a close look at the only life species capable of seeking truth on the big questions of life— human beings.

All humans share two basic truths:

First, we had no choices coming into this world. Nobody asked, do you want to be born? Do you want to be a boy or a girl? In what country do you want to be born? Do you want rich or poor parents? Do you want to be born into a religious family or one with no religion? Science has documented 3.1 million life species. We had no choice as to which life species we would be given. We could have entered this world as a cockroach.

The second absolute truth that all mankind shares is that we all have to die.

Why should all people seek the truth?

The search for truth is part of man's nature. In Pope John Paul II's, *The Splendor of Truth*, he says this about man:

> In the depth of his heart there always remains a yearning for absolute truth and a thirst to attain full knowledge of it. This is eloquently proved by man's tireless search for knowledge in all fields. It is proved even more by his search

for the meaning of life. The development of science and technology, this splendid testimony of the human capacity for understanding and perseverance, does not free humanity from the obligation to ask the ultimate religious questions. Rather, it spurs us on to face the most painful and decisive of struggles, those of the heart and of the moral conscience.

—Pope John Paul II's Encyclical Letter
The Splendor of Truth, Electronic copyright 1999 EWTN, http://www.EWTN.com.

We are all compelled to live this life we didn't ask for, and we all have to die. The need to know is in our self-interest. The truth our head and heart accepts will determine how we live our lives. If one concludes that there is no God or afterlife, his motto may be "Eat, drink, and be merry, for tomorrow we die."

If we believe there is a God and an afterlife following judgment of our present life, we'll live differently and with a hope. Guessing wrong can have eternal consequences. Searching for truth means objectively examining all the evidence, for and against, to help us make a decision that for us is "beyond a reasonable doubt." Before making the search, it is important to recognize that there are two kinds of truth: First, there are those truths that can be nailed down with complete certainty. Second, there are those truths that cannot be nailed down with complete certainty.

Examples of the first truth are the certainties of mathematics and musical notes, facts of history, discovered laws of the universe, sport statistics, etc. We can find sources that will nail those truths down with certainty.

The second kind of truth, big ones like God's existence, revelation, and afterlife, are more difficult, if not impossible, to nail down with certainty. Here's why. Science's best theory of existence is the big bang theory that everything began with a large explosion from a single point. All that we can see, measure, and study came after the big bang. The pre–big bang cause is an invisible mysterious power that we cannot see, measure, or study. There are limits to human reason. Distinguished philosopher Immanuel Kant (1724–1804) believed that science should be understood as applying to the world of data rather than the "other world." In showing the limits of reason, Kant said he did "make room for faith."[2]

Thus, for the second truth, we gather all the available evidence, pro and con, to the limits of our reason. If the evidence points to one conclusion, "without a reasonable doubt," we make a "leap of faith" decision. Life/death courtroom truth decisions are made this way.

Dinesh D'Souza, best-selling author of *What's So Great About Christianity,* wrote:

> Faith is a statement of trust in what we do not know for sure. Faith says, "That even though I don't know something with certainty, I believe it to be true." The purpose of faith is to discover truths that are of the highest importance to us, yet are unavailable to us through purely natural means.
>
> —Dinesh D'Souza, *What's So Great About Christianity,* (Washington, D.C.: Regnery Publishing, Inc., 2007), 95

D'Souza points out, "If there is a Divine being who has created the universe with special concern for us as human beings, then it is entirely reasonable to suppose that, absent our ability to find him, he would find his way to us."[3]

Why will knowing the truth set us free?

I've been living in Florida for the past twenty-five years. When I drive to the store, place of worship, or restaurants, I'm free from anxiety and concerns on my journey. There are traffic lights, stop signs, and white or yellow lines separating the lanes of traffic. There are rules of the road. If I follow the rules, no problems. It's a peaceful drive. I'm free.

But Florida also gets its share of hurricanes and their aftermath. Try driving to familiar places the day after a major hurricane with trees or large limbs on the road. Or at the biggest intersections, traffic lights are out, street lights are out, street signs are gone or covered up. You are playing "chicken" at busy intersections as to who goes next. Suddenly, everything is different. There's confusion and danger. All the guides we relied on are gone. Anxiety and concerns take away our freedom.

Life is a journey. Feelings and emotions are a part of our human nature. While not good or evil in themselves, they have to be controlled by our intellect and will. We need reliable guides that are there all the time; reliable guides that can tell us when to stop and when to go; a guiding light, which never darkens on our big journey of life. That's what the search for truth is about. The search is to find which guide we can entrust our lives to. If God has revealed his laws on how to make the journey, relative to him and our neighbors, aren't we freer and safer knowing when to stop and when to go?

Nobody can be indifferent in the search for these truths. One can be evasive only until death. Blaise Pascal (1623–62) was an eminent French scientist, mathematician, and philosopher. One should recall his famous Pascal's Wager. He affirmed that at a certain point, a leap into faith must be made. He called it a wager. It became known as Pascal's Wager, which is described below:

If God does not exist, and there is no hereafter, the atheist will have gained nothing because after death, he will disappear into the void, and his life will be as if it never had been. The Christian will have lost nothing because he will no longer be able to remember the pleasures he has foregone.

If God exists, and there is a hereafter, the atheist will have been deprived of him forever, which will be an infinite loss. The Christian, on the other hand, will be united with him forever. By deciding to live as though God and the hereafter do exist, man has nothing to lose and everything to gain.

Notes

1. *The New Lexicon Webster's Dictionary*, (New York: Lexicon Publications, Inc., 1989).
2. *Routledge Encyclopedia of Philosophy*, http://routledge.com/article/dbo47sect4.
3. D'Souza, What's So Great About Christianity, 95.

Knowing God Exists by Reason Alone

You and I are at the end of a long process from nothingness to our present exalted existence as human beings. This chapter will connect, in chronological order, the necessary stages to support and produce an irreplaceable you and me. It will make clear how each scientific event or stage of existence supports the existence of God.

Science tells us that once, there was nothing. Nothing plus nothing equals nothing. Nothing times nothing equals nothing. If ever there was nothing, we'd still have nothing. But we do have something. You exist. I exist. Everywhere we look, we see existence. There are two major kinds of existence: First, there are man-made kinds like houses, furniture, clothes, cars, and toothbrushes. Second, there are those mysteries of nature—people, trees, the sun, the moon, and the oceans.

Both kinds have one thing in common. They all had to depend on something else, outside of themselves, for their existence. Nothing gives itself existence. If it did, it would have to precede its own being. That's illogical and impossible.

My son, Don, lives in Colorado. My wife Theresa and I were visiting with him and his family one summer and made a day trip to a ski resort. There was an architecturally beautiful hotel where one could swim from the outside pool to the pool inside the hotel. My granddaughter, Amy, who was eight at the time, admired the beauty of the building and exclaimed, "Look at the beautiful building God made."

Her father replied, "God didn't make it. Man made it."

She quickly replied, "But God made man." This was wisdom beyond her years.

In the instance of man-made things, man was responsible for their existence, but where did man get his existence? He got it from his parents. His parents, in turn, got it from their parents. It's not an infinite series. Eventually, it would get back to the first parents who started the series. But those first parents couldn't have given themselves existence. There had to be an existence initiator, an uncaused cause, who always had, has, and will have existence. The sun, the earth, and the moon also had a beginning. They once did not exist. Let's go back to the very beginning.

Existence had a beginning. The great philosopher, Soren Kierkegaard, once said that a person lives his life forward, but understands it backwards.[1] So let's go backward to the very beginning of existence, using science as our resource.

There were three major preparatory stages for the coming of humans:

14 billion years ago, the big bang;

4.5 billion years ago, the earth, sun, and moon;

3.7 billion years ago, the first life;

50 to 100 thousand years ago, humans.

The first stage, the big bang. About five hundred years ago, the scientific world was shocked to discover that the earth orbits around the sun. People always believed that the earth was the center of the universe and that the sun orbited the earth. About ninety years ago, the scientific world received an even bigger shock. Astronomers discovered that the entire universe had a beginning, that there was a time when there was no earth, no sun, no moon, and no stars. Here's what happened.

In the early 1920s, astronomer Edwin Hubble (1889–1953) was working at the Mount Wilson Observatory in California with the most advanced technology of the time. He was about to make an amazing discovery. Some of the numerous, distant faint clouds of light were not just distant parts of our own Milky Way galaxy but entire other galaxies much like our own. Our Milky Way was not alone!

But Hubble's greatest discovery came in 1929, when he determined that the farther a galaxy is from the earth, the faster it appears to move away. The impact on science's perception of the world was shattering. The universe was not static but evolving. This idea of an expanding universe formed the basis of the big bang theory, which states that the universe began with an intense burst of energy at a single moment of time and has been expanding ever since.

Until NASA's Hubble telescope was repaired and upgraded in 2009, the farthest back in time that astronomers could see was 900 million years after the big bang. Since the upgrade, they have been able to see back to just 600 million years after the big bang. They still don't see the first galaxies. For that, NASA will have to rely on a new observatory, the $4.5 billion James Webb telescope, which is set to launch in about four years.[2]

Stephen Hawkings, world famous physicist, wrote in his *A Brief History of Time,*

> If the rate of expansion one second after the Big Bang had been smaller by even one part in a hundred thousand million million, the universe would have re-collapsed before it reached its present size."[3]

Odds are astronomically against us being here. Yet we are here. Who is responsible for this? How did the earth come from the big bang?

Barry Parker, retired professor of physics and astronomy and author of *Vindication of the Big Bang* explains,

Initially it was pure radiant energy, but as it expanded, it congealed into a gas cloud of particles. And as it continued to expand, tiny ripples developed, which over billions of years condensed into galaxies, stars, and planets."[4]

Whoever triggered the big-bang event was the father of all existence that was to come. It was the first stage that made possible the next three. Galaxies, stars, and planets were dependent on the "big banger." We call him God.

In 1996, Charles Townes, cofounder of the laser, said, "Before the 1960s, the Big Bang was just an idea that was hotly debated. Today, there is so much evidence supporting the idea that most cosmologists take it for granted."[5] The important point is this: the best of scientists agree that at one time, there was no earth, sun, and moon. Now they are here. Their existence had a cause!

The second stage, the earth, sun, and moon. Let's fast forward from the big bang, 14 billion years ago, to the next stage, 4.5 billion years ago, when the earth, sun, and moon began their operable existence in an awesome, purposeful, orderly way. Their coming seemed to defy the second law of thermodynamics that simply states that left to themselves, things break down. Cars not taken care of will eventually stop running. Most athletes in professional contact sports start fading out in their late thirties. Metal things rust. Bridges corrode. But when the earth, sun, and moon sprang into action, it was an upgrade from the big bang.

From this disorder came a purposeful, enduring, working relationship between the earth, sun, and moon, which is responsible for the continued existence of everything on earth. This amazing trio are not close neighbors. The moon is 238,857 miles from the earth. Man has been there. The sun is 93 million miles from the earth. Man will never get there, not just because of the heat but because of the distance.

For example, if there were a highway from the earth to the sun, and you drove sixty miles an hour, twenty-four hours a day, it would take 176 years to reach the sun. Despite this tremendous distance, the sun and the earth have an amazingly close and designed relationship. The power responsible for their existence knew what it was doing. Just as a baby's continued existence in the mother's womb depends on the mother carrying it, so the earth is dependent for its existence on the presence of the sun. Without the sun, life on earth would be unable to exist. Earth would be a frozen dark ball, drifting dead in space. We need the sun for light, warmth, and energy. With the sun, plants can grow; animals and humans can eat.

Here's how the earth, sun, and moon work together. We are on spaceship earth with six billion fellow passengers. We are traveling at a speed of 1,000 miles per minute in an orbit around the sun. It takes 365.24 days to make a round trip. However old you are, that's how many round trips you've made. At the same time, the earth is rotating at the speed of one thousand miles an hour. It takes twenty-four hours to make a complete rotation. When our side of the earth is facing the sun, it's daytime. When we're on the other side, it's nighttime. Thus, with the spinning earth movement around the sun, we have a calendar and a clock in space. We also have night and day. This was the beginning of using tools for measuring time. Rev. Matthias Premm writes:

> Everyday we hear the exact time given over radio and television, but where does the announcer get the time? From astronomy. When the astronomer sees the sun pass over the meridian, it is twelve noon. We all measure the time of day by the position of the sun. There are no hinges, pegs, and screws. Hanging freely in the air, it has been going now for billions of years, and has never needed repairs. Whoever planned and produced it must be millions more intelligent and powerful than mere man, in order to put its gigantic works into proper position and make it go. The world watchmaker is God.
>
> —Rev. Matthias Premm, *Dogmatic Theology of the Laity*, (Staten Island, NY: Alba House, 1967; Rockford, IL:

Tan Books and Publishers, Inc., 1977) 14.
Citation is to the Tan Books edition.

Think what our life would be like without time. We would not be able to make doctor appointments, tee times, or schedule all our activities in an orderly way. Chaos would reign. Humans need a supporting structure to exist in space. The earth/sun/moon team provides time to perfection. But there are many other needs, provided separately, or together.

For example, the moon shares this long distance dance and will make its contributions. While the earth is orbiting its path around the sun, the moon is orbiting the earth, with a purpose, which is to support life on earth. The moon is the perfect size and distance from earth for its gravitational pull. Without the moon, it would be impossible to live on this planet. God has provided the moon as a maid to clean up the oceans and shores of all continents. Without the tides created by the moon, all our harbors and shores would become one smelly pool of garbage, and it would be impossible to live anywhere near them.

Also because of tides, continuous waves break upon the shores of the ocean, providing plankton, which is the very foundation of the food chain. Plankton provides more than 50 percent of the earth's oxygen supply. Without oxygen, man can't live. Tides follow their scheduled times, which are reported in our daily newspapers. This is order with a purpose. Greek sages taught that where there is order, there is a mind. This is another example of the involvement of a divine mind and power.

Humans need a firm place to stand, work, play, and live out their existence. The earth provides this essential need. Humans need light to see, or everything would be in darkness. The sun provides light. We need air to breathe. The moon helps provide oxygen. We need livable temperatures. The earth is located just the right distance from the sun. Temperature swings are roughly –30 to +120 degrees Fahrenheit. Much further away from the sun, we'd freeze; much closer, we'd fry.

The third stage, appearance of first life. Man would need a support system to sustain his existence on earth. He would need energy. He would need food. When the earth settled and was ready, we had the primitive beginnings of life forms for providing a food chain. There is a flow of energy that comes from the sun to the earth.

It begins with the sun shining on green plants giving them transferable energy for the rest of the living organisms on earth. This process of loading energy in the plants is called photosynthesis. That energy is then passed on to plant-eating animals, like cows, cattle, and sheep when they munch grass and plants. Then there are those animals that eat plant-eating animals in the jungle to get their energy.

All this was preparatory to the coming of man who would eat both plants and animals. Wheat would give him bread. Tomato plants would allow him eventually to enjoy pizza and pasta, among other things. Cows give milk. Hens lay eggs providing man's most popular breakfast staple. Cattle, chicken, and fish are also in that food chain. When man would come, food needs were available.

The enormous variety of plant seeds is amazing! They perpetuate their kind over and over, generation after generation, keeping a constant food supply. But seeds are not limited to plant perpetuation. Non-plant species also use seeds to perpetuate their species. All creatures, whether it's a rhino, rabbit, or human, have a male/female relationship with a seed-dispensing mechanism. Who could possibly have created all these different seeds? Certainly not man. And they didn't come about randomly. But they exist. This is another example of a providential mind with a plan of bringing man into existence, preparing all the necessary support materials to achieve his plan.

Life could not exist without water. Just as seed systems provided for the renewal of plants, humans, and creatures, so water and a renewal process for it was provided. Science says that oceans formed on this planet 3.8 billion years ago. There is a limited amount of water that continually goes around and around. It is called a water cycle and has four phases—evaporation, condensation, precipitation, and collection. Evaporation happens when the sun heats up the rivers, lakes, and ocean, and turns it into vapor or steam, which goes into the air. Condensation happens when the water vapor in the air gets cold, changing back into liquid and forming clouds. Precipitation happens when so much water has condensed that the clouds can't hold it. Water falls back to earth as rain, sleet, or snow. The final phase is collection. When the water falls back to the earth as liquid, it may fall back into the oceans, lakes, or rivers. Or it may end up on land. It soaks into the earth and becomes part of the groundwater that provides water for plants, humans, and other creatures. And that cycle continually repeats.

Was this coincidence or part of a master plan with a purpose? The complexity of our planet points to a deliberate designer who not only created our universe but sustains it today. All things point to God. Human beings are the crown of God's creation.

Dinesh D'Souza describes it this way:

> The universe is fine tuned for human habitation. The entire universe with all its laws appears to be a conspiracy to produce, well, us. Physicists call this incredible finding the "Anthropic Principle," which states that the universe we perceive must be precisely such a nature as will make possible living humans who can perceive it.
>
> —D'Souza, *What's So Great About Christianity*, 129

The fourth stage, human beings. Let's look at why humans are so special. Science has documented 3.1 million life species. They say there could be millions more. Not one life species existed prior to the earth settling in its orbit around the sun. Humans have four major faculties that separate them from all other life species:

1. Humans have intelligence. We can think. Only man has an awareness of the ultimate questions: Does God exist? Is there a meaning and purpose to life? What happens when we die? To man's intellect, objects are not just what they are. Man can reflect, analyze, and generalize on what he sees. Because he can do these things, he dominates the material universe. Humans have the power of abstract thought and reasoning. They can discuss ideas, concerns, and ask questions. No other creature in the world can do this. Is it because humans have a bigger brain? Horses, hippos, and elephants have bigger heads and room for bigger brains.

    The very nature of thought shows the soul to be immaterial and not subject to the laws of disintegration and destruction, which governs all material things. All corruption is disintegration of parts. The soul has no parts. Man is the only creature capable of knowing, thanking, and praising his creator in prayer. Evidently, the intelligent super power that caused all existence had a reason for giving this special gift only to man.

2. Humans have an inner law. It's a law of right and wrong, a moral law, which we know we have to obey. Somebody wants us to behave in a certain way. We each have a conscience. It's that little voice inside us, prepackaged in our human nature, which warns us when we are tempted to do the wrong thing or to let us know after we've done the wrong thing. We must assume it has a mind because we know the only other thing is matter, and we know matter can't give advice. There are two important pieces of evidence about that somebody:

    First, just look at the designed order and beauty of the universe he has made out of nothing. It had to be caused by somebody who was a great architect and artist.

    Second, reflect on the moral law he has put in our minds.

This is a very important clue about God and his expectations. All the other clues came from observation. This is inside information. It tells us much more about God than just observing the ordered universe he built.

Now because of this moral law, which is within us, we must conclude that the God who built the universe is interested in people doing the right thing like fair play, unselfishness, good faith, and truthfulness. This is a moral universe.

3. Humans have free will. We can know that an action is wrong and choose to do it anyhow. Or we can know the right thing to do and choose not do it. But we are answerable for our choices. That's why we have jails. But people in jails aren't there for all the wrongs they did, only for the times they got caught. Now if there is a God who revealed how we should behave and provided warning mechanisms like conscience and truly knows every little thing about us, won't his evidence for a judgment be complete? Many individuals who were blameworthy for actions in the holocaust may have escaped detection in this life, but did they in an afterlife?

How did the human species get here? The two competing theories are creation and evolution. Did God create man instantly, or did he use a drawn-out process as he did to get the earth, sun, and moon from the big bang? *Radio Replies* is a three-volume work by Fathers Rumble and Carty. They were on radio in the early thirties, answering questions about the Catholic faith. Here's how they answered the evolution question:

Did man himself evolve from lower beings? It is absolutely certain that his soul did not. The soul is an intelligent spirit, and an intelligent spirit cannot evolve from matter. Did man's body evolve from lower animals, creating the rational soul when some lower animal had sufficiently evolved toward manhood? Despite conjectures in favor of this notion, the evidence is against it. The missing link is still missing, and reason discounts the probability, that a purely animal soul could develop an animal body beyond its own powers, lifting it to the higher stage needed for a rational soul.

—Leslie Rumble and Charles M. Carty, *Radio Replies* (St. Paul, MN: Radio Replies Press Society, 1938)

Evolution cannot explain the beginning of life. Darwin didn't even try. He assumed the first living thing and then tried to show how one living thing could be transformed into another, like a human coming from an animal.

F. J. Sheed, in *Theology for Beginners*, adds,

"What they must not deny is the immediate creation, for the first man and every subsequent man, of the soul. The soul, being a spirit, having no parts, cannot evolve from some lower form; it can exist only if God creates it."[6]

Dinesh D'Souza wrote,

Christians should not be afraid of the evolution debate, because there is nothing that threatens their faith. The Christian position is that God is the creator of the universe and everything in it, and the evolution debate is about how some of these changes came about. For the Christian, the evolution debate comes down to competing theories of how God did it.

—D'Souza, *What's So Great About Christianity*, 153

4. Big picture of belief in God. Greek sages always believed that where there is order, there must be a mind. Everywhere you look, there is order:

Order in the sky. There is an amazing order of stars and planets that observe their appointed courses. The Big Dipper of my youth still appears nightly in its original form.

An astronomer is able to forecast to the minute and to the inch when and where a certain planet will appear. An astronomer can tell us when and where an eclipse of the sun will happen hundreds of years from now, and he can tell us to the second how long it will last. Astronomers tell us that there are as many stars as there are grains of sand on the seashore. If we may put it in human terms, think of the traffic problems of the heavens; and yet the heavenly bodies keep their appointed courses and travel their appointed way."

—William Barclay, *Daily Bible Study Series, Book 5* (Edinburgh, UK: St. Andrew Press, 1955; Philadelphia, PA: Westminster Press, 1975). Citation is to the Westminster Press edition, 57.

Man's mind has no power to make stars or planets and set them in perpetual motion. It required a mind and power greater than man. It required God.

Order on the earth. Tides appear at their appointed times. On March 2, 2012, the *Sun Sentinel* newspaper reports on what the tide times will be today in Boca Raton. Note the precision of times—high tides (from 1:34 a.m. to 1:37 p.m.), low tides will be 8:04 a.m. to 8:32 p.m.[7] Night and day, summer and winter, seed times and harvesting, all follow in natural order. Man cannot make night and day, summer and winter, or create seeds that have within them the power of growth of food to perpetuate the food it bears for all generations. Clearly, we see an order in nature and conclude that there is a great mind and power behind it all.

Order in music. We all enjoy our favorite songs, singers, and musical instruments and take them for granted. Music consists of different tones, represented by musical notes, which a songwriter can arrange in sequence and timing to produce harmonious melodies. Voices and musical instruments can all be "in tune" because they work from the same musical arrangement with its keys, tones, and timing. Musical tones are mathematically precise. They are so orderly that only a supernatural mind and power could have provided this amazing gift to humanity.

We must look within ourselves and ask, who gave us the power to think, ask questions, and reason? Who gave us our awareness of right and wrong? Why do we feel remorse and guilt for doing bad things? Who do we answer to for what we've done? We didn't give ourselves life nor did we give ourselves guides and directions for living it. Both had to come from a power outside ourselves. Many years ago, Emmanuel Kant (1724–1804), a famous German philosopher, said that two things convinced him of the existence of God: the stars in the heavens above him and the moral law within him.[8] No man can understand himself apart from the existence of God.

What is the purpose of living? Bishop Sheen created an audio tape album called, *Ye Shall Know the Truth*. I'd like to quote a section in which he discusses the meaning and purpose of life:

> This universe of ours is a free universe. It is a universe of character making, of soul making. Almighty God has placed into our hands the power to make ourselves saints or devils. It is up to us.
>
> There are some laws we cannot disobey—the law of gravitation and certain biological laws like circulation of blood. But, in a moral universe, we are free either to obey the laws of God, or disobey them, just as we are perfectly

free to obey the laws of health, or disobey them. What makes a thing good? What makes a thing bad?

What makes a thing good? A thing is good when it attains the purpose for which it was made. I have before me a watch. Is it a good watch? How will I know whether it is good? What is the purpose of a watch? To keep time. Does it keep time? Then it is a good watch.

Let us apply that to our ultimate end.

Why were we made? What is the purpose of living? The purpose of living is to become supremely happy. How do we become supremely happy? By attaining the life, the truth, and the love which is God. Anything I do therefore that helps me attain that goal or purpose is good. I have an organ in my home. As I talk to you, I'm looking at the notes. Which note is good? Which note is bad? Which note is right? Which note is wrong? One cannot say that any particular note is right or wrong. What makes any note right or wrong? Its correspondence to a standard. Once I have a piece of music before me, I know what I ought to do, what note I ought not to hit.

So, too, we have a moral standard within us which is the conscience. What is good and bad is in relationship to that standard that is not of our own making. We do not draw our own maps and decide that the distance between New York and Chicago will be so and so. We do not arbitrarily set our own watches. We set them by a standard outside of us. When we buy material, we don't decide that a yard will be 24 inches instead of 36 inches. So a good, therefore, is that which helps us in relationship to the attainment of goals and destinies which are in accord with right reason.

What makes a thing bad? Here's a pencil. Is it a good pencil? Yes, it writes. That is why it was made. Is it a good can opener? It certainly is not. Suppose I use it as a can opener. What happens? First of all, I do not open the can. I do not attain the purpose for which I used the pencil. And secondly, I destroy the pencil. I do not attain the purpose that I hoped to attain.

For example, becoming an alcoholic does not make me happy. And furthermore, I destroy myself just as I destroyed the pencil in opening the can. When I disobey God, I do not make myself very happy on the inside and certainly destroy any peace of soul that I ought to have.

—Bishop Fulton J. Sheen, *Ye Shall Know the Truth*, (Audiocassette. Montvale, NJ: Catholic Historical Society in cooperation with Keep the Faith Inc., 1980).

What happens after death? We've covered nonexistence to existence. But what happens when earthly existence ends? At this point of our search, we can't know. The only way we could know is if God revealed himself to humanity through specially selected human messengers. There are claimants who say he has, which is the field of religion. This brings us to the next chapter, where we will take a close look at the Judeo-Christian religions, asking each three simple questions: What is your story? What is your belief about God? What is your belief about an afterlife?

Notes

1. Soren Kierkegaard, *Journals* IV A 164 (1843).
2. The Florida *Sun Sentinel* 1/6/2010.
3. Stephen Hawkings, *A Brief History of Time*, Bantam Trade paperback ed., (New York, NY: Bantam Books, 1998), 126.
4. Barry Parker, *Vindication of the Big Bang*, (New York, NY: Plenum Press, 1993), 1.
5. Charles Townes, *Perspectives on Science and the Christian Faith*, 55, no. 3 (2003).
6. F.J. Sheed, *Theology for Beginners*, (Ann Arbor, MI: Servant Books, 1958), 58.
7. The Florida Sun Sentinel 3/2/2012.
8. William Barclay, *Daily Bible Study Series*, Book 5, (Edinburgh, UK: St. Andrew Press, 1955; Philadelphia, PA: Westminster Press, 1975, 58.

What Do the Christians and Jews Believe About God?

God exists. Our reason has shown us that, but what is he like? Is there any meaning to life? Has God revealed the answers to the big questions of life and death?

Since God created humans distinct from all creation by giving us minds to think, understand, and question, it's perfectly reasonable and doable that he would reveal what life is about by using special human messengers who would relay his messages to all humanity. Has he done it? If God created man for a purpose, why keep it hidden? Is there a messenger for us with the authentic fullness of truth that will set us free? The purpose of this chapter is to closely examine claimants in a search for truth.

Judaism

What Is Their Story?

Unlike other ancient religions and cultures, Judaism is rooted in history, not mythology. It is the first recorded monotheistic faith. Their history began about 4,000 years ago with a man named Abraham, who was a Hebrew warrior and a tribal chieftain. He is their founder. His story, and what followed, and what went before, appear in the Hebrew scriptures, which Christians refer to as the Old Testament. The Old Testament contains thirty-nine books, which detail a continuous 1,500-year historical journey from Abraham to the last Jewish prophet, Malachi, about 450 years before the birth of Jesus. That was the cutoff point Jews used for their scriptures.

From that point to the present day, the many prophecies of a coming Messiah have not been fulfilled by the Jews.

The time before the coming of Abraham is considered early world history. It is covered in the first eleven chapters of Genesis. Some of it is from very early traditions, and other parts, like the creation stories, which had no eye witnesses, are considered truths that were divinely revealed to the sacred authors. For instance, Genesis begins with "In the beginning, when God created the heavens and the earth" (Gen 1.1, NAB). It's interesting that less than 100 years ago, science's big bang theory affirmed that the heavens and the earth did have a beginning.

The Old Testament includes many key names and events in their history as a chosen people—names like Abraham, Isaac, Jacob, Joseph, Moses, Joshua, David, Isaiah, etc. and also a continuous line of historic events from Abraham to the death of their last prophet. It's quite amazing that in such a small, remote part of the world, one man, Abraham, would become not only the founder of Judaism but would also provide the religious foundation for the two largest religions in the world, Christianity and Islam. Each look to Abraham as their founder.

Who was Abraham? Judaism does make claims that the unseen, unknown God, did reveal himself to Abraham and others, as we shall see in Judaism's long story. Foremost among these was the promise that Abraham would become the founder of a new nation and would father its first citizen. Abraham was seventy-five years old, and his wife Sarah, sixty-five, when this promise was made. This nation would have a purpose. Three times in the book of Genesis, God tells Abraham that this nation will be the "light" to all the nations of the world. Thus God's revelations to the Jews through the Law, Psalms, and prophets were meant for all mankind.

Jews and Christians believe in the same one God who revealed himself to Abraham almost 4,000 years ago. Isaiah, the Jewish prophet, speaking for God, said to Israel, "'I will make you a light to the nations that my salvation may reach to the ends of the earth'" (Is 49:6, NAB).

Why do Christians believe in Abraham? Christians believe the whole Old Testament story. If there were no Old Testament, there would be no New Testament. There would be no need for a savior. There would be no need for a Messiah, which Jesus claimed to be. Christianity is often correctly referred to as Judeo-Christianity. That's why the next chapter, "Judeo-Christian Connections," will be a historical journey, connecting in chronological order key people and events from Adam to Jesus. For Christians, the coming of Jesus in the New Testament was not the replacement of the Old Testament story, but its fulfillment.

The first five books of the Old Testament are called the Torah. It has other names, including the Mosaic Law. The name of Abraham's chosen nation was Israel. It was named for Abraham's grandson, Jacob, whose name had been changed to Israel by God. We'll put all names and events in chronological order in the next chapter as we trace the Biblical journey from Adam to Jesus.

Judaism has no dogma, no formal set of beliefs that one must hold to be a Jew. In Judaism, actions are far more important than beliefs, although there is certainly a place for belief within Judaism. The closest that anyone has come to creating a widely-accepted list of beliefs was by a man named Maimonides (1135–1204 AD). He was a Spanish Jew and considered to be the foremost Jewish philosopher and expert of Jewish law. He believed that his thirteen principles of faith were the minimum requirements of Jewish belief. They are:

1. God exists.
2. God is one and unique.
3. God is incorporeal.
4. God is eternal.
5. Prayer is to be directed to God alone, and no other.
6. The words of the prophets are true.
7. Moses' prophecies are true, and Moses was the greatest of the prophets.
8. The written Torah (first five books of the Bible) and oral Torah (teachings now contained in the Talmud and other writings) were given to Moses.
9. There will be no other Torah.
10. God knows of the thoughts and deeds of men.
11. God will reward the good and punish the wicked.
12. The Messiah will come.
13. The dead will be resurrected.

As basic as these principles are, the necessity of believing each one has been disputed at one time or another and the liberal movements of Judaism dispute many of these principles.

Jewish Belief about God

Jews believe in the one God who revealed himself through the Law, Psalms, and prophets.

Jewish Belief in an Afterlife

For the most part, the Torah describes the afterlife in vague terms. Later in the Torah, the concept of a conscious life after death began to develop. Daniel 12:2 (NAB) declares, "Many of those who sleep in the dust of the earth shall awake, some shall live forever, others shall be an everlasting horror and disgrace."

More developed concepts of the resurrection of the dead and afterlife seemed to have entered Judaism under Hellenistic influence after the Torah was completed. It became one of the fundamental beliefs in Rabbinic Judaism. The rabbis were the intellectual successors of the Pharisees. Readers familiar with the New Testament will recall that the Sadducees were the Jewish group that denied the resurrection. Pharisees believed in it. *Olam Haba* is a Hebrew phrase which means "the world to come."

According to the *Encyclopedia Judaica*, "In the Rabbinic period, the doctrine of the resurrection of the dead is considered one of the central doctrines of Judaism" and "is to be distinguished from the belief in…immortality of the soul."[1] Today, however, while the immortality of the soul is accepted by all factions of Judaism, the resurrection of the dead is not.

Orthodox Jews maintain the tenet of bodily resurrection of the dead, including traditional references to it in their liturgy. Conservative Jews have generally retained it also, including it in their liturgy. Reform Jews have altered traditional references to the resurrection of the dead from "Who gives life to the dead" to "Who gives life to all."

I found these interesting comments on the subject by Rabbi Shraga Simmons:

> The creation of man testifies to the eternal life of the soul. The Torah says, "And the almighty formed the man of dust from the ground, and he blew into the nostrils the soul of life" (Gn 2:7, KJV). The soul is actually part of God's essence. Since God's essence is completely spiritual and non-physical, it is impossible that the soul should die.
>
> For anyone who believes in a just and caring God, the existence of an afterlife makes logical sense. Could it be that this world is just a playground without consequences?

> No. There is obviously a place where good people receive reward and bad people get punished.
>
> —http:www//Judaism.about.com/library/3_askra

The rabbi also had these thoughts about heaven:

> Heaven is where the soul experiences the greatest possible pleasure - the feeling of closeness to God. Of course not all souls experience that to the same degree. It's like going to a symphony concert. Some tickets are front row center; others are back in the bleachers. Where your seat is located is based on the merit of your good deeds, like, giving charity, caring for others, prayer.
>
> A second factor in heaven is your understanding of the environment. Just like at a concert, a person can have great seats but no appreciation of what is going on. If a person spends their lifetime elevating the soul and becoming sensitive to spiritual realities (through Torah study), then that will translate into unimaginable pleasure in heaven. On the other hand, if life was all about pizza and football, well, that can get pretty boring for eternity.
>
> —http:www//Judaism.about.com/library/3_askra

Christianity

What Is Their Story?

The Old Testament was the story of a nation—Israel. The New Testament is the story of a man—Jesus.

Jesus' appearance on earth is the central event of all history. The Western world calendar measures all other events, before and after his coming, from his birth. Today, Christianity, with 2.1 billion followers of Jesus, is the largest religion in the world. The Old Testament set the stage for his coming. The New Testament described what he is all about.

Jesus was a Jew born over two thousand years ago in the little town of Bethlehem. Born of poor parents in a stable, he lived thirty-three years on earth. His mission was only three years. What could one man possibly accomplish in a brief three-year ministry to merit such continuing world respect and loyalty?

Without the Old Testament, Christianity would not exist. Christianity considers the New Testament as the fulfillment of the Old Testament. If there were no Old Testament, there would be nothing to fulfill. Christians believe Jesus fulfilled two major roles—that of the Savior of the world and that of the Messiah.

Why is Jesus considered the Savior of the world? It's because he saved all mankind from the major consequences of Adam and Eve's disobedience to God, which is called original sin. Adam was not just the first man; he was the whole human race and our representative. God had created man in his image, blessed him, and gave him dominion over the earth. Man was the crown of God's creation. There was unity and harmony between God and the human race in a holy relationship.

What did Adam do? Adam's disobedience destroyed that unity for him and for all future members of the human race. This was the fall. There were additional consequences. Work, pain, suffering, and death would now be the lot of mankind. Heaven was closed to the human race after death. A given man might be virtuous, but he was a virtuous member of a fallen race.

Newborn babies are affected by original sin, which, on the surface, seems unfair. Why should an innocent baby be guilty of Adam's sin? A Christian might respond this way: Say there was a man of great wealth. He goes to Las Vegas and gambles all his wealth on one roll of the dice. He loses it all and becomes poor. His kids became poor. They became poor because of the consequences of their father's actions.

Adam had a human nature, but God had given him and the human race two supernatural gifts above his human nature—sanctification (his divine relationship with man) and freedom from concupiscence, which is protection against temptations of the flesh. After the fall both were taken away. These losses were the consequences of Adam's disobedience. Only their human nature remained. Things looked dark.

Suddenly, there was hope. Genesis 3:15 is considered by Christians as the first good news promise that what was destroyed by Adam would one day be restored. It basically promised that the "seed of a woman" will crush the head of the serpent. The seed is Jesus. The woman is Mary. And the serpent is Satan who successfully tempted Adam. The Old Testament was a preparation for the coming of the seed who would be Jesus, the Savior of the world.

What did Jesus do? Jesus was one person with two natures—one divine, one human. It was his divinity that could offset Adam's offense against divinity. Jesus' obedient death on the cross brought atonement for Adam's disobedience. Atonement can be viewed as "at-one-ment," meaning that the unity and holy relationship lost with Adam was restored by Christ in his holy church on earth. Heaven was reopened after his crucifixion. Before his resurrection, Jesus descended to the abode of the righteous dead to give them the good news that heaven was now open for them. The doctrine of original sin is, so to speak, the "reverse side" of the good news that Jesus is the savior of all men, that all need salvation, and that salvation is offered to all through Christ.

Jews do not believe in the Christian concept of original sin. The Catholic catechism gives this explanation:

> With the progress of revelation, the reality of sin is also illuminated. Although to some extent the people of God in the Old Testament had tried to understand the pathos of the human condition in the light of the history of the fall narrated in Genesis, they could not grasp the story's ultimate meaning, which is revealed only in the light of the death and resurrection of Jesus Christ. The supreme truth about the Savior, for which the chosen people were

wholly unprepared, was that Jesus was God. To affect the redemption of the world, God became man.

—Catechism of the Catholic Church,
(Liguori, MO: Liguori Publications, 1994), #388.

Why are Jews looking for a Messiah? Why do Christians believe that Jesus is that Messiah? Since Jews do not believe in original sin, they are not looking for a savior. What they are looking for is the Messiah, who has no connection to original sin. The Messiah has to do with their history. God had promised Abraham the land of Canaan as the home for his chosen nation. But it wasn't a free "walk-in gift." The Israelites had to battle seven pagan nations that occupied it. From the time of Joshua to the time of King David, about 250 years, there were constant battles to keep and gain land. Under King David (1,000–960 BC), the Israelites enjoyed their golden years of peak power. After his reign, things went downhill because people were disobedient to the covenant God made with Moses.

Prophetic links to Jesus abound in the OT. Starting with "the seed of a woman" in Genesis 3:15, over three hundred Messianic prophecies over hundreds of years were fulfilled in the coming of Jesus. Peter Kreeft, prolific Christian author, says that the odds of that happening are so astronomical, that it's like hitting the lottery every day for one hundred years. So Jesus was pre-announced. No founder of any other major religion was ever pre-announced.

In addition, when Jesus came, he did things no man in history ever did, always with witnesses. He raised three people from the dead, changed water into wine, fed five thousand people with a few loaves of bread, walked on water, and cured the deaf, the blind, the lame, and lepers. However, his most awesome miracle was his own resurrection from the dead. If he didn't rise, he wasn't God.

The chief witnesses to the resurrection were the remaining eleven apostles who were with him throughout his three-year ministry and had been eyewitnesses to all his miracles and teachings. However, on Good Friday while he was being crucified, only John had the courage to be there. The other ten apostles were hiding.

Yet on that first Easter Sunday, the apostles witnessed the risen Christ. They were in his company for forty days before he ascended before their eyes to the Father. History shows that the ten who had not been there on Good Friday, died horrible deaths witnessing to Jesus' life, death, and resurrection. Nobody dies for what he knows is a lie. So Christians believe that Jesus was not only the Savior not only the Messiah but the God of the universe, who would fulfill the worldwide blessing promised to Abraham.

Christian Belief about God

Christians believe in the Trinity, which means that there is one God, with three divine persons— the Father, the Son, and the Holy Spirit. This claim came out of the New Testament revelations of Jesus. For instance, Jesus made statements like these, claiming to be part of the Trinity.

> "I and the Father are one." (Jn 10:30, NAB)

> "Whoever has seen me has seen the Father." (Jn 14:9, NAB)

> "Before Abraham came to be, I am." (Jn 8:58, NAB)

Also, statements like this for including the Holy Spirit:

> "The advocate, the Holy Spirit that the Father will send in my name…He will teach you everything and remind you of all I told you." (Jn 14:26, NAB)

Plus this in the Old Testament:

> God said: "Let us make man in *our* image, after *our* likeness." (Gn 1:27, NAB) (Emphasis added)

In the Trinity, God's life consists of the infinite interflow of knowing and loving among three persons who are one God.

Christians believe the Trinity always was, is, and always will be. For the purpose of salvation, the second person of the Trinity came down and became Jesus in the flesh. Jesus would be one person with two natures—a divine and a human. St. Paul described it this way:

> One man's trespasses led to condemnation (loss of original justice) for all men, so one man's (Christ's) act of righteousness leads to acquittal and life (grace) for all men. For as by one man's disobedience many (mankind) were made sinners (sharers in Original Sin) so by one man's obedience many will be made righteous. (Rom 5:18, NAB)

Jesus made some powerful claims about truth:

> "I came into the world to testify to the truth" (Jn 18:37, NAB).

> "I am the way, the truth, and the life" (Jn 14:6, NAB).

> "You shall know the truth, and the truth shall set you free" (Jn 8:32, NAB).

Interestingly, if the Christian claim of Jesus' divinity as the second person in the Trinity is true, then it would follow that Jesus was present at all the Old Testament events where God was present. Here are some major ones:

> In the beginning, when God created the heavens and the earth (Gn 1:1, NAB);

When God created Adam and gave him instructions, "The Lord God formed man out of the clay of the ground and blew into his nostrils the breath of life, and so man became a living being" (Gn 2:7, NAB);

When "The Lord gave man this order: 'You are free to eat from any of the trees of the garden except the tree of knowledge of good and bad. From that tree you shall not eat; the moment you eat from it you are surely doomed to die'" (Gn 2:16–17, NAB);

In justice, applying the consequences of Adam's fall (Gn 3:14–19, NAB);

In mercy, promising a savior, which would be fulfilled by himself in the flesh, "I will put enmity between you and the woman, and between your offspring and hers; he will strike at your head, while you will strike at his heel" (Gn 3:15, NAB);

In judgment with a flood, warning Noah (Gn 7, 9, NAB);

In love, unveiling his plan with Abraham which would reach all mankind, in all generations, in the whole world (Gn 12:2–3, NAB);

In wisdom and love, gracing leaders like the patriarchs Moses, Joshua, David, and the prophets, which prepared for his coming as savior, Messiah, and eternal king of the universe;

and in loving guidance, establishing his church with a leadership structure to provide guidance and aids for all people to live their lives to recapture the paradise originally intended at the creation of man. Jesus promised his presence and that of the Holy Spirit until his second coming, guaranteeing the truth of his church's teachings.

Christian Belief in an Afterlife

Christians believe in heaven and hell. At an individual's death, there will be a judgment of heaven or hell by Jesus on how that individual lived the life he/she was given. Those who merit heaven will be reunited with loved ones who have been saved. More importantly, they will see God face-to-face. At the second coming of Jesus, the time of which is unknown, all who have been saved and merit heaven will receive physical glorified bodies.

Catholics believe in purgatory. They point to Revelations 21:27, "But nothing unclean will enter it, nor anyone who does abominable things or tells lies."

> All who die in God's grace and friendship, but still imperfectly purified, are indeed assured of their eternal salvation; but, after death, they undergo purification, so as to achieve the holiness necessary to enter the joy of heaven. The Church gives the name *purgatory* to this final purification of the elect, which is entirely different from the punishment of the damned. *Catechism of the Catholic Church*, (Liguori, MO: Liguori Publications, 1994), #388

The supreme happiness of heaven is totally different from any happiness we know on earth. "Eye has not seen, nor ear heard... what God has prepared for those who love him" (1 Cor 2:9, NAB).

"An eternity of the things we know here, and life as we experience it here would soon become blank misery, and not heaven at all. God himself tells us that we shall see him face to face."[2]

Notes

1. *Encyclopedia Judaica*, rev. ed., 22 volumes, Macmillan Reference USA, 2006.
2. *Catechism of the Catholic Church*, #1030, #1031.

Judeo-Christian Connections

This will be a fast time journey, connecting chronologically key events in the Old Testament from creation to the coming of Jesus in 1 AD.

Creation?—2000 BC

We begin with creation. We have no beginning date. The time period will extend from the creation event to about 2000 BC when Abraham comes on stage. Genesis chapters one to eleven cover this time period. These chapters were written to establish religious truths and not to dabble in natural history or prehistory. But they are a necessary preface to the history that is to follow. God made a covenant with Adam and Eve, creating a sacred family bond relationship between God and man. God created man in "his image and likeness." So God is our father. We are his children. We are family. We were created to know, love, and serve God in this world and to be eternally happy with him in the next.

A covenant is not a contract. A contract is an exchange of property or services: "You paint my house, I'll give you money." A covenant is like a marriage: "I'll give you me, and you give me you." It's an exchange of persons. Promises of love and faithfulness are exchanged in this binding relationship. God said, "I will be your God. You will be my people" (Jer 7:23, NAB). God blessed them saying, "Be fruitful and multiply and fill the earth" (Gn 9:1, NAB). The Lord gave Adam this order, "You are free to eat from any of the trees of the garden except the tree of knowledge of good and bad. From that tree you shall not eat: the moment you eat from it you are surely doomed to die" (Gn 2:16, NAB). Adam disobeyed. That was the fall for all mankind.

With the fall came consequences. Heaven was closed. Men were never supposed to work or suffer or die. All these things came as a result of the sin of disobedience, along with our present sinful nature. But here, we have Genesis 3:15, the first good news promise that man's peace with God, lost by Adam, would be restored. The promise was that the seed of a woman would crush the head of the serpent. The seed is Jesus. The woman is Mary, and the serpent is Satan who caused the fall by Adam. Our peace with God was lost. Five more family covenants would be required by God to restore that peace. They would be ever widening in size.

After Adam, we move on to Noah. He is the second covenant. In the time of Noah, God was very displeased with his human creation and man's misuse of free will. Mankind had lost two supernatural gifts because of the fall—sanctifying grace and freedom from concupiscence. Now man had to struggle against temptations without them. Jesus would later come to restore graces and provide the spiritual aid of confession to help man live according to God's will and bring his temptations under control. People today, who don't take advantage of what Jesus has brought, end up like the people at the time of Noah. The same sins they committed then are the sins these people commit now. Sin was rampant, so he destroyed everything. Only a small remnant remained. That's the story of the ark. There were eight people on the ark—Noah and his wife, three sons (Shem, Ham, and Japheth), and their wives. "God blessed Noah and his sons and said to them: 'Be fertile and multiply and fill the earth'" (Gn 9:1, NAB).

The journey continues.

The Patriarchs (2000–1700 BC)

Our third major figure is Abraham. Abraham is a descendant of Noah's oldest son, Shem (Gn 11:10–26, NAB). There were four primary patriarchs—Abraham, Isaac, Jacob, and Joseph.

Abraham is the founder. He will receive the third of the six covenants that God will make with representatives of his family. God told Abraham that his descendants would become a great and mighty nation, and through him, God would bless all nations. God made three promises to Abraham: He will give land to this promised nation (this will be fulfilled by Moses and Joshua around 1250 BC); he will give it a royal dynasty (this will begin with David around 1000 BC and lead to Jesus); and he will give it a worldwide blessing (this will be fulfilled by the coming of Jesus in 1 AD).

When Abraham heard these promises, he was seventy-five years old and his wife Sarah sixty-five. They had no children. He obviously needed descendants to begin this promised mighty nation. At eighty-six, he still had no children. So Sarah asked him to go to her slave woman, Hagar, saying maybe that's how God intends to get the promised nation started. Abraham did and had a son named Ishmael. The religion of Islam, which came into existence about 610 AD, considers Abraham their founder through the line of Ishmael.

When Abraham was ninety-nine, he and Sarah finally had their very own son, Isaac. The Bible traces its covenant promises through Isaac. We will follow his line chronologically through history right to the coming of Jesus. Abraham died in his 175th year.

Isaac married Rebecca. They had twin sons who were struggling in the womb.

> "She went to consult the Lord and he answered her: 'Two nations are in your womb, two peoples are quarreling while still within you: But one shall surpass the other and the older shall serve the younger.'" (Gn 25:23, NAB)

Esau, the older, deserved the important firstborn blessing. Isaac was old and blind and ready to bless Esau. Rebecca, favoring the younger Jacob, tricked Isaac into believing Jacob was Esau. Jacob received the blessing. Jacob knew he was in for trouble when his brother, Esau, came home. So he took off for the north country where his uncle Laban lived.

Laban had flocks of sheep and goats. He also had a beautiful daughter, Rachel. Jacob wanted to marry Rachel. Since Jacob had fallen in love with Rachel, he told Laban, "I will serve you seven years for your younger daughter Rachel" (Gn 29:18, NAB). Jacob worked seven years. There was a big party on the night of the honeymoon. The tent was dark. Jacob woke up the next morning and discovered he was with Leah, the older daughter.

He cried out:

> "How could you do this to me! Was it not for Rachel that I served you? Why did you dupe me?" "It is the custom in our country," Laban replied, "not to marry off a younger before an older one. Finish the bridal week for this one, and then I will give you the other too, in return for another seven years of service to me." (Gn 29:25–27, NAB)

Jacob would go on to have twelve sons—two with Rachel, six with Leah, and four more provided by servants of the sisters.

Earlier, God had changed Jacob's name to Israel. A name change in the Bible has meaning. For example, if you take the last two letters of the word, Israel "el," that means God. So the name Israel means "God flourishes." This name change was important because all his descendants will be now called Israelites from that name on. If the name hadn't been changed, they would have been called Jacobites. And today, instead of calling Israel "Israel" we would be calling it Jacob.

One of the sons was Joseph, who was Jacob's favorite because he was the firstborn of Rachel, the woman he loved. The other sons resented Joseph and decided they would kill him. They reconsidered and sold him to a gypsy caravan on its way to Egypt. Now Joseph had a gift of interpreting dreams. The king in Egypt had a dream nobody could interpret. Somebody knew about Joseph. He was summoned. Joseph said the dream meant seven good years of crops and then seven bad years, so save up during the good years. The king made Joseph governor to set up and manage this program.

When the seven bad years came, Joseph's brothers and his father, Jacob, were starving in Canaan. They heard about the food in Egypt. So Jacob sent ten of his sons over to Egypt. When they got to Egypt, Joseph recognized them, but they didn't recognize him because he was young when they sold him. The end result was that Jacob and all his sons were reunited with Joseph in Egypt. Ten sons would become heads of ten of the twelve tribes of Israel. Levi would become the priestly tribe and not get territory. Joseph's sons, Manasseh and Ephraim, in place of Joseph, would round out the twelve tribes.

The journey continues.

Israel in Egypt (1700–1290 BC)

Jacob, his eleven sons and their families, seventy people in all, went to Egypt to rejoin Joseph. This was the Israelite nation. They settled in the area of Goshen. There would be good times and bad times. These were the good times. Joseph was a big man in Egypt. They had land. They had food. And they lived in their own family community.

Time passed. Jacob died in his 147th year. Joseph, his brothers, and the rest of that generation also died, but their descendants, the Israelites, had many children and became numerous. A new king, who knew nothing about Joseph, came into power. He viewed this Israelite nation as a threat within his borders in case of war. Now came the bad times. The Israelites were forced into cruel slavery, but they continued to grow, and the king ordered that every newborn Hebrew baby boy be thrown into the Nile. Baby Moses now came on stage. He survived the "kill order" and was raised by the king's daughter with the help of Moses' mother and sister.

When Moses had grown, he saw how his people were forced to do hard labor. He saw an Egyptian kill a Hebrew. Moses killed the Egyptian. Knowing he had been discovered, he fled and went to live in the land of Midian. Moses married the daughter of Jethro, who owned a flock of sheep and goats. One day, while tending the flock, Moses saw a bush on fire that would not burn up. Curious, he moved closer. A voice said, "Do not come any closer. Take off your sandals. You're standing on Holy ground. I am the God of your ancestors, the God of Abraham, Isaac, and Jacob" (Ex 3:5, NIV).

God said, "I have seen how cruelly my people are being treated in Egypt. I am sending you to the Pharaoh so that you can lead my people out of his country to a spacious land, rich and fertile" (Ex 3:7–9, KJV).

Moses was afraid to go, making excuses. Then he agreed. God gave Moses instructions on what he should do.

Moses returned to Egypt, talked to the pharaoh, and requested a three-day journey for the Israelites into the desert "to sacrifice to our God." Pharaoh refused. He called them "lazy" and increased their workload.

> Moses and Aaron went and assembled all the Elders of the Israelites. Aaron told them everything the Lord had said to Moses, and he performed the signs before the people. The people believed and when they had heard that the Lord was concerned about them and had seen their affliction, they bowed down in worship." (Ex 4:29–31, NAB)

Nine plagues were sent by God to help change the Pharaoh's mind. Egyptians worshiped many nature gods like cattle, sheep, goats, frogs, the Nile, etc. The plagues were directed against those gods to show the Egyptians that the Israelite God was God of the universe. Pharaoh remained stubborn. Finally, the tenth plague would be the Passover. If the pharaoh didn't let the Israelites go, all Egyptian firstborn males would die. The Israelites were to eat a special meal to include an unblemished lamb whose blood was to be sprinkled on their doorposts. When the angel of death came that night, it would pass over the homes of the Israelites and not kill their firstborns.

The next morning, the firstborn sons of the Egyptians were found dead. Pharaoh was considered divine. Firstborn sons were divinized in a ceremony. They represented in a sense the political power of the pharaohs. There would be a power vacuum. Pharaoh finally allowed the Israelites to leave.

The journey continues.

Escape from Egypt (1290–1250 BC)

Moses led the exodus of the Israelite nation. But pharaoh changed his mind and pursued them with warriors and chariots. Moses parted the waters of the Red Sea, and the waters that parted for the Israelites closed over the Egyptians. When the Israelites first went into Egypt, they were a nation of seventy people. When they come out over 400 years later, they had 600,000 men, not counting women and children. The "chosen nation" of Abraham, Isaac, and Jacob had grown.

The fourth covenant, the most important OT covenant will be made with Moses at Mt. Sinai. God would give Moses his law, highlighted by the Ten Commandments. When Moses told the people all that God expected, they responded, "We will do everything that the Lord has said" (Ex 24:3, NIV). This covenant would be the foundation of Israel's relationship with God during the subsequent history of the chosen people.

Moses went up to Mt. Sinai for forty days, fasting. When he came down with the Ten Commandments, he was horrified to find that the Israelites, who had just been saved by God from

Egyptian slavery, had made a golden calf, which Egyptians worship. Moses "stood at the gate of the camp and cried, 'Whoever is for the Lord, let him come to me!' All the Levites then rallied to him" (Ex 32:26, NAB). All were silent except for the Levite tribe that rallied to Moses. At Moses' command," they took swords and killed 3,000 of their own Israelite kinsmen. This would cause a major shift in worship responsibility. Up until that time, a father was the king and priest of his household. His firstborn son was the prince and heir apparent. Under them, animal sacrifices and dietary regulations had not been required. Their priesthood was taken away and given to the Levites. Now, every day, there would be sacrifices of goats, cattle, and sheep ceremonially renouncing the gods of Egypt. God had taken the Israelites out of Egypt. These constant ceremonies would help take Egypt out of the Israelites.

God wanted the Israelites to enter the promised land of Canaan. Twelve scouts were sent. Ten of them had fearful reports about the power of the enemy. The Israelites rebelled against God's command and would not enter the land. God said, "not one man of this evil generation shall look upon the good land I swore to give your fathers except Caleb, son of Jephuuneh" (Dt 1:35, NAB). Joshua was the second loyal scout.

After forty years of desert wanderings, that generation of warriors died. Finally, Moses was leading them toward the promised land. Canaan was on the west side of the Jordan. While on the east side, the Israelites under the leadership of Moses defeated two Amorite kings. Their lands were allotted to two and one-half tribes—Reuben, Gad, and one-half of the tribe of Manasseh. This began the fulfillment of God's promise of land to Abraham. The men from these tribes were told that they must leave their families and livestock in their new lands and cross the Jordan to conquer land for the remaining nine and one-half tribes. Canaan was the target. Moses will not enter the promised land. He will die.

The journey continues.

Conquest of Canaan (1250–1220 BC)

Joshua, the faithful scout, will be the new leader. Land was needed for the remaining nine and one-half tribes. But this land was occupied by seven pagan nations. It must be conquered by force. The first city they attacked was Jericho. Forty thousand Israelite troops were available. God's instructions were to have a line of Israelites circle the city once each day for six days. The lineup would be: First, picked troops followed by seven priests with ram's horns, blowing them continuously. Next, priests carrying the Ark of the Covenant providing God's presence in their midst. The Ark would be followed by a rear guard of soldiers. On the seventh day, they marched around the city seven times. Then Joshua said to the people, "Now shout, for the Lord has given you the city and everything in it" (Jo 6:16, NAB). And the walls collapsed and Jericho was theirs. This strange military strategy was intended by God as a test of the people's obedience and of their faith in his promise.

Joshua would continue to lead them in battles in which they conquered much but not all of the promised land. At Shiloh, they divided the land by lots for the nine and one-half tribes and let the tribes from the east side go home. The land promise by God to Abraham for his chosen people had been fulfilled. Joshua had played a major leadership role in the conquest of Canaan. He would die about 1220 BC.

The journey continues.

The Judges (1220–1050 BC)

The death of Joshua began a new stage in the life and history of the Israelites. It was the period of the Judges, which lasted about 200 years. It filled the time gap between the leadership of Joshua and the leadership, which will be provided by their first king, King Saul, about 1050 BC.

There were twelve Judges. Judges were charismatic military leaders whom God would provide to rescue the Israelites when they were in trouble. Israel's problem was this: after Joshua and his generation died, the next generation forgot the Lord and what he had done for them. They were living amongst people they conquered and began to worship the gods of the peoples around them. God became furious and let raiders attack and rob them. The Israelites could no longer protect themselves, and in seven different times there is a sin cycle repeated. They sin and disobey God. Then they are in servitude to the enemy. When they repented, God raised judges to deliver them. One of the examples was Gideon. Here's what happened.

The Midianites were giving the Israelites a bad time. They were stealing their crops. They were stealing their livestock. When Sarah died, Abraham remarried and had a son by the name of Midian.

So God came to Gideon to solve the problem. Gideon protested that he was from an insignificant family and that he was the most insignificant member in his father's house. He asked for a sign and said,

> "If indeed you are going to save Israel through me, as you promised, I am putting this woolen fleece on the threshing floor. If dew comes on the fleece alone, while all the ground is dry I shall know that you will save Israel through me, as you promise.'" (Jgs 6:36–38, NAB)

This is what took place. Gideon then said to God,

> "Do not be angry with me if I speak once more. Let me make just one more test with the fleece. Let the fleece alone be dry, but let there be dew on all the ground." That night God did so; the fleece alone was dry, but there was dew on all the ground." (Jgs 6:39–40, NAB)

Gideon was convinced. So Gideon had to go to the tribes to get some manpower. He got about 32,000 soldiers to go. God said to him,

> "You have too many soldiers with you for me to deliver Midian into their power, lest Israel vaunt itself against me and say, 'My own power brought me victory.' Now proclaim to all the soldiers, If anyone is afraid or fearful, let him leave." When Gideon put them to this test on the mountain twenty-two thousand of the soldiers left but ten thousand remained. (Jgs 7:2–3, NAB)

So now God said,

> "You still have too many. Go to the river and make a test. Tell them to drink water. The ones who cup their hands and bring it up to their mouths and lap it like a dog. Those are the ones you want. They are ready for action." (Jgs 7:5–7, NAB)

There were 300 of those. That became the force that prevailed over the Midianites who had numerical superiority. God caused such confusion in the Midian camp that they killed each other.

The journey continues.

United Kingdom (1050–930 BC)

Time moves on. The last judge would be Samuel, who was also considered a prophet and a priest. During the period of the judges, when a problem arose, the Israelites were dependent on God providing them with a charismatic leader, a judge, to rescue them. Israelites wanted to be like other nations, with a king and an army ready to protect them in times of trouble. So they got a king. Samuel selected and anointed Saul, the first king over the twelve tribes of Israel. They were now a kingdom. This kingdom would remain united for 120 years. It would have three kings—Saul, David, and Solomon. Each would reign forty years.

Saul was a good king at the beginning. He defeated the Ammonites and the Philistines. Wherever he fought, he was victorious. Later, Samuel told Saul that God wanted him to attack the Amalekites and completely destroy everything they had. Saul disobeyed. He spared the king's life and saved the best sheep and cattle. God was disappointed in Saul. After the David/Goliath incident, Saul made David an officer in his army. David was very successful. The women played and sang, "Saul has slain his thousands, and David his ten thousands" (1 Sm 18:7, NAB). Saul was jealous. He could see the writing on the wall. He was trying to kill David, and David had opportunities to get rid of him, but David respected his position and didn't do it. Eventually, Saul was killed by the Philistines.

Now David was made king. He conquered Jerusalem. David is the fifth covenant, an eternal royal dynasty. One day, David said to his prophet, Nathan,

> "I'm living in a palace here, and God is living in a tent. I want to build a temple for him." So Nathan said, "Go ahead and do it." During the night, Nathan conversed with God. The next morning Nathan told David, "Your house and your kingdom shall endure forever before me; your throne shall stand firm forever." (2 Sm 7:16–17, NAB).

A dynasty is a kingdom in which as long as there is a family successor, the kingdom continues. When there is not a successor, the dynasty dies. Thus David's kingdom will last forever. We will trace David's descendants for 1,000 years right to the birth of Jesus, the eternal king. It's right there in scripture.

David, before he died, made one of his younger sons, Solomon, king. In the beginning, Solomon was a great king. God asked him what he wanted, and he replied, "Give your servant, therefore, an understanding heart to judge your people and to distinguish right from wrong. For who is able to govern this vast people or yours" (1 Kgs 3–9, NAB)? God liked that. So people came from all over to listen to his wisdom. As promised by God, David's son Solomon built a fantastic temple, along with many fortifications. But later on, he accumulated 700 wives and 300 concubines. These were the kind of political alliances in which territories were acquired along with sisters and daughters. Solomon would build pagan altars to their gods. This would lead him to worship foreign gods and lose God's favor. There was trouble ahead.

Divided Kingdom (930–722 BC)

Solomon died. For 120 years, under three kings—Saul, David, and Solomon—the kingdom had been united. Things are about to change. When Solomon died, Rehoboam, his son, was to be the next king. Now Jeroboam, who had been a general in the army of Solomon, came to Rehoboam and said, "Your father put on us a heavy yoke. If you now lighten the harsh service and the heavy yoke your father imposed on us, we will serve you'" (1 Kgs 12:4, NAB).

Rehoboam spoke to the white-haired counselors of his father, and they advised, "If today you will be the servant of this people and submit to them, giving them a favorable answer, they will be your servants forever" (1 Kgs 12:7, NAB).

Then he went to the young men like himself. They advised him what to say, "My little finger is thicker than my father's body. Whereas my father put a heavy yoke on you, I will make it heavier. My father beat you with whips, but I will beat you with scorpions" (1 Kgs 12:10–11, NAB).

This is what happened. The kingdom divided. There would be ten tribes in the north called Israel with Jeroboam as their king, and there would be two tribes in the south called Judah with its capital in Jerusalem. Rehoboam would become king of

Judah. David's promised line to Jesus will continue through the kings of Judah.

Prophets began to arise. Prophets spoke in place of God. They were telling the people that trouble was happening because of their unfaithfulness to God's covenant with Moses. So for a period of about 400 years beginning around 800 BC, these prophets not only were warning the people, but they were providing all kinds of clues about a special person that God would send one day—a Messiah.

The journey continues.

The Exiles (722–538 BC)

Now the problems began. In 722 BC, Assyria (present day Iraq) was the powerhouse nation at that time. Under the leadership of Sargon II, they came down and conquered the ten northern tribes and exiled them from the country. They became known as the "ten lost tribes of Israel" because they never came back. Only Judah with its two tribes was all that remained of the chosen people.

In 586 BC, Babylon was the big powerhouse ruled by Nebuchadnezzar. King Zedekiah was king of Judah. His royal line of succession reached back 400 years to King David. Babylon had been tolerating Judah with its two tribes, but when Babylon discovered that Judah was negotiating with Egypt to help remove the Babylonian influence, Babylon slammed down on them. They came and destroyed the beautiful temple that Solomon had built, and they took the major part of the remaining two tribes, Judah and Benjamin, into Babylonian captivity.

It's about 600 miles from Jerusalem to Babylon. Babylon is in Iraq where we're still having trouble. But can you imagine how we would feel if we were Jews at that time, and we had been the chosen people, and in our national memory, we knew that 400 years earlier, under King David, Israel had been the most powerful nation on earth. Now Solomon's temple had been completely destroyed. Their ten brother tribes were gone. And now they, the two remaining tribes, would be going into captivity with no chance of ever coming back. Their nation was to be the light to all nations. The promised land was in darkness.

The journey continues.

The Return (538–430 BC)

In 539 BC, after fifty years of captivity, Babylon was conquered by Cyrus of Persia (present day Iran). One year later, he let the Jews return saying, "The Lord, the God of Heaven, has given me all the kingdoms of the earth, as he has charged me to build a house at Jerusalem, which is in Judah" (Ezr 1:2, ESV). Gold, silver, and supplies were given the Jews to help them rebuild. Cyrus even gave them all the sacred utensils, which the Babylonians looted when they destroyed the temple in Jerusalem fifty years earlier. Zerubbabel, with 42,000 exiles, led the first wave back. What's important about him is that he is in the kingly line of David. Without a Babylonian captivity, he would have been king. Matthew traces Zerubbabel's genealogy right down to "Joseph, the husband of Mary, the mother of Jesus" (Mt 1:12–16, NAB). Thus, the family link from David to Jesus, the eternal king, is established. God's promise to David was fulfilled.

The king in Persia wouldn't allow Zerubbabel to become king, so he became governor. With the task of rebuilding, they began to rebuild, starting with the altar where it existed in Solomon's temple. They renewed sacrifices like the old days. They also restored four religious feasts before beginning work on the temple. The foundation for the temple was laid in 536 BC. Progress was slow with many complaints, especially from people old enough to remember the first temple destroyed by the Babylonians. Other opposition developed. Work ceased from 536 to 520 BC. In 520 BC, because of encouragement from two prophets, Haggai and

Zechariah, rebuilding of the temple resumed. Finally, it was completed in 515 BC. It took them about twenty years from the time they returned to get the temple rebuilt.

The second group's return was eighty-one years later. In 457 BC, Ezra led a group of about 2,000 men. He was an expert in the law. The Jewish Talmud regards him as a second Moses. God used Ezra to rebuild the people spiritually and morally. When Ezra discovered intermarriage with foreign women, he offered a great intercessory prayer for them. The people made a solemn promise to put away their foreign wives and to live in accordance with God's law.

The third group would return fourteen years later, in 444 BC. This was led by Nehemiah, a Jew, who was a wine steward for King Artaxerxes in Persia. Nehemiah was concerned that Jerusalem had no defense. He wanted to return to Jerusalem and rebuild the walls of the city. The king let him go. Nehemiah returned and rebuilt the walls against all kinds of opposition. It is said that workers had a sword in one hand and a trowel in the other trying to rebuild the walls. Built in fifty-two days, it was a miracle. Later, Nehemiah became governor. He accomplished for the political community what Ezra accomplished for the religious spirit of Israel. Together, they were an effective team.

The journey continues.

Other Invasions (430 BC–1 AD)

Ezra and Nehemiah's restored order and sense of unity among the Jews would last only one hundred years. In 332 BC, Alexander the Great, a twenty-two-year-old Greek, had conquered the then known world. He wanted everything to be Greek—Greek culture, Greek language, everywhere. When he died, four generals took over all his territory. There were two in the west and two in the east. General Ptolemy seized Egypt in the southeast and had control over the Holy Land. Later on, the northern empire in Syria took control, and that meant trouble.

In 168–165 BC, Antiochus Epiphanes IV, the leader in Syria, decided that he was going to come down to Jerusalem and make everything Greek. He built a gymnasium outside the temple area, where naked athletes would compete. He then took control of the temple. He put a statue of Zeus in there. Swine were sacrificed on the altar. Rooms of prostitution were put in the temple. It became a crime punishable by death to have your child circumcised. It was a crime punishable by death if you were caught with any scripture. Over 80,000 Jews were killed or sent into slavery. Those were bad times.

Then the Maccabees, who were Jewish zealots, organized and, against great odds, drove them out. And now, because the rebuilt temple had been desecrated, it had to be rededicated. There was only enough oil to burn for one day, but miraculously, it burned for eight days. This is the feast of Chanukah, which Jews celebrate in December even though interestingly, they do not recognize in their Hebrew scriptures the book of Maccabees where this story is told.

More problems were to come. In 63 BC, General Pompey of the Roman Empire invaded and occupied the Holy Land. This means that when Jesus was doing his three-year ministry, the Romans had been there almost one hundred years.

In the Old Testament, prophets had been giving clues that a Messiah would be coming and that he was going to be a savior of some kind. Jews, conditioned by the reality of the Romans in town and their history, wanted a Messiah who would save them from the political bondage of the Romans. Jesus came to save all people from the spiritual bondage of sin.

Jesus (1–33 AD)

Let's briefly review the covenants between God and his family.

The first was with Adam. Adam's fall destroyed our peace with God.

The second was with Noah. His household would begin the restoration of that peace as they repopulated the world.

The third was with Abraham, a tribal chieftain. Through him, a chosen people, the Israelites would be created. This nation was to be "a light to all the nations."

The fourth was with Moses. He would lead Israel, this chosen nation, out of Egypt to the promised land. Israelites were saved by the "blood of the lamb" in the tenth plague. Catholics see this as a foreshadowing of Jesus in their Eucharist.

The fifth was with King David. He would be the royal link to Jesus, the eternal king. God's promise to Nathan that David's kingdom would last forever was about to be fulfilled. The OT traces David's kingly descendants through twenty-one kings of Judah to the Babylonian captivity in 586 BC. Fifty years later, when they were freed by the Persians and allowed to go back to Jerusalem, Zerubbabel, a descendant of David, led the first wave of Jews back to Jerusalem.

Jesus was the sixth Covenant. Jesus was the New Covenant. He would be the light to all the nations. This Covenant would be universal and last until his second coming. How would he implement this final age of salvation history? He would establish a church.

The next chapter will be about Jesus' church.

Jesus' Church

The First 400 Years

The Jews closed their scriptures about 450 BC with the death of their last prophet, Malachi. During their 1,500-year history, major promises by God and his prophets had been made. When Malachi died, at least four major prophecies had yet to be fulfilled:

1. "The seed of a woman" prophecy, which would redeem all mankind from the consequences of Adam's fall (Gn 3:15, NAB);
2. God's many promises to Abraham and Isaiah that their chosen nation would be the "light" to all nations. Judaism is not a missionary religion;
3. God's promise that David would have an eternal royal dynasty (2 Sm 7:16, NAB); and
4. The Messiah hadn't come (over 300 prophecies).

If fulfillment of the Old Testament prophecies hadn't happened by the death of Malachi, who would fulfill them? Fortunately, it would be someone from the Hebrew tradition. Jesus, a Jew, was born in 1 AD. Jesus talked about fulfillment: "Do not think that I have come to abolish the law or the prophets. I have come not to abolish, but to fulfill" (Mt 5:17, NAB). Also, after his resurrection, Jesus said to his apostles, "These are my words that I spoke to you while I was still with you, that everything written about me in the

Law of Moses and in the prophets and psalms must be fulfilled" (Lk 24:44, NAB).

How did Jesus fulfill these prophecies? The first good news prophecy that the seed of a woman will crush the head of the serpent (2,000 years old) was fulfilled on Good Friday, 33 AD, when Jesus died on the cross, redeeming mankind from major consequences of Adam's fall. The promises to Abraham and Isaiah that Israel would be the "light" to all the nations of the world (two thousand years old) were fulfilled when Jesus established his church as his instrument to bring the good news of salvation to the whole world. The Davidic eternal dynasty prophecy of Nathan (one thousand years old) was fulfilled with the birth of Jesus, the eternal king. Twenty-one kings from the tribe of Judah and blood relatives of David are traced in scripture from David to the birth of Jesus, the eternal king. Finally, Jesus is the Messiah, as discussed in the previous chapter, fulfilling over 300 prophecies (450 to 1,000 years old).

In addition to Messiah Jesus made an awesome claim! More important than being the Messiah, Jesus made the astounding claim that he was God! We read about that in chapter three's discussion on Christianity, "The Father and I are one" (Jn 10:30, NAB); "Whoever has seen me has seen the Father" (Jn 14:9, NAB); "Amen, Amen I say to you. Before Abraham came to be, I am" (Jn 8:58, NAB). We'll hear more about challenges to that claim shortly in a major heresy.

Jesus knew his ministry would be three years. He had much to do and much to tell. His present audience was very localized in space and time. There were no radios, TVs, or tape recorders. His target audience would be the whole world and all generations. His church would be the perfect instrument to overcome time and media limitations. Jesus would establish a church to achieve three major purposes:

First, it would proclaim his good news message to the whole world. His salvation message was universal. The consequences of

Adam's disobedience had negatively affected all mankind. Jesus' obedience to the cross had positively affected all mankind. Forty days after his resurrection, Jesus prepared to return to his father. It was the ascension event. He gathered his remaining eleven apostles and gave them the great command:

> All power in heaven and earth has been given to me. Go, therefore, and make disciples of all nations, baptizing them in the name of the Father, and of the Son, and of the Holy Spirit, teaching them to observe all that I have commanded you. And, behold, I am with you always, until the end of the age. (Mt 28:18–28, NAB)

Ten days later, on Pentecost, the Holy Spirit came. Peter spoke. Three thousand persons became Christians that day.

I've heard that Coca-Cola has a mission statement to make their product available to all inhabitants of the civilized world. This goal cannot be accomplished by sitting in an office in Atlanta, Georgia. While directions come from headquarters, a worldwide organization is needed to accomplish that goal. The goal of Jesus' church was to reach the whole world with his good news message. Its headquarters are in Rome. His church is a worldwide organization.

Second, it would safeguard the Apostolic deposit of faith. These were the eye-witness accounts, writings, and traditions of a living church from that important first century when Jesus and his apostles were at the very beginning of what is today a two-thousand-year-old church. Three of the four Gospel writers were eyewitnesses of his three-year ministry of words and deeds. John, the apostle, died about 100 AD. His writings closed the New Testament scriptures.

Safeguarding the scriptures means not changing them, but with time and challenges from heresies, the church would come to a deeper understanding of what they meant. There have been twenty-one world church councils. The successors of Peter and the apostles (the bishop of Rome and the various bishops) would lead these councils. Working together, they would come to be referred to as the magisterium of the church. Of the magisterium, Christ said, "Whoever listens to you, listens to me. Whoever rejects you, rejects me. And, whoever rejects me, rejects the one who sent me" (Lk 10:16, NAB).

What was learned from each council became important belief foundation stones for the church's deeper understanding of the truths of the Christian message. The church also preserved the important writings of what Jesus did and said and writings by apostles and others that eventually became the New Testament. The church preceded the New Testament writings. The New Testament scriptures contained warnings that safeguarding the apostolic deposit of faith was an absolute necessity against heresies that would follow. Here are some of those warnings:

Jesus said, "Beware of false prophets, who come to you in sheep's clothing, but underneath are ravenous wolves. By their fruits you will know them" (Mt 7:15, NAB). He also said, "Many false prophets will arise and deceive many" (Mt 24:11, NAB). St. Paul wrote, "But even if we or an angel from heaven should preach to you a gospel other than the one we preached to you, let that one be accursed" (Gal 1:8, NAB). Also "And no wonder. For even Satan masquerades as an angel of light. So it is not strange that his ministers also masquerade as ministers of righteousness" (2 Cor 11:14, NAB). These warnings were prophetic. The church has had many heresies trying to change the apostolic deposit of faith right to our present day.

Jesus claimed to be "the truth." He took every precaution in setting up his church so that truth could be communicated to all peoples in all times. Truth doesn't change. That's why the church needed unity in leadership and truth in the message proclaimed. Jesus said,

> "I pray not only for them (apostles), but also those who will believe in me through their word, so that they all may

be one, as you, Father, are in me and I in you, so that they also may believe in us, that the world may believe you sent me." (Jn 17:20–21, NAB)

"I have other sheep that do not belong to this fold. These also I must lead, and they will hear my voice, and there shall be one flock then, one shepherd." (Jn 10:16, NAB)

Thus, Paul wrote, "But if I should be delayed, you should know how to behave in the household of God, which is the Church of the Living God, the pillar and foundation of truth." (1 Tm 3:15, NAB)

Third, the church was to provide the full means of salvation. As a consequence of the fall, two important supernatural gifts to humans were lost—sanctifying grace (man's close relationship with God) and freedom from concupiscence (strong desires of the flesh). Losing these two gifts dealt a serious blow to a person's efforts, unaided, to live in a way that would merit heaven. Jesus gave his church the full means of salvation by providing spiritual aids that would give humans graces for their earthly journey. Graces are "muscle food" for our souls. These graces would help restore the power of the two supernatural gifts lost in the fall. They would get us closer to God (sanctification) and help our battle against sin. The church later would call these aids "sacraments." There are seven. These gifts given by Jesus are what make Jesus' church holy. Statistics put our present life expectancy at seventy-eight years. We are body and soul. We eat three meals a day to provide nourishment for our physical bodies, which will eventually become dust. Our souls will live forever. Our body is temporal. Our soul is eternal. Our souls should rule our bodies.

Jesus brought the kingdom of God to the earth. People who accept him and his claims are part of a community called the mystical body of Christ. They are God's kingdom on earth. To enter this kingdom, Jesus gave his church the following spiritual aids or sacraments.

Baptism. It signifies a rebirth of our spirit, forgiving original sin plus any sins we may have. It is a one-time only sacrament. Early in his ministry, Jesus had said, "No one can enter the kingdom of God without being born again of water and Spirit" (Jn 3:5, NAB). And again, at his ascension, when he commanded the apostles to go and "make disciples of all nations, *baptizing* them in the name of the Father, and of the Son, and of the Holy Spirit'" (emphasis added) (Mt 28:19, NAB). Baptism is referred to as the "gateway" sacrament to the other six. Jesus was looking for disciples, not followers. Disciple comes from the word *discipline.* Jesus wanted disciples who would seriously embrace and spread his message.

Reconciliation. This important sacrament is called confession, penance, or reconciliation. It enables one to regain his peaceful relationship with God, lost through sin. We are at peace with God when we are obedient to his will. We lose that peaceful relationship when we sin. Despite good intentions, sin happens. Remember how the gift of freedom from concupiscence was lost in the fall? Jesus provided a remedy on the evening of his resurrection, giving the apostles the power to forgive sins.

> Jesus said to them again, "Peace be with you. As the Father who sent me, even so I send you." And when he had said this, he breathed on them, and said to them "Receive the Holy Spirit. If you forgive the sins of any, they are forgiven. If you retain the sins of any, they are retained." (Jn 20:21–23, NAB)

The penitent, in the confessional, confesses his sins to the priest after which the priest gives him absolution making the sign of the cross and saying, "I absolve you from your sins, in the name of the Father, and of the Son, and of the Holy Spirit." It is Christ Jesus through the priest who forgives our sins. As the penitent must make restitution or satisfaction for his sins, the priest gives a penance to the forgiven one, usually prayer, fasting, or almsgiving.

I have been doing prison ministry for many years. One year, a psychiatrist was one of the volunteers in our group. Before the Mass begins, the priest hears confessions in a very small room. One day, as the psychiatrist and I watched the relieved faces of penitents as each exited the confessional, the psychiatrist whispered to me, saying, "In my work, I could never get the results that priest is getting in just a few minutes." Confession gives one a wonderful sense of freedom and peace from the burden of sin.

Some people believe we can confess our sins privately to God. In setting up the sacrament of confession, Jesus said, "If you retain the sins of any, they are retained" (Jn 20:23, NAB). This suggests that there are situations when sins may not be forgiven. How would one who confesses directly to God know if his sins have been truly forgiven or have been retained?

Eucharist. The supreme sacrament Jesus gave his church was the Eucharist, which is described in the sixth chapter of John's Gospel. Teaching in a synagogue in Capernaum, Jesus said:

> "Amen, amen, I say to you, unless you eat the flesh of the Son of Man and drink his blood, you do not have life within you. Whoever eats my flesh and drinks my blood has eternal life, and I will raise him on the last day. For my flesh is true food, and my blood true drink. Whoever eats my flesh and drinks my blood remains in me and I in him. Just as the living father sent me and I have life because of the father, so also the one who feeds on me will have life because of me." (Jn 6:53–57, NAB)

He mentioned this four times, and people walked away. At the Last Supper, it all came together: "Then he took the bread, said the blessing, broke it, and gave it to them, saying, 'This is my body, which will be given for you; do this in memory of me'" (Lk 22:19, NAB).

Memory meant to "represent the event." What event? Death on the cross that saved all humanity from the consequences of Adam's sin. The high point of worship in Jesus' church is the reception of the consecrated bread and wine, which is Jesus' body and blood. At the ordained priest's words *this is my body* the substance of bread is replaced with the substance of Jesus' body. And likewise, at the words *this is my blood*, the substance of wine becomes the substance of his blood. This transfer of substances, bread to body and wine to blood is called transubstantiation. There are no signs in the Eucharist proving that he is bodily present. It is a mystery of faith. All external appearances remain as before the consecration. Jesus' church has had many substantiated Eucharistic miracles. The reason we believe is because Jesus, who is God, said so.

The Eucharist is the source of unity for all Catholics in the world. I've been to Mass in different countries, and while I didn't know their language, I knew exactly what was going on. I also knew what the person sitting next to me believed. Peter Kreeft, prolific Catholic author, wrote, "Every detail in the great medieval cathedrals was for the Eucharist. They were built first of all for the Eucharist: to celebrate the Eucharist and to house the Eucharist. Eucharist is the most intimate union between us and Christ that exists in this world."[1]

Confirmation. Confirmation is the sacrament of the Holy Spirit whom Jesus Christ sent. "But I tell you the truth, it is better for you that I go. For if I do not go, the advocate will not come to you, but, if I go, I will send him to you" (Jn 16:7, NAB). Jesus had instructed his Apostles "But you will receive power when the Holy Spirit comes upon you, and you will be my witnesses in Jerusalem, throughout Judea and Samaria, and to the ends of the earth" (Acts 1:8, NAB). At Pentecost, the Apostles were "filled with the Holy Spirit, and began to speak in different tongues, as the spirit enabled them to proclaim" (Acts 2:4, NAB). *The Acts of the Apostles* is often referred to as the Gospel of the Holy Spirit.

At confirmation, the confirmed receives the seven gifts of the Holy Spirit. "A spirit of wisdom and understanding, a spirit of counsel and of strength, a spirit of knowledge and of fear of the Lord, and his life shall be the fear of the Lord" (Is 11:2–3, NAB). The effect of the grace of the sacrament gives the recipient the strength and character to witness for Jesus Christ.

Holy Orders. The sacrament of holy orders began at the Last Supper when Jesus summoned his Apostles to continue the Eucharistic celebration in memory of him. "Do this in memory of me" (Lk 22:19, NAB). Before his ascension event, Jesus had gathered his Apostles together and commissioned them to be his witnesses to the ends of the earth.

> Jesus approached and said to them, "All power in heaven and on earth has been given to me. Go, therefore, and make disciples of all nations, baptizing them in the name of the Father, and of the Son, and of the Holy Spirit, teaching them to observe all that I have commanded you. And behold, I am with you always, until the end of the age." (Mt 28:18–20, NAB)

Popes are successors of Peter, and bishops are the successors of the other Apostles. Priests and deacons provide services for their bishops. Men are ordained to the priesthood in the Catholic and Orthodox churches as the sacrament confers upon the priest the character to act in the person of Christ—*in persona Christi*. It is important to note that Jesus gave these powers to baptize, forgive sins, and preside in the Eucharist, plus the other sacraments *only to the Apostles*. The Apostles themselves, at the proper time, had the authority to transfer these powers to an approved person by the "laying on of hands," such as Paul to Timothy: "Do not neglect the gift you have, which was conferred on you through the prophetic word with the imposition of hands of the presbyterate" (1 Tm 4:14, NAB).

The Old Testament also used this method when Moses transferred the authority given him to Joshua. To this day, priests get their authority to administer the sacraments by the laying on of hands by a bishop. This sacrament is called holy orders. Kreeft says, "Christ is present not just at the origin of the sacraments, two thousand years ago, but really present and active in them now."[2]

Matrimony. The sacrament of marriage is a covenant by which a man and woman establish in the presence of God and his church a lifetime partnership, which by nature is ordered for the good of the spouses and the procreation of children. God established a marriage and blessed it. As is written in Holy Scripture, "God created man in his image, in the divine image he created him; male and female he created them; God blessed them, saying: 'Be fertile and multiply; fill the earth and subdue it" (Gn 1:27–28, NAB).

Genesis also adds, "That is why a man leaves his father and mother and clings to his wife, and the two of them become one body" (Gn 2:24, NAB).

The Trinity revealed this to the inspired sacred author. The second person of the Trinity became Jesus two thousand years ago. It is no wonder then that Jesus made marriage a sacrament. Just when he did so, during his public life, we do not know. Some think that it may have been at the marriage feast at Cana where he performed his first miracle. Others think it may have been at the time Jesus instructed the Pharisees on divorce.

> "Have you not read that from the beginning the Creator made them male and female, and said, 'For this reason a man shall leave his father and mother and be joined to his wife, and the two shall become one flesh'? So, they are no longer two, but one flesh. Therefore, what God has joined together, no human must separate." (Mt 19: 4–6, NAB)

"However, such speculations as to the exact time at which Jesus made marriage a sacrament are rather fruitless. It is enough for us to know, by the constant and unbroken tradition of the Church, that Jesus did so transform the marriage bond."³

Sacrament of the Sick. The anointing of the sick is the sacrament given to seriously ill Christians, and the special graces received unite the sick person to the passion of Christ. While on earth, Jesus healed the blind and the sick, as well as commissioning his Apostles to do so. So they (the twelve Apostles) went off and preached repentance. They drove out many demons, and they anointed with oil many who were sick and cured them (Mk 6:12–13, NAB), and

> "Is anyone among you sick? He should summon the presbyters of the church, and they should pray over him and anoint him with oil in the name of the Lord, and this prayer of faith will save the sick person, and the Lord will raise him up. If he has committed any sins, he will be forgiven." (Jas 5:14–15, NAB)

The effect of this sacrament is incorporation into the healing body of Christ with a spiritual healing of the soul and, at times, the healing of the body. The sacramental grace helps us to accept sickness as a purifying cross sent by God and the grace even to accept death if that is God's will.

Jesus prepared for the establishment of his church. While Jesus was performing miracles and teaching people about life, he would need credible eyewitnesses for all generations and places throughout the world. He handpicked twelve apostles. They were with him daily. It was on-the-job training because when Jesus would return to the Father, they would have the responsibility for managing and fulfilling the purposes of his church, which would need a strong ongoing foundation that would last until his return. Jesus hinted at this in a parable about building your house on rock rather than sand.

> "Everyone who listens to these words of mine and acts on them will be like a wise man who built his house on rock. The rain fell, the floods came, and the winds blew and buffeted the house. But it did not collapse; it had been set solidly on rock" (Mt 7:24, NAB).

Jesus gave his church a strong foundational leadership structure. Jesus said to Simon,

> "And so I say to you, you are Peter, and upon this rock I will build my church, and the gates of the netherworld shall not prevail against it. I will give you the keys to the kingdom of heaven. Whatever you bind on earth shall be bound in heaven; and whatever you loose on earth shall be loosed in heaven." Mt 16:18 (NAB)

This was awesome authority! No king, emperor, or dictator ever received authority like this. With these words, Jesus provided his church with a leadership authority, whose decisions on important church matters, properly exercised, would be recognized and approved in heaven! All would have equal powers, but Peter and his successors would have the primacy because he was the only Apostle who was given "the keys to the kingdom of heaven."

With these words, Jesus promised that his church would never die. The winds of heresies and persecution would never destroy his church. His church would be the new Israel, connected in time and events to the Old Testament. This leadership structure survives to the present day. The present bishop of Rome, Pope Francis I, is the 265th successor of Peter!

Jesus gave his church the continuing presence of the Holy Spirit. Before his ascension, Jesus had given the apostles several important promises about the Holy Spirit, "I have told you this while I am with you. The advocate, the Holy Spirit that the Father will send in my name — he will teach you everything and remind you of all I told you" (Jn 14:25–26, NAB). Ten days after Jesus' ascension back to the father, the Holy Spirit came at an event called Pentecost. Those who accepted his message were baptized, and about 3,000 persons became Christians that day.

Our previous chapter covered the 2,000-year history of Judaism from its founder, Abraham, to the coming of Jesus. This history had fulfilled its purpose, which was to prepare for the coming of Jesus. With the brief but crucial thirty-three-year life of Jesus on earth, salvation history now entered its final stage—the age of the church. It too is now almost two thousand years old!

After the ascension, Jesus was gone. The apostles were now in charge. Blood ran early. Stephen, a deacon, was stoned to death. Present at that gory event was a man named Saul, who looked favorably on what was happening. Saul of Tarsus, a devout Jew, who had been a pupil of the famous rabbi Gamaliel was totally dedicated to the law as the way to salvation. He could see that Christianity had the seeds of doctrinal divergence from Judaism. Saul accepted the task of crushing the Christian movement. He "entered house after house dragging out men and women, and he handed them over for imprisonment" (Acts 8:3, NAB).

Saul, in his zeal, had gone to the high priest asking him for letters to the synagogues that if he should find any men or women who were Christians, he might bring them back to Jerusalem in chains. It was on this journey that an event happened that would soon change the fortunes of the church. Nearing Damascus,

> a light from the sky suddenly flashed around him. He fell on the ground and heard a voice saying to him, "Saul, Saul, why are you persecuting me?" He said, "Who are you, sir?" The reply became, "I am Jesus whom you are persecuting. Now get up and go into the city and you will be told what you must do." Acts 9:3–6, NAB

He was blinded and led by his companions into Damascus. He would regain his sight, be baptized, and become—despite beatings, imprisonments, and shipwrecks—the greatest evangelizer of the early church, establishing Christian communities from Damascus to Rome.

Saul's name was changed to Paul. He was the church's first theologian. Generation after generation of theologians study his deep understanding of the Christian faith. Half of the New Testament was written by him. A great obstacle had become a great blessing. God can do amazing things with "bad" people after they have seen the light.

What did the apostles do? At his ascension, Jesus had commanded his apostles to go to the whole world. But Jesus had an order of priority,

> "You will receive power when the Holy Spirit comes upon you, and you will be my witnesses in Jerusalem, throughout Judea and Samaria, and to the ends of the earth.'" (Acts 1:8, NAB)

They were to go first to the Jews in Jerusalem, Judea, and Samaria, and then to the whole world. They did go first to the Jews in the Holy Land. When they finally started reaching out to the whole world, they had several things working for them. The Romans were organized and built roads connecting the various large cities of the empire. Romans also enforced the peace that provided the whole Mediterranean area with a unity of government, language, and culture. These same roads would soon be paths for spreading the faith.

There were two major languages—Greek in the east and Latin in the west. The Greek went back to the time of Alexander the Great 400 years earlier, who had conquered the then known world and wanted Greek spoken throughout his empire. This made it easier to communicate, especially in the east. The apostles always went first to the great cities located on the trade routes. These would be major cities like Ephesus, Corinth, Philippi, and Rome. They would go first to the Jewish ghettos, which housed descendants of Jews who had been banished from their homeland or had fled for safety because of different Holy Land invasions. Once they had preached to the Jews, the apostles would then reach out to the gentiles in those city or towns.

What did each apostle do? We have the Acts of the Apostles, which was written by St. Luke. But this book does not tell us what each apostle did. Only two apostles are featured: Peter and Paul. There is a brief mention of James, the brother of John, being killed and a story about Philip's evangelization and baptism of an Ethiopian eunuch, a court official of Candace, the queen of the Ethiopians. But for what happened with the others, we have to rely on traditions. These traditions show that ten of the remaining eleven apostles met horrible deaths following the command of Jesus to go to the whole world. John was the only apostle who died a natural death about the year 100 AD. Peter's death by crucifixion upside down, and Paul's beheading in Rome are not mentioned in any scripture but are part of that tradition.

Despite martyrdoms, the church grew, spread throughout the whole of Jerusalem, Judea, and Samaria. It then leaped to Antioch in Syria, which in the first century was the third largest city of the Roman Empire. Tradition says that Peter had been bishop of Antioch for seven years before moving to Rome.

Eventually, reaching out to the gentiles would create a problem that had to be solved. The question was did gentile converts have to become fully Jewish, including male circumcision, in order to become a follower of Jesus? This problem would require a special council in Jerusalem to resolve it. Peter, Paul, and the apostles were present. After much debate, they sent Judas and Silas to deliver this message to the assembly in Antioch:

> "It is the decision of the Holy Spirit, and us, not to place on you any burden beyond these necessities, namely, to abstain from meat sacrificed to idols, from blood, from meat of strangled animals, and from unlawful marriage. If you keep free of these, you will be doing what is right. Farewell." (Acts 15:28–29, NAB)

This removed any Jewish obstacles to obtaining converts. The experiences of Paul, later recorded in Acts, may have served as a catalyst to make the apostles decide it was time to go to the whole world and preach the Gospel. Eusebius, famous early church historian, says that the apostles "divided the world" and set forth to all points of the compass.

In the summer of 64, Rome suffered a terrible fire that burned for six days and seven nights, consuming almost two-thirds of the city. Nero, the emperor, was a lunatic, who fancied himself a great artist. He wanted to destroy drab, old wooden buildings in the working-class district, enjoy the beauty of the flames, and "fiddle while Rome burned" (en wikipedia.org/wiki/nero). That popular expression came from sources who said he had a lute, a primitive fiddle, and was mouthing dribble, trying to rival Homer as a poet in the *Iliad* when Troy burned. Nero wasn't a good man. He killed his mother and an aunt. He had several wives, and he had the first executed. The fourth, he kicked to death.

The fire and the subsequent building of Nero's golden palace on the destroyed property was wildly unpopular in Rome. The people accused the emperor Nero of setting the fire. Needing a scapegoat, he looked for the most unpopular people, who were the Christians. He accused them of setting the fires. Heavy persecutions of Christians began. As part of these persecutions, Peter and Paul were killed in 67 AD, but Nero's persecution only affected the Christians in Rome. Afterward, there was a relative period of calm that the network of churches used to organize and grow.

In 70 AD, the Romans destroyed the temple in Jerusalem. This ended animal sacrifices as a worship ritual for the Jews. The temple and its animal sacrifices have never been restored. When Jesus established the Eucharist as a sacrifice back in 33 AD, animal sacrifices for Jews ran parallel to the Eucharist "bloodless" sacrifice for the Christians. Since 70 AD, the Eucharist has been the sole sacrifice for the Judeo-Christian tradition. Animal sacrifice in the temple ran for about 1,000 years, the Eucharist, almost 2,000.

By 70 AD, all the Apostles were dead except for John, who tradition says lived to the year 100 AD. What would the church do? Jesus was gone. The apostles were gone. Would the preparation and promises Jesus made in establishing his church work? The historical sources let us down. Between the years, 70–90 AD, the sources are silent, but in the early 90s, what emerged was that in every major Christian community (Ephesus, Corinth, Antioch, Philippi, Rome, etc.), the leadership structure was the same. There was a bishop who had presbyters, elders, and deacons to assist him. The bishop had three chief responsibilities. He would preside at the Eucharist, preach the Gospel, and settle disputes when they arose. The original apostles had no spatial limitations, but as apostolic authority was transferred from the apostles to successors, these successors would have territorial limitations. The church borrowed a word from the Roman Empire to describe these limited areas. The word was *diocese*, and to this day, that designation has remained.

In 96 AD, Clement was the fourth bishop of Rome. He wrote a letter to the church at Corinth, occasioned by a dispute in their church, which had led to the ejection of several presbyters from their office. Their dismissal was regarded by Clement as high-handed, unjustifiable, and a revolt of the younger members of the community. It is interesting that in 96 AD, the bishop of Rome was exercising his prerogative as successor to Peter. He was commanding, in a gentle and fatherly way, the members of the church at Corinth to reinstate the presbyters whom they had removed without authority. John the Apostle was still alive, living in Ephesus, which was a lot closer to Corinth than Rome was. He was the only remaining apostle with the apostolic authority to go anywhere. He didn't. Was it because he recognized the primacy of Peter's office, or was he just too old? "It is interesting that it shows the fourth pope interfering to put another apostolic church in order."[4] This letter was circulated to all the churches and almost made it into the New Testament.

Another important letter in the progression of the church history was written in 106 AD. The Romans had captured Ignatius, the bishop of Antioch, and were taking him as a prisoner to Rome to put him with the wild beasts in the coliseum. He was allowed by his captors to meet with Christian communities along the route to Rome. He wrote six "thank you" letters to those communities as he neared Rome. In one of the letters was the earliest use of the word *Catholic* to describe the church of Peter. "Wherever the bishop shall appear, there the multitude of the people also be; even as, wherever Jesus Christ is, there is the Catholic Church."[5] Catholic means "universal"—the everywhere church.

Jesus had given his church a command to spread his good news of salvation to the whole world. Two major obstacles arose to seriously challenge fulfillment of that goal— Roman emperors and heresies.

Within thirty-seven years of Jesus' departure, his message had reached the key population areas along the Mediterranean of Rome, Africa, Spain, and India. It was inevitable that this sudden worldwide (at the time) growth would attract the notice of the imperial powers. The empire was worldwide. The church was worldwide. Emperors feared that in secrecy, under the pretext of divine worship, Christians could plan a rebellion. In addition, emperors were getting complaints from livestock dealers because Christianity was hurting their business. Livestock dealers' biggest customers were the different pagan temples where animals were sacrificed. As Christianity grew, the livestock dealers' customers dwindled.

Religions normally have three parts—what they believe, a code of conduct, and a worship ritual. Pagan religions had only the third part. They might believe in gods or goddesses or mythological ones like Aphrodite, Venus, and Ishtar. Pagans believed that the powers of nature could be hostile. For example, you can drink and bathe in water, but, you can also drown in it. Fire is good for cooking and keeping warm, but it can burn your house down. The sun gives us light and warmth, but it could cause drought and famine. These pagan religions wanted to appease these gods, so they sacrificed animals to them to keep the gods on their side.

After Nero, there would be ten separate Roman persecutions, extending from the late first century to 312 AD, trying to destroy Christianity. These persecutions were identified with the name of the emperor who was promoting the persecution. There would be times of peace, creating an ebb and flow of one escalating persecution. Here are some of the worst.

Domitian (81–96). According to many historians, Christians were heavily persecuted toward the end of Domitian's reign. He was the first of the emperors to deify himself during his lifetime by assuming the title of "Lord" and "God." The book of Revelation was written during his reign when many of the Christians had already perished with more to follow. Rome, "the great Babylon" was drunk with the blood of saints and martyrs of Jesus (Rv 17:5–6, NAB).

Trajan (98–117). Between 109–111, Emperor Trajan sent Pliny the younger to the province of Bythynia as governor. Pliny encountered Christians, and he wrote to the emperor about them.

> I considered that I should dismiss any who denied that they were, or ever had been Christians, once they had repeated after me a formula of invocation to the gods, and had made offerings of wine and incense to your statue, and, furthermore, they had to curse the name of Christ.[6]

The governor then indicated that he had ordered an execution of several Christians. However, he was unsure what to do about those who said they were no longer Christians.

Trajan responded that Christians should not be sought out. Anonymous tips should be rejected as "unworthy of our times" and if Christians recanted and "worshiped our gods," they were to be freed. If not, the punishment of death should follow. The emperor issued an edict to all governors, saying that anyone who identifies someone as a Christian, cannot do it anonymously. The Christian must be arrested and brought to the tribunal. Here he would be given a test. He must sacrifice to the pagan gods. If he did, he was released. If not, he would be killed. Trajan's most distinguished martyr was Ignatius of Antioch, whom we mentioned earlier.[7]

Marcus Aurelius (161–180). Marcus considered the Christian doctrine of the immortality of the soul, with its moral consequence, as vicious and dangerous to the welfare of the state. A law was passed under his reign punishing with exile everyone who should try to influence people's minds by fear of the divinity. The law was aimed at Christians. Marcus's reign was a stormy time for the church, although the persecutions cannot be directly traced to him. The law of Trajan was sufficient to justify the severest measures against the founders of the "forbidden religion." Later, there is a record of a "new decree" making it easier for Christians to be accused and have their property confiscated.[8]

Septimus Severus (193–211). The church was gaining power and making many converts. This led to popular anti-Christian feelings and persecutions in Carthage, Alexandria, Corinth, and Rome between 202–210. In 202, Septimus enacted a law prohibiting the spread of Christianity and Judaism. This was the first universal decree forbidding conversions to Christianity. Violent persecutions broke out in Egypt and North Africa. The famed Perpetua, a noblewoman, and Felicitas, her slave, were martyred during this time. They held hands and exchanged a kiss before being thrown to wild animals at a public festival.[9]

Decius (249–251). The reign of the Emperor Decius brought the most organized persecution to date of Christians across the empire. Its purpose was to stamp out Christianity as an assault on Roman traditions. All Christians were ordered to worship the

Roman gods by offering a pinch of incense before a statue and eating sacrificial meat. Many persecutions arose against the name of Christ, causing a great slaughter of believers. The writings of Cyprian, bishop of Carthage, explain how it was carried out. He wrote that the persecution under Decius was the first universal and organized persecution of Christians, and it would have lasting significance for the Christian church. In January of 250, Decius issued an edict requiring all citizens to offer sacrifice to the emperor in the presence of a Roman official and to obtain a certificate (*libellus*) proving they had done so. Forty-four of these certificates survive. Here's one:

> To the officers in charge of the sacrifices
> of the village of Alexander's Isle,
> from Aurelius Diogenes,
> the son of Satabus, of the village
> of Alexander's Isle, aged about 72,
> with a scar on his right eyebrow.
> I have always sacrificed to the gods;
> And now in your presence, according
> To the commands,
> I have sacrificed and made a libation
> And tasted of the victims;
> And I desire you to subscribe.
> Fare ye well. (June 26, 250)
>
> —http://www.earlychurchtexts.com/publiclibellus_from_time_of_decius.htm

In general, public opinion condemned the public violence and admired the martyrs' passive resistance, and the Christian movement was thereby strengthened. Tertullian, noted church apologist, said, "The blood of martyrs is the seed of the church."[10] The Decian persecution ceased in 251, a few months before his death. The Decian persecution had lasting repercussions for the church. How should those who had bought a certificate or actually sacrificed be treated? It seems in most churches those who had lapsed were accepted back in the fold. A century and a half later, Augustine would battle with an influential group called the Donatists, who broke away from the Catholic church because the church had accepted those who lapsed.

Valarian (253–260). Under the Emperor Valarian, nobles were forbidden to join the church. Church leaders were compelled to acknowledge the pagan gods or face death. The most savage phase of his persecutions and, perhaps of all early persecutions, began in 257. Imprisonment, torture, loss of property, exile, and reduction to forced labor and chains were the punishments. In 258, the punishment became death. Pope Sixtus II was beheaded, and the great theologian, St. Cyprian, was martyred. Valarian himself, though in his sixties, led the imperial legions in the east. Incompetent, he surrendered to the Persians. The Persian king Sapor kept him as a slave, using him as a step to mount his horse. When Valarian died, Sapor stuffed him as a trophy.[11]

Diocletian (284–311). The last major persecution of Christians occurred under Diocletian, and it was the worst of all. It is known as the Great Persecution. He published the edicts of 303–304, which ordered the burning of scriptures, destroying of churches, enforcement of sacrifices to the pagan gods, execution of clergy who refused to submit, and the depriving of noble citizens of their rights as Roman citizens. The edicts eventually outlawed Christianity entirely under pain of death.[12] The Diocletian persecution turned out to be extremely violent. It became the most detailed, forceful, and coherent plan for the extermination of the church. *Encyclopedia Britannica* writes that it "did not succeed in annihilating Christianity but caused the faith of the martyrs to blaze forth instead." Diocletian seems to have relented as he approached his own deathbed. He ordered the discontinuation of his aggressive policy, if only Christians would pray to their God in his behalf.[13] Diocletian's most important reform was to divide the empire's administration between an Augustus of the west and one of the east, each supported by a Caesar. He also divided Rome's provinces into a system of dioceses, which would be inherited in the fullness of time by the Catholic Church with the decline of the empire.[14]

Galerius (303–311). Galerius had been the Caesar for Diocletian before becoming Augustus of the east. He had a bitter hatred of the Christians and encouraged Diocletian in the persecution of the Christian sect. The persecution of the Christians raged in the east as they were hunted down like wild beasts from one end of the empire to the other. Galerius died of a horrible disease during which he was filled with remorse for his cruelties to the Christians. He entreated Christian prayers and stopped the persecutions. It is interesting that the last two savage Roman emperors repented as they approached their deathbeds begging prayers from the very Christians they had persecuted.

Emperor Constantine (306–337). Roman persecutions would end with Emperor Constantine. These persecutions were the backdrop of the challenges the church had to face during its first three hundred years. In 311, Constantine became emperor of the west. He and Emperor Licinius in the east agreed that the persecutions should stop. A general edict of religious toleration was issued in Constantine's Edict of Milan in 313. You could no longer persecute or kill Christians. Pope Miltiades, thirty-first successor of Peter, was the pope. Twenty-six of his predecessors had been martyred in the persecutions. Jesus' promise that "the gates of hell would never prevail against his church" had been kept. We'll come back to Constantine shortly and see what happened after 313 AD when the persecutions stopped. The reason for the interruption is to catch up with heresy challenges that were active during the Roman persecutions.

Heresies challenged the authority of the apostolic deposit of faith.

> Without Rome's central authority, it might have been impossible for the church to defeat the early heresies. One of the first organized assaults, in the late first century, came from the Gnostics, who promised a specialized "higher" knowledge that would offer the elect-few who could understand its mysteries—the promise of salvation. The secret knowledge held by the Gnostics was supposed to be the ultimate distillation of the truth of every religion, Christianity included.
>
> —H. W. Crocker,
> *Triumph*, (Roseville, CA: Prima Publishing, 2001), 39

The church responded by dismissing gnosticism for what it was—esoteric theorizing, appealing to human vanity. The church affirmed *"that faith is not a thing to be refashioned by any human intelligence, but something to be safeguarded by the church's authority against any refashioning."*[15] (Emphasis added)

Among the early heretics were the Marcionites. They held that the God of the Old Testament was incompatible with the message of Jesus. Marcion rejected the Jewish Bible. He compiled his own, consisting mostly of Paul's letters, heavily edited. He had his own church with many adherents. Then there were the Docetists, who denied Jesus was a man; and the Theodotians, who denied Jesus was God. The important point to grasp is that heresy has been a challenge to the church from the beginning, and though they have been defeated, they never truly go away.[16]

Irenaeus against heresies (180). Irenaeus had been a disciple of Bishop Polycarp, who had been a disciple of John, who wrote the fourth Gospel. So Irenaeus had a direct pipeline to what happened in the church from its very beginnings. His most famous work, *Against Heresies,* is an anti-gnostic treatise in five books, fully preserved. In it, Irenaeus teaches that there is no secret doctrine apart from the rule of faith, publicly handed down and guaranteed by the continuous succession of bishops. In response to heresies that were happening, he had this to say:

> We must obey the elders in the church, who hold their succession from the apostles...who with the Episcopal succession have received the sure grip of truth. As for the rest, who are divorced from the principal succession and gather where they will, they are to be held in suspicion, as heretics and evil thinkers, faction makers, swell-headed and self-pleasing.
>
> —Irenaeus, *Adversus Heresus*, IV 26, 2

In other words, Catholics (members of the universal church to which St. Ignatius, in 107 AD, gave Catholics their name), were to be submissive to church authority, teaching, and tradition and to be stubborn in defense of it. Certainly, by the second century, as noted by H. W. Crocker III in his previously quoted book, *Triumph*:

> Rome was recognized as the plumb line to keep Christianity straight. Without Rome's central authority, it might have been impossible for the church to defeat early heresies.
>
> The belief in objective authority...based on the testimony of the apostles, and guarded by the veneration of tradition...has made the historic faith of the Catholic Church, and kept it alive and triumphant through persecutions, schisms, wars, and rumors of wars...outlasting every empire, constitution, and philosophy born of man.
>
> —Crocker, *Triumph*, 33

Irenaeus, with his link to the beginning church, also listed the first thirteen bishops of Rome. Incidentally, Peter's successors would later be called popes, which means "papa" in Latin. In earlier centuries, the title was used for any bishop in the west and in the east for priests as well. In 1073, Pope Gregory VII formally prohibited its use for all except the bishop of Rome.

Constantine came on the scene in 312. In a way, it was like the parable Jesus told about the Good Samaritan, who stopped to help heal an enemy of his people, who had been beaten and left for dead. Constantine stopped the killing of Christians and helped heal a beaten and battered church.

Who was Constantine, and why did he do it? Constantine was born about 273 AD from a one-night stand in Serbia between a young army officer Flavius Constantius and an innkeeper's daughter named Helena. Nine years later, Flavius became governor of Dalmatia, where unknown to him, his son Constantine was growing up. When two Roman soldiers hit the young boy for annoying their horses, Helena rebuked them, saying that they had struck the governor's son. As proof, she produced Flavius's military cloak. The soldiers reported the incident. When Constantius heard about this, he married Helena and was reunited with his son.

When Diocletian was emperor, he had divided the empire into two, east and west. He gave the west to his friend, Maximian. Constantine's father, Constantius, was appointed Caesar (junior emperor). That meant that he would inherit the title of emperor of the west when Maximian died or stepped down. In 303, Diocletian and Maximian abdicated, and a battle began as to who should succeed them. There was all-out civil war. When Constantius died soon afterward in 306, the troops hailed Constantine as the new Augustus.

One of his challengers would be a man named Maxentius, who was also Constantine's brother-in-law. In 312, the showdown battle was to be at the Milvian Bridge in Rome. The night before the battle, Constantine had his soldiers paint crosses on their shields. There are various stories as to why. One was that Constantine claimed that the night before the battle, he saw in the sky a cross with writing in Latin underneath: "*In hoc signo vinces,*" which means "in this sign conquer." Constantine won and was now the emperor of the west. Christians became his friends. One of his first official acts after the Milvian Bridge battle was to give the bishop of Rome the Lateran Palace as his official residence.

The following year, 313, Constantine signed the Edict of Milan, which gave religious toleration for all citizens of the empire. He convinced Licinius, his emperor counterpart in the east, to also agree. Several years later, Licinius broke his promise and resumed persecutions. In 324, Constantine brought an army emblazoned with Christian banners and defeated Licinius and, after a short period, had him executed. Now Constantine was the head of the whole Roman empire.

Council of Nicaea (325). Twelve years after Christians were free, a major heresy erupted. This time, it was within the church. Arius, a priest in Alexandria, Egypt, had been teaching for several years that Jesus was not God. He was a good man, the best God ever created, but he wasn't God. His bishop, Alexander, told him that although he was a brilliant man, his explanations were difficult to follow, and that what he was teaching was not what had been passed down to him from the beginning of the church.[17] The bishop told Arius to stop. Arius continued to teach and was excommunicated.

There was turmoil in the empire with good men on both sides of the issue. Emperors don't like turmoil. Constantine told Pope Sylvester (314–335) to call a council at the emperor's summer palace in Nicaea to resolve the issue. Over three hundred bishops attended. The pope didn't attend. He was old and sickly, but he sent two legates to represent his office to make the council official. The result was the Nicene Creed, named for the city. In the part related to Jesus' divinity, it says:

> We believe in one God, the Father Almighty, maker of heaven and earth, of all that is seen and unseen. We believe in one Lord, Jesus Christ, the only Son of God, eternally begotten of the Father, God from God, Light from Light, true God from true God, begotten, not made, one in Being with the Father. Through him all things were made.
>
> —Thomas D. McGonigle and James F. A. Quigley, *A History of the Christian Tradition, Volume I* (Mahweh, NJ: The Paulist Press, 1988), 100–101

The authority given by Jesus to Peter and the apostles was now being exercised by their successors to settle this most important question. The vote was 316-2 for the creed. But was it settled? On the day after the signing, three eastern bishops of Nicaea, Nicomedia, and Chalcedon, revoked their signatures condemning Arius. They were promptly banished, and the emperor replaced them.

In 328, the bishop of Alexandria, Egypt, died. Athanasius, his advisor, became bishop. That same year, Constantine recalled the three bishops who had been banished and reinstated them. Why? What we do know is that Eusebius, the bishop of Nicomedia, would, until his death in 341, be the leading figure in trying to undo the work of Nicaea. His actions would unsettle the Nicene Creed for over fifty years.

Eusebius never attacked the work of Nicaea directly. His strategy was to destroy the leading bishops who had supported *Homoousios*, meaning that Jesus was of the same substance as God the Father, which meant that Jesus was equal to the Father, therefore, truly God. The word *homoousios* had a bad history. A nonbiblical term, it had been used in the previous century in a controversial and heretical way. Eusebius's plea was that these bishops were heretics.

His first victim was the bishop of Antioch, Eustathius, who may have presided at Nicaea. A carefully chosen council of bishops met at Antioch, condemned and deposed him. The emperor followed up with exile. Nine other bishops were similarly removed (330–332). The Arian party began to go after Athanasius, concocting all kinds of charges trying to discredit him.

Founding of Constantinople (330). Rome was the capital of Constantine's empire. Its physical location, at the western extremity of his empire, had serious control disadvantages. His ships had no direct access to control the lands bordering the Mediterranean. There was a much more strategic location for control of his empire. It was called Byzantium. Centrally located, with access to the Mediterranean, he would make this the new Rome. He changed its name to Constantinople to honor himself. Today, it is called Istanbul. This move would eventually cause a major problem for the church.

There were four important church centers: Jerusalem, Alexandria, Antioch, and Rome. Constantine wanted Constantinople to be number one because its capital had been moved from old Rome to New Rome. The church said no. Constantinople would eventually settle for number two as a fifth church center. In time, it would split the church into a Greek east and a Latin west. Constantine died in 337. Now what will happen? Before he died, Constantine began to do strange things. He was arranging to bring the excommunicated Arius back into the church. On the day, Arius was happily making his way to the re-induction ceremonies, he became violently ill on the street, went into a public rest room, and died. Constantine also exiled Athanasius, bishop of Alexander, in 336. Athanasius had been a great hero for the church in the fight against Arianism. His enemies had tried to discredit him, having him exiled five times. Constantine seemed to be moving closer to the Arian position. When Constantine learned that baptism takes away all your sins, he always had a priest nearby until the day he was on his deathbed. In this way, he could continue to live a loose moral life until it was time to die. He was baptized on his deathbed by an Arian bishop.

Upon Constantine's death, five relatives divided the empire. Three were his sons. With greed for power, this was a certain recipe for bloodshed. In a short time, two were eliminated. His three sons remained, splitting the empire three ways. Here's the surviving lineup:

1. Constantine II, a firm Catholic and the church's strong hope. In the West, he ruled Britain, France, and Spain;

2. Constans, also Catholic and subordinate to his elder brother. He ruled Italy and North Africa; and
3. Constantius II, an Arian. He ruled in the east.

Who would survive?

Constantine II decided he would conquer Italy while Constans was busy fighting barbarians on the Danube. Constans heard about it and cleverly had his brother ambushed and killed by archers. Two key players now remained—Constans the Catholic in the west and Constantius II the Arian in the east. Constans was weak. Constantius II took his legions west and crushed Constans and became the sole emperor of the east and the west. The last emperor left standing was the only pro-Arian among them. St. Jerome wrote a famous comment that the whole world woke one morning, lamenting, and marveling to find itself Arian. Things looked black for Jesus' church and the Nicene Creed.

The year was 350, Constantius II would rule for eleven years. The anti-Nicene radicals could now take off their masks. They had control. Arianism was not popular with the people, but it was with the schools and theologians. This would be Constantius's first thrust on the bishops of the west. Bishops gave up wholesale, fearing the consequences. Eventually Constantius died and was baptized by an Arian. Some years before his death, a partial blood relative of Constantine came into the picture. His name was Julian.

Julian, the Apostate (361–363). Julian was the son of Constantine's half-brother, Julius Constantius, whose killing had been ordered by Constantine's sons to avoid future family rivalries after their father's death. Julian was a bright man, showing promise. Constantius II had appointed him Caesar of the west to fight the barbarians. Eventually Julian's troops would declare him Augustus of the west. Constantius asked him to resign. He wouldn't. Constantius put together an army and set off to remove him by force. On the way, Constantius died. Julian was now the last remaining royal blood member of Constantine's male descendants.

Julian always hated his cousins for having killed his father. They were Christians, so he hated Christianity. This helped nurture a desire to restore the honor of the old pagan gods against the church, replacing Christianity and Arianism. In doing this, he earned the name Julian, the apostate. Now the whole world would awake to find the pagan gods returning to imperial favor and religious supremacy.[18]

Julian encouraged popular pagan resentment to end Christianity's status as the official imperial religion. Constantine's policy of state support for Christian clerics was revoked so that Christians were now obliged to repay what they had previously received. Julian's attempt at reviving paganism was a failure. He met his end in battle in the always turbulent east, fighting the Persians. He had been so involved in trying to undo Christianity during his two-year rule that some sources say his last words were, "Galilean, thou hast triumphed." Jovian, a Catholic, won a battlefield promotion to emperor.

Jovian (363–364). Jovian restored Constantine's laws, including the Edict of Milan, insuring religious tolerance for pagans and Christians. He returned the aged and exiled Athanasius to his bishop's post in Alexandria from where he would never be banished again and in which post he would serve another ten years. Jovian, however, served only nine months before dying in his sleep at the age of thirty-three. How he died remains a matter of dispute.[19]

Valentinian I (364–375). Though openly Catholic, Valentinian was adamant about ruling with religious impartiality, granting benefits equally to pagans and Catholics alike. His statement on the Arian versus Catholic controversy was, "I am a layman. It is no business of mine to scrutinize Christian dogma. That's the bishop's affair."[20] Valentinian was emperor of the west. He appointed his brother Valens as emperor of the east. This increased the cultural divide between the east and the west because Valens supported the Arian cause. Valens's most famous atrocity occurred when eighty Catholic bishops and priests came to him, petitioning for tolerance. He assembled them on a ship, sent it out to sea, and set it afire. His own death came in a war against the barbarians in 378. In the west, Gratian succeeded Valentinian.

Gratian (367–383). With Theodosius in the east, Gratian stamped the Christian religion firmly and forever in the empire. He was sixteen years old. He abolished all the pagan privileges from the state without persecutions. Gratian was guided by St. Ambrose, the great doctor of the church and bishop of Milan. After Gratian was killed trying to put down rebellious legions in Gaul, Ambrose became religious advisor to his eventual successor, Valentinian II. The new emperor dabbled in Arianism but returned with Ambrose's influence to the Catholic faith.

Ambrose (339–397). In the late 300s, Ambrose was a governor in northern Italy and a very popular political figure. There was a deep conflict in the diocese of Milan between Catholics and Arians. In 374, the bishop of Milan, Auxentius, an Arian, died and the Arians were concerned about who would be his successor. As governor, Ambrose went to the church where the election was to take place. His concern was to help prevent any riots, which could happen. His opening address was interrupted by a call, "Ambrose, bishop!" which became the cry of the whole assembly. At first, he strongly refused acceptance of an office, for which he was in no way prepared. To refuse was to risk inciting the mob to riot. He reluctantly accepted. He was not baptized and not trained in theology. In fact, he was still a catechumen. Within a week, he was baptized, ordained, and duly consecrated bishop of Milan.

Using his excellent knowledge of Greek, he studied the Hebrew Bible and some Greek authors. He applied this knowledge as preacher, concentrating especially on the Old Testament. This knowledge and his oratorical abilities impressed Augustine of Hippo, who until then had a poor opinion of scriptures and Christian preachers. In confrontation with Arians, Ambrose sought to theologically refute their propositions, which he considered heretical. Ambrose also guided the thought of the greatest emperor since Constantine, Theodosius, the august of the east, and finally of all the empire.

Theodosius (379–395). Theodosius dealt the deathblow to paganism and the Arian heresy. He was Catholic and made sure when he was baptized that the ceremony was performed by an orthodox Catholic bishop. Heretical churches were restored to the Catholic faith. Pagan practices, including witchcraft, were officially outlawed. In the fifty-five years from Nicaea to Emperor Theodosius, there had been Catholic emperors, but none had the ability or the will to get the Nicene Creed nailed down. Theodosius did. He initiated a church council.

Theodosius called for the Council of Constantinople in 381, with mostly eastern bishops in attendance. Philip Hughes, author of *The Church in Crisis*, points out that this council was

> summoned primarily as a solemn demonstration of the unshaken loyalty of the Eastern bishops to the faith as set forth at Nicaea, a demonstration that the church of the East had never gone over to Arianism; that the Arians were no more than a heretical faction; had never been anything more, despite their power…and were now finally discredited.
>
> —Philip Hughes, *The Church in Crisis,*
> *A Popular History of the Catholic Church*,
> (Garden City, NY: Hanover House), 37

At this council, a question was raised concerning the divinity of the Holy Spirit. Was the Holy Spirit divine? Was the Holy Spirit of the same substance as the Father or merely like the Father and the Son? The bishops added the phrase, "We believe in the Holy Spirit, the Lord and giver of life, who proceeds from the Father, who with the Father and the Son is worshiped and glorified."[21] This seemed to finalize the creed. It was now referred to as the Nicene-Constantinopolitan Creed, recited every Sunday, by standing congregations in every Catholic Church around the world. For short, it is called the Nicene Creed.

But it still wasn't in its present form. Three little words were missing. Those three words *and the Son* were added in 589 AD to show that the Holy Spirit proceeds from the Father and the Son. Those three words are called the *filioque* and would eventually be one of the main causes for the division of the western and eastern church that continues today. Crocker writes:

> That the Holy Spirit came from both the Father and the Son was traditional Christian belief. What made it controversial was its insertion by the Roman Church into the Nicene Creed in order to make the point clear to the newly converted tribes to the West. Even in Rome, the insertion was controversial, as it meant a change in the established formula. It was accepted, however, because it clarified Church doctrine, rather than altered it.
>
> —Crocker, *Triumph*, 115

From this council came four canons. The third was quite interesting. It said that the bishop of Constantinople shall have the primacy of honor after the bishop of Rome because Constantinople is "new Rome." It acknowledged that Rome had the primacy. Previously, Constantinople wanted to be number one. This claim was denied by Rome. It was pointed out that papal authority rested on scriptural and apostolic grounds, not because Rome was "the imperial city."

However, the real target of the eastern Bishops was not Rome, but Alexandria, Egypt, which was traditionally second in precedence to Rome. Most interesting was that Rome and Egypt had not been invited to this local council, yet it is considered one of the twenty-one general church councils. In its final form, it officially became known as the Nicene-Constantinopolitan Creed. In short, it is called the Nicene Creed.

In 394, Catholic Christianity's every opponent within the empire had been subdued by the emperor's sword. However, one famous incident occurred during the reign of Theodosius. In 390, a Roman general was killed by a mob in Thessalonica. The mob was incensed because the officer had jailed their favorite charioteer. Theodosius ordered a swift punishment on the city. The Thessalonians were called, in the name of the emperor, to the circus where they missed their hero. A detachment of soldiers recruited from barbarian tribes plunged their swords in the unsuspecting crowd, killing about seven thousand Thessalonians.

> St. Ambrose, the confessor of emperors, would not let Theodosius escape responsibility for this. In a letter, the Saint told the emperor that his hands were stained with blood; that he had no place before Christ's altar; that he was unworthy, in his current state of sin, to receive the body of Christ in the Eucharist, and that he should commit himself to a regimen of prayer to make a beginning of his penance.
>
> Theodosius appeared in Ambrose's Church in Milan, stripped of all symbols of imperial power, begging forgiveness, which was granted him after a penitential period of 8 months. The 4th century, which opened with Diocletian's anti-Christian persecutions, closed with their mighty, warlike successor to the imperial purple prostrating himself in penance before a saintly bishop.
>
> —Crocker, *Triumph*, 74

Ambrose had enforced his position that the emperor was not *above* the church but within it and, thus, subject to its discipline. Ambrose turned out to be one of the most influential ecclesiastical figures in the early church, being considered one the four original doctors of the church. Doctors were early church fathers with extraordinary achievements.

New Testament Canon

We close out the first four hundred years of the church with the final selection of the twenty-seven books of the New Testament. In the Council of Rome in 382, these were the books that made the final cut. In 393, the Council of Hippo, reaffirmed this listing. And in 397, the Council of Carthage reaffirmed it again. The church once again exercised its power "to bind and loose."

Msgr. George Agius wrote:

> The great persecutions of the first three centuries had one good effect. They confirmed the divinity of the Church. Hell and heresy had gone their limit to uproot from the earth the tree which Jesus Christ and the apostles had planted and sprinkled with their blood. The combination of evil forces was so formidable that the Church would have succumbed were it not that it is the work of God. The victory of the Church, however, was so complete that peace was at last granted to her throughout the whole Roman Empire. The Cross surmounted the temples of the false Gods.
>
> —Msgr. George Agius, *Tradition and the Church,* (Rockford, IL: Tan Books and Publishers, Inc., 2005), 176

As the church completed its first four hundred years of existence, Anastasius I (399–401), the thirty-eighth successor of Peter, was its leader.

Notes

1. Peter Kreeft, *The Luke E. Hart Series Basic Elements of the Catholic Faith*, Part Three, Section Four of "Catholic Christianity," (New Haven, CT: The Knights of Columbus, 2001), 7.
2. http://www.servantofchrist.info/apologetics-church.php.
3. http://www.beginningcatholic.com.
4. Joseph Brusher, S.J., *Popes Through the Ages*, (New York, NY: D. Van Nostrand & Company, 1959), 8.
5. Ignatius, *Apologeticus*, Carthage, 197.
6. http://www.mesace.edu/~thoqh49081/handouts/pliny.html.
7. Ibid.
8. John J. Burke, *Characteristics of the Early Church*, (Baltimore, MD: McCormick Press, 2008), 101.
9. http://en.wickipedia.org/wiki/Persecution-of-Christians-en.
10. http://www.servantofchrist.info/apologetics-church.php.
11. H. W. Crocker III, *Triumph*, (Roseville, CA: Prima Publishing, 2001), 39.
12. Ibid, 40.
13. http://www.unrv.com.
14. Crocker, *Triumph*, 40.
15. Philip Hughes, *The Church in Crisis, A Popular History of the Catholic Church*, (Garden City, NY: Hanover House), 37.
16. Crocker, *Triumph*, 32.
17. Rev. Marvin O'Donnell, *Two Critical Moments in Church History* (audiovisual, AMCN 31463-31474 Group), (Notre Dame, IN: International Catholic University, Lecture Series, 1997).
18. Crocker, *Triumph*, 65.
19. Ibid, 70-71.
20. Hughes, *The Church in Crisis*, 224.
21. McGonigle and Quigley, *A History of the Christian Tradition, Volume 1* 101.

Jesus' Church

400–800 AD

The church has had some great leaders and teachers in its two-thousand-year history. One of the greatest was St. Augustine.

St. Augustine (354–430)

Augustine was born November 13, 354, in North Africa to Monica, a Christian. At eighteen, he took a concubine. Faithful for the next fifteen years, he had a son in 373. A scholar with a restless mind, Augustine explored every philosophical school. As a young man, he was finally considering his mother's Christianity. His attitude was, "Give me chastity, but not yet!" Augustine objected to the Bible. To read it was only to prove its absurdity. But the great St. Ambrose told him it was not to be read literally but symbolically. Reading the Bible under Ambrose's sophisticated guidance brought Augustine closer to Christianity, but it was not enough. He said, "I wanted to be just as certain about things I could not see as I was certain that seven plus three make ten."[1]

Augustine, deeply influenced by Ambrose, finally decided to join the church of his mother. In 387, he was baptized by Ambrose at Easter in the same year Augustine's mother died. Abandoning his profession as a teacher of rhetoric, Augustine eventually returned to his African home, which today is Tunisia.

One of the best-educated Christians of his day, he soon was prevailed upon to become a priest. He was consecrated bishop at the nearby town of Hippo in 395. The last thirty-five years of his life were spent there, writing *Confessions* (397–401), which is considered as one of the most famous books of western literature, "and one of the most profound and emotional examinations of conscience."[2]

The other famous book written by Augustine is the *City of God*, which he considered his masterpiece. It was begun by him in 412 and was completed in 427. It began in response to charges arising from Alaric's sack of Rome in 410. Pagans alleged that Rome had fallen because the pagan imperial religion had been discontinued. Augustine replied that the rise and fall of empires was nothing unusual in the course of human history.

> In the book, Augustine argued that during our time on earth, the Christian inhabits two realms, the earthly city and the heavenly city. To each of these realms the Christian has duties, but they are not the same duties. The Christian gives his ultimate devotion to the heavenly city. Claims of the earthly city are limited. There is a sanctuary of conscience inside every person that is protected from political control, and that kings and emperors, however grand, cannot usurp authority that rightfully belongs to God.
>
> —D'Souza, *What's So Great About Christianity*, 48–49

Three important heresies arose in Augustine's lifetime, and he played a crucial role in addressing each.

Manichaeism

During his twenties, Augustine had sought religious guidance in the strange teaching of the Persian prophet, Mani (216–276). To the Manichees, the material world was the creation of the powers of evil, and procreation was to be shunned. Augustine taught the opposite—the goodness of the creator and of creation. Marriage was a positive good, and that even if virginity is a higher ideal, married persons may be more virtuous than their celibate counterparts. Further, he taught that the origin of evil is not to be located in a mystic realm of eternal darkness but is to be found in the perversity of the individual created will, which freely turns away from God.[3]

Donatism

Upon Augustine's ordination to the priesthood, he became immediately involved in the Donatist controversy, a dispute of long-standing in the African church. The Donatists argued that the consecration of Caecilian, as bishop of Carthage, was invalid because one of the bishops consecrating him had handed over scriptures to the Roman persecutors.

> Donatists insisted that the sacraments, especially baptism and ordination, were valid only if the ministers of them were free of sin. Against this rigorist view of the church as a society of the pure, Augustine argued that the sacraments belong to Christ and his church, and that, as such, their validity does not depend upon the holiness of the minister, who may in any event have secret sins impossible to know, and that the church is a mixed body of sinners, some progressing toward holiness, some lapsing always. In 412, Donatists were declared heretical.
> —Richard P. McBrien, general ed.,
> *HarperCollins Encyclopedia of Catholicism,*
> (San Francisco, CA: HarperSanFrancisco, 1995), 116

Pelagianism

Pelagianism was a major heresy in 411. Pelagius, a British monk, denied original sin, believing that faith alone is sufficient for salvation. With these ideas, the logic of Christianity began to unravel. By denying original sin, he necessarily cast doubt on the sacrament of baptism, on the practice of prayer, perhaps even on the role of priesthood and, most fundamentally, on the redemptive nature of Christ's sacrifice.

When informed of Pelagius's ideas, Augustine responded,

> The sin of Adam had weakened human nature to such an extent that, although freedom of choice is retained, people are free only to sin, unable to love the good unless God's grace frees them. It is God's grace, the Holy Spirit shredding charity abroad in people's hearts that moves them to take delight in God such that they are freed to love and thus enjoy the good.
>
> —Crocker, *Triumph*, 85

The Council of Carthage was convened in 418. It condemned Pelagianism as heretical. By the early sixth century, the heresy disappeared everywhere.

Augustine, bishop of Hippo, was one of the greatest Christian teachers and bishops of all time. His massive body of written work remained the central influence on Catholic thought for the next eight hundred years until Thomas Aquinas wrote the *Summa Theologica*. William Jurgens, in the third volume of his *Faith of the Early Fathers* wrote this,

> If we were faced with the unlikely proposition of having to destroy completely either the works of Augustine, or the works of all the other fathers and writers, I have little doubt that all the others would have to be sacrificed. Augustine must remain.[4]

St. Jerome (340–420)

St. Jerome was a church father and the greatest Biblical scholar of his age. In 379, he was ordained a priest. In 382, he became secretary to Pope Damasus, the thirty-seventh pope. Following Damasus's death in 384, Jerome left Rome. Eventually, he established a monastery in Jerusalem. There he completed work on the Bible, which included translation of the Old Testament directly from the Hebrew that superseded the old Latin version, which had been based on the Greek Septuagint. The resultant Bible, the Vulgate, became the standard of the Roman Catholic church and Jerome's most important achievement. His correspondence, especially with Augustine, is of profound historical interest. He has been honored as one of the four great doctors of the Western church.

A lot of things happen in a four-hundred-year period of history. Just think of America. If America began with the Mayflower and Jamestown, we're about 400 years old. We've had wars with the Indians, with ourselves (civil war), participation in two world wars, and other wars, including two at the present. We've had up and down economic conditions; inventions like electricity, cars, airplanes, telephones, radio, TV; medical discoveries; weather disasters; various religions, old and new; homegrown sports; politics, etc. Each category could fill volumes of books. So the problem is, how do we cover this two-thousand-year history of the church in a simple, organized, meaningful way, showing its continuity from Jesus and the apostles to us?

There are two main things going on—first, the church and all its activities fulfilling its mission, including heresies, within their own ranks; second, everything else, including imperial interference in church matters, power struggles, and barbarian invasions, which significantly impacted the church and its mission. Taking a cue from Augustine, we'll divide this 400-year period into two segments: the city of God and the city of man.

The city of God will focus on the actions and growth of the church. The city of man will focus on major things happening in the political area impacting the church's mission.

The City of God

First, we'll look at church councils. In its two-thousand-year history, the church has had twenty-one general councils. Two were in the first four hundred years—in 325, the First Council of Nicaea, and in 381, the First Council of Constantinople. In the second four hundred years, (400–800) there were five—in 431, Ephesus; in 451, Chalcedon; in 553 the Second Council of Constantinople; in 680, the Third Council of Constantinople; and in 787, the Second Council of Nicaea.

Nearly all Christians, of whatever church, acknowledge the authority and truth of the teachings of the first four great councils of early Christianity. This is because the councils clarified what the Christian scriptures taught and what the early church believed about God, Jesus, and Mary. Some of the great leaders of early Christianity affirmed the importance of these councils such as Augustine (354–430) who compared the authority of the ecumenical councils with that of the apostles and St. Gregory the Great (540–604), who said, "I confess that I accept and reverence the four councils as I do the four Gospels…for they are founded on universal consent."[5]

Let's look at the first four councils as a group and see their importance. In the earlier segment, we reviewed the first two—Nicaea in 325 and Constantinople in 381.

The Council of Ephesus in 431

In April 428, Nestorius, a monk in Antioch, was appointed bishop of Constantinople by Emperor Theodosius II. His selection as bishop by the emperor spelled trouble for the church, and it surfaced early. In the beginning months of his administration, Nestorius wrote several letters to Pope Celestine (422–432), complaining about heresies. Nestorius said that:

> One very serious matter is the unconscious heresy of good Catholics, of monks, and even some of the clergy, about the meaning of the belief that Christ is God. They talk, for example, of God having been born, of God being buried, and invoke the most holy virgin as "the God bringing forth," the mother of God, the Theotokos. They should be more careful in their speech, and say she is Christotokos, the mother of Christ. "The virgin," he told the Pope "is certainly Christotokos, and not Theotokos."
>
> —Hughes, *The Church in Crisis*, 50

Nestorius also taught that there were two natures and two persons in Jesus Christ, completely dividing the human person from the divine person. His views reached Cyril, bishop of Alexandria, who was a first-rate theologian. Cyril wrote a theological defense against this heresy for his monks, which was a severe denunciation of Nestorius. Cyril also wrote to Nestorius in February 430 condemning his views.

Cyril contacted the emperor. Next, Cyril had a council in Egypt with his bishops about the matter. He then sent a copy of the synod's results, copies of Nestorius's speeches, his errors, and the opinions of classic theologians of the past on the subject to Pope Celestine. When the package reached Rome, the pope summoned a gathering of bishops. The pope wrote his judgment. Nestorius was to be summoned to make a written retraction of his errors and to declare his belief that the birth of Christ is what the church believes. He would be given a ten-day notice to comply. If he didn't comply, he would be excommunicated and removed from office.

The pope wrote to Nestorius notifying him of what had been decided and advised him that papers concerning the process were being sent to Alexandria, and Cyril would be acting with the authority of the pope. Cyril did not go in person but appointed four bishops to carry out the work.

The emperor called a council for all bishops to be held in Ephesus on June 7, 431. A problem developed. Forty-six bishops from Antioch, Nestorius's hometown, so to speak, still hadn't arrived. In addition, the three legates sent by the pope as his representative also had not arrived. What would they do? Alexandria was traditionally the first See of the east. (A See is the official seat, center of authority, or jurisdiction of a bishop.) The weather was hot. Bishops were getting impatient.

Two weeks later, on June 21, Cyril of Alexandria, made the decision to start without them. There were protests. Count Candidian, charged by the emperor with safety of the council, demanded a delay until the bishops from Antioch would arrive. He said the emperor's will was that there should not be a "fragmentary council." Sixty-eight bishops also demanded a delay, but the majority of bishops remained firm.

The council began. A notary read a summary of the case. Nestorius was sent for three times. He ignored all three calls. Next they read the Creed of Nicaea and then the letter of Cyril to Nestorius. There was a call for a mass vote. All called for anathema for Nestorius. The notary read the long collection of classic theologians on the matter. They voted. One hundred ninety-eight bishops signed, depriving Nestorius of his episcopate. Not one voice defended his views of the faith. The Council of Ephesus was over in one day.

Then something happened. The next day, the bishops from Antioch arrived. They had been delayed by an accident. When they heard what happened, they formed a group and protested. Count Candidian supported it. The emperor declared that all bishops must stay. In the beginning of July, the three legates showed up. They allied themselves with Cyril. There would be six more sessions for the month of July and agonized waiting in the heat for a decision before the process worked out.[6]

Supported by the emperor, the majority of the fathers of the council agreed that the teaching of the Catholic faith was that Christ was perfect God and perfect man by union of two natures in one person. The title of Mother of God (*Theotokos*) was accorded to Mary since she was the mother of the one divine person existing in two natures.[7] Cyril died in 444. Several years after his death, another heresy arose, which would eventually lead to the fourth general council.

In 448, Eutyches, a seventy-year-old monk, was the leader of a group of 300 monks in a monastery just outside Constantinople. His heresy would be the opposite error from that of Nestorius, who saw Christ as two separate beings. Eutyches held that the two natures in Christ, the divine and the human, were so intimately united that they became one divine nature because his human nature was completely absorbed by the divine. The result was one Christ, not only with one personality but also with one divine nature (monophysitism). If this were true, there would be no human component in Jesus, and the Apostolic deposit of faith story of our redemption would be destroyed.

In November of 448, Bishop Flavian of Constantinople called a synod of bishops to the capital city to discuss some local problems. At this meeting, Eusebius, bishop of Dorylaeum, produced evidence denouncing Eutyches as a heretic and demanded he be summoned to explain his heretical view. He came and was heard. After many arguments, Eutyches would not agree that there were two natures in God incarnate. The synod proclaimed him a heretic. Removed from his post at the monastery, he was forbidden to exercise his priesthood, and he was forbidden to have any contacts. Two high-placed men disagreed—Emperor Theodosius II of Constantinople and Bishop Dioscoros of Alexandria.

When Eutyches appealed to Rome about his sentence, Emperor Theodosius sent a letter supporting him. Dioscoros, to whom an appeal also had been sent, called a synod of his own and annulled the synod's decision. Pope Leo the Great (440–461) asked for a full report. When the pope received Bishop Flavian's report, he confirmed the sentence.

On March 30, 449, the emperor called a general council to meet once again at Ephesus. The pope was invited to come, but he chose to be represented by three legates. In his reply to the emperor, the pope stated his view that Eutyches had been justly condemned. The pope also wrote a letter to the council, accrediting his legates and making it clear that while he left it to the council to decide the fate of Eutyches, the doctrinal issue had been decided in his letter to Bishop Flavian, and he expected the council to accept it. The letter to Flavian is also known as Leo's Tome, which declared that Jesus was one divine person, with two natures—a human nature and a divine nature.

On August 8, 449, The Robbers' Council opened at Ephesus with 130 bishops. Bishop Dioscoros, by Emperor Theodosius's command, presided. The legates asked for Leo's tome to be read. They were ignored. Dioscoros passed to another matter. Eutyches then came forward to read his appeal against the synod in April. The legates made a second attempt to have Leo's Tome read. Again, they were ignored. After Eutyches read a statement of his belief, a vote was taken. There was a great uproar. The name of the accuser Eusebius was greeted with, "Burn him alive!" One hundred bishops agreed Eutyches had good Christian doctrine. However, by the emperor's orders, no bishop who voted Eutyches's condemnation earlier was allowed to vote this time.

Dioscoros now proposed punishment for Eusebius and Flavian with bishops voting their condemnation. Flavian asked for an appeal. The Roman legate also protested. With a signal from Discoros, the doors of the church were thrown open, and thugs rushed in. Bishop Flavian was dragged off to prison. Legates feared for their lives. The bishops then voted Flavian's condemnation, 135 signing the decree, many of them through fear and inability to escape. Before Flavian died, he managed to draft an appeal to the pope and get it into the hands of the helpless delegates. Bishops ended with acclamations, "Hail, Dioscoros! God has spoken through Dioscoros!" Bishop Flavian died three days later from his beatings. The council of 449 came to an end. Pope Leo called it "The Robbers' Council."

Pope Leo wrote a letter of protest to the emperor saying that what had happened at Ephesus was "an insult to the faith, an injury to all the churches of the world."[8] The pope said that a more authoritative council should be held with bishops from the whole world, and it should be held in Italy. The reason for this council was that Bishop Flavian's appeal to Rome, made at Ephesus, had been ignored. The pope said that appealing to Rome was a fundamental right for all bishops. Emperor Theodosius II never replied. On July 28, 450, the emperor fell off his horse and died.

His successor as emperor, Marcian, was a loyal Catholic, who agreed to have a fourth ecumenical council. The emperor picked a convenient location, Chalcedon, which was close to Constantinople, and he wanted the pope to lead it. The principal reason for this council was to assert the orthodox Catholic doctrine against the heresy of the monophysites.

The Council of Chalcedon (Modern Turkey) in 451

The council opened on October 8. Five hundred bishops met in the great church of St. Euphemia. Pope Leo sent legates headed by Paschasinus, a bishop from Sicily, who would preside in his place.

> Paschasinus opened the proceedings, explaining as he said, the instructions sent to the council by "him who is the head of all the churches." Firstly, Dioscoros was not to be given a place among the bishops. If he resists this ruling, he must be expelled. Such are our instructions, and "if Dioscoros is allowed to sit as a bishop, we leave. Dioscoros is here only to be judged."
>
> —Hughes, *The Church in Crisis*, 80

Dioscoros was given a place in the nave of the church.

Bishop Eusebius, who had earlier denounced Dioscoros, opened the case against him by readings from the minutes of the Robber's Council and of Bishop Flavian's synod, which had condemned Eutyches in 448. The council acclaimed Flavian's statement of 448 as orthodoxy itself. One bishop said, "The pope has given us a ruling about Eutyches. We follow the pope." All agreed. To clinch the matter, the classic documents were again read out—the creeds of Nicaea, the council of 381, and the letters of Leo to Flavian, (Leo's Tome.) At this last, the bishops called out, "It is Peter who says this through Leo. This is what we all of us believe. This is the faith of the Apostles. Leo and Cyril teach the same thing."[9]

On October 13, the bishops returned to Dioscoros. What he had done was recalled. Paschasinus, with the authority of the pope, passed sentence on Dioscoros. He was stripped of his rank as bishop and all of his episcopal functions and was immediately notified of his fate. Reports went out to the emperor and the pope. The emperor confirmed the sentence, promptly banishing him to Gangra, a mountainous town, two hundred fifty miles away. "The emperor's will," commissioners said, "is that in all business between bishops, the pronouncements of the court shall have no force if they are contrary to the canons laid down by the councils."[10] This gave the bishops bold independence.

A suggestion kept recurring for a new creed that would satisfy everyone. A third time the commissioners came out with one they prepared. The majority of bishops liked it. The papal legates would have nothing to do with it. Their instructions were simple. The Tome of Leo had been set for the council's acceptance as the official teaching about the incarnation. Paschasinus said, "If you will not accept the letter of the blessed pope, Leo, make out our passports, that we may return to Italy, and the general council be held there."[11]

The following week, the council enacted twenty-eight canons or disciplinary laws, the twenty-eighth being the most controversial. They began by recalling the act of the council of 381, making Constantinople number two and confirming it. They then spoke of the see of Rome and of how "the fathers" always recognized its special privileges as something due to that city's imperial state. In this canon, they defined and declared the same about the privileges of the see of Constantinople, the new Rome. They pointed out that the city, now honored with the presence of the emperor and the senate, Constantinople, should enjoy the same state privileges as the old royal Rome. Constantinople should be as great as old Rome in what relates to the church and rank second to her. They added,

> And for the future, all the 26 metropolitans of the three civil dioceses of Thrace, Asia, and Pontus are to be consecrated by the bishop of Constantinople—he is to be definitely their overlord. And, it is he who will consecrate the bishops of the churches among the barbarian people beyond the frontier.
>
> —Hughes, *The Church in Crisis*, 88

The legates had missed that session. When Paschasinus heard about it, he protested strongly. A legate read a passage to the commissioners that warned the legates "not to allow anything that violated what the holy fathers decreed or that lessened the dignity of the Roman see. Should any bishop, relying on the importance of the capital, attempt any usurpation, he was to be opposed."[12] There were hot discussions. The commissioners declared the canon carried, saying that the rights of old Rome had been safeguarded, but that it is only right that the bishop of New Rome should have the same rights and honors and also the rights to consecrate in the three civil dioceses mentioned. And the bishops again applauded.

Lucientius, one of the legates, said to the commissioners,

> The holy see ought not to be basely treated while we look on. And therefore, all that was done yesterday, in our absence, to the prejudice of the canons and laws, we demand of your highness (the set of commissioners) to order that it be annulled. Otherwise, our appeal in law against the canon will be attached to the minutes, that we may know what it is we must report to the apostolic bishop who is the leader of the whole church, so that he may be able to pronounce sentence on the unjust act against his see, and on the overthrowing of canon law.
>
> —Hughes, *The Church in Crisis*, 89

With this rupture between the bishop and the Pope, the council came to an end.

The bishops, before they left, wrote a letter to the pope, trying to butter him up with compliments. They said that "since in you the apostolic light shines in all its splendor, you will often, with your customary care, see that Constantinople benefits from that brightness."[13] They begged the pope to confirm what they had placed in canon twenty-eight.

In reply, Pope Leo protested strongly against canon twenty-eight and declared it null and void as being against the prerogatives of the bishops of Alexandria and Antioch and against the decrees of the Council of Nicaea. Otherwise, the pope ratified the acts of the Council of Chalcedon but only inasmuch as they referred to matters of faith.

> The Eastern bishops' attempt to ratify their power only showed their faulty presumption. As in 381, Constantinople based its claim on being a city of wealth and power. But the pope ruled from the see of St. Peter, not the see of Caesar, and papal authority rested on scriptural and apostolic grounds, not on the fact the Rome was "the Imperial city."
>
> —Crocker, *Triumph*, 92

In summary, these four ecumenical councils were most important in nailing down basic beliefs of Jesus' church:

325 Nicaea: the Father and Jesus are of the same substance (the Nicene Creed);

381 Constantinople: the Holy Spirit is a divine person and part of the Trinity (added to the Nicene Creed);

431 Ephesus: Jesus is one divine person with two natures—one human, one divine. Mary bore one divine person in her womb. Therefore, she is the mother of God (Theotokos);

451 Chalcedon: the defeat of the heresy of monophysitism, which claimed that Jesus was one person with a single divine nature that swallowed up his human nature.

> These were the first four important ecumenical councils where the Holy Spirit guided the popes and the bishops to develop the authentic expression of many of our core doctrinal beliefs. These teachings were necessary to settle theological disputes in the Church in order for harmony and unity to reign. Over the centuries many theological works have been written on the teachings first articulated in this time period.
>
> —Steve Weidenkopf & Dr. Alan Schreck,
> *Epic: A Journey through Church History*,
> (West Chester, PA: Ascension Press, 2008), 31

There would be three more councils in this 400–800-year period. We'll discuss each briefly, noting the issues and solutions.

Second Council of Constantinople (553)

This fifth general council would be called a little over one hundred years after the previous council. Justinian was the emperor. Pope Vigilius (537–555) was the fifty-ninth pope. This council was called by the emperor, and it consisted mostly of Eastern church leaders. It would last a month (May 5 to June 2, 553). The council dealt mainly with the emperor's wish to produce a condemnation of the "three chapters." This designation as chapters referred to three writers long dead. The emperor hoped that the public rejection of these supposedly Nestorian writings and their authors would help reconcile the empire's monophysites with the Council of Chalcedon, which had determined that Christ had two natures, divine and human, and seen by many as opening the door to Nestorianism.

The council was resisted by Pope Vigilius, who had been brought to Constantinople against his will several years before, after he refused to condemn the three chapters because he feared it could undermine what had been achieved at Chalcedon. Taken by imperial agents to a ship, he left Rome in November 545 but did not reach Constantinople until late 546 or early 547. Still refusing to agree to the condemnation of the three chapters, Vigilius was kept in Constantinople against his will for eight years, sometimes under great pressure.

The pope questioned whether the writers in question were truly heretics and feared that their condemnation would weaken Chalcedon and encourage monophysitism. When the Roman clergy and civil leaders requested the emperor to permit Vigilius to return to Rome, Emperor Justinian agreed to do so only on condition that the pope would accept the decisions of the council.

Vigilius finally bowed to the emperor's wishes in a letter of December 8, 553, to the Patriarch Eutychius, accepting the decisions of the council, which he had so long opposed. At the end of a sorrowful residence of eight years, the pope was finally allowed to start his return to Rome in the spring of 555. While on his journey back, he died at Syracuse in Sicily.

> The Second Council of Constantinople faced serious opposition in the West even after the endorsement of Vigilius. In northern Italy, the Church provinces of Milan and Aquileia, believing that the papacy had become a

tool of the Eastern emperor, broke off communion with Rome. The schism would last for several decades around Milan, and for more than a century in Aquileia. Today, the Second Council of Constantinople is accepted as a legitimate council by the Eastern Orthodox, the Roman Catholics, and a number of Western Christian groups."

—*New World Encyclopedia*,
s.v. "Second Council of Constantinople,"
http:// www.newworldencyclopedia.com/ (accessed) July 7, 2013

Almost a hundred years later, came a new doctrine from the east meant to end the lingering monophysite heresy by rallying every Christian to the idea that Jesus had two natures that acted as one. This doctrine was presented to Pope Honorius (635–638) for his approval. To him, it seemed like an affirmation of the church's belief in the human and divine unity of Christ. He accepted it. However, with closer scrutiny, it became clear that it was a heresy because it claimed that Christ did not possess a human will or act with a force that was human. If that were true, then Christ was not really a man because it defined Jesus' will as being purely divine without a human element. After Pope Honorius died, the Emperor Constans II defined the doctrine as law. The papacy condemned it. This heresy would become known as monothelitism, which was a variation of the monophysite heresy. The emperor was upset. In retaliation, his troops raided and looted the Lateran palace and arrested the pope's ambassador to Constantinople. This was a virtual war between the emperor and the papacy.

A new pope, Martin (649–653), joined the war in 649. He bravely called a synod of more than 100 Western bishops, who condemned the monothelite heresy. The pope presented their decision to the Emperor Constans II, pointing out that this was a correction of an error made by the emperor's patriarchs. Greatly angered, the emperor wanted the pope's submission to the heresy or his death. The pope was arrested, beaten, flogged, and finally convicted of treason and exiled to Crimea, which was suffering from a horrible famine. In fact, it was a death sentence for the pope for refusing to surrender the authority of St. Peter to that of the emperor. The emperor moved his troops into Rome, stripping the city of everything of value it could find and sending it back to Constantinople. However, justice would soon prevail. Constans was murdered in his bathtub. His son, Constantine IV would replace him.

Constantine wanted to reconcile with Rome. Agatho (678–681) was now pope in Rome. The emperor wanted to work with the pope to reject monothelitism and return the empire to Catholic orthodoxy. This would be the objective of the sixth general council.

Third Council of Constantinople (680)

The purpose of the council was to deal with the monothelitism heresy over the question of whether Christ had one will or two. The heresy claimed that Christ did not possess a human will nor did he ever act with a force that was human. If that were true, then Christ was not really a man. Pope Agatho sent delegates to represent him at the council. They brought with them and read a long dogmatic letter from the pope, plus one from a Roman synod held in the spring of 680.

> Both letters insisted on the Roman faith as the living and stainless tradition of the apostles of Christ and therefore, authoritative for the Universal (Catholic) Church. Pope Agatho and his successor, Pope Leo II (682–683), would succeed. Monothelitism was officially anathematized. But, it came at a cost. The East wanted more. It wanted Pope Honorius, who had been dead for 42 years, condemned as a monothelite for his hasty, ill-judged apparent approval of the doctrine. The accusation was unjust. It struck at

the heart of what even the Eastern church conceded was the proper pride of Rome. Pope Leo II reluctantly complied though he made it clear publicly that he believed Honorius' crime was not committing heresy, but failing to stamp it out.

—Crocker, Triumph, 109–110

The Second Council of Nicaea in 787

The Second Council of Nicaea had nothing to do with the nature of Jesus, but its purpose was to put an end to the iconoclastic controversy. Iconoclasm developed as Christians began to question whether the use of icons violated the Ten Commandments and emperors felt that their military setbacks, which began in 632, were the results of God's displeasure.

This controversy was about an edict and enforcement made by an Eastern emperor, Leo III (717–741). That edict made it unlawful to display and venerate images and relics and to pray to the saints. Remember, Leo was an emperor, not a religious figure. He was meddling in religion, usurping the rights of the true authority in these matters, which belonged to the bishop of Rome. In the west, Pope Gregory III (731–741) condemned the emperor's actions resulting in a new schism between Rome and Constantinople. Some monasteries in the east, however, became strongholds of icon veneration. John of Damascus, a Syrian monk, emerged as the main opponent of iconoclasm. The conflict over images remained a doctrinal argument until in 726, Emperor Leo enforced iconoclasm. His edict enforced the removal of all icons from churches. Between 726 and 730, Leo ordered the removal of an image of Jesus over the imperial palace gate in Constantinople.

Emperor Leo died in 740. His son, Constantine V (741–775), took over and ruled for thirty-five years. Destruction of images continued more vigorously under his reign. "All prayers to saints were forbidden, and all veneration of their relics. From the great basilica of Chalcedon, the body of the martyr to honor whom it was built, St. Euphemia, was thrown into the sea."[14]

When Constantine died, his son, Leo VI (775–780) took over. He lasted only five years. When he died, his wife Irene became empress and regent for their infant son, Constantine VI. Irene was a loyal Catholic and wanted to restore images. She informed Pope Adrian I (772–795), the ninety-fifth pope, that she was going to summon a council to restore images, statues, mosaics, and relics. She had to be careful because much of her army was still iconoclast.

The council was initially convened in the capital, but soldiers, loyal to the two previous emperors on iconoclasm, burst into the meeting and kicked out all the bishops. The meeting was then moved to Nicaea, which had been the site of the first ecumenical council 462 years earlier. This new council declared the propriety of the "images of Jesus Christ, the Virgin Mary, the holy angels, as well as those of the saints, and other pious -and holy men."[15] It also deposed all bishops and clergy who refused to allow such things. Among other things, the council declared that icons deserved reverence but not adoration, which was due to God alone. The council condemned the iconoclasts. This statement was confirmed by Pope Adrian. Nicaea II, the seventh council, was the last ecumenical council accepted as such by both the Eastern Orthodox and Roman Catholic churches.

What was interesting was the reaction of Charlemagne when he was notified by the pope about this council. At this point in time, the western Roman empire had been gone for over three hundred years. Charlemagne, a good Catholic, was now the church's protector and regarded the Byzantine emperor as a rival. He wrote:

> "Whenever a dispute arises about matters of belief, we must consult the holy, Roman, catholic, and apostolic church, which is set in authority over the other churches, and not a synod of Greek bishops." For the note that

sounds throughout this polemic "is not so much as one of hostility to the doctrine set out at Nicaea, but as to the fact of these Greeks sitting in council and giving forth as though they are the infallible rulers of Christendom."

—Hughes, *The Church in Crisis*, 161

Jesus had established his church with the responsibility and authority to safeguard the truths of the Christian faith. These councils were fulfilling that purpose. But the other major responsibility was to get the good news of the Christian message to the whole world. We'll begin with the monks.

Monks played a critical role in saving Western civilization. Who were they? In the third century AD, the monastic tradition in the church began its development in the Egyptian desert. St. Antony (251–356), a young Christian, received a call from God to sell all that he possessed and give its proceeds to the poor. He responded to Christ's call to follow him. After long years of solitary existence, Antony found himself surrounded by a number of disciples. He became a model for hermits and those who wanted to live a community type of monasticism. They believed that Christ and a life led in strict conformity to the ideals of the Gospel were the only realities that could bring true happiness. By the time Antony died, thousands of hermits were living in the area.

Next came Pachomius (290–347), a contemporary of Antony, who began his monastic career as a hermit. He had great organizational skills. Over the years, his monastery grew into a small town where several thousand monks resided. They divided into small groups according to their skills for the essential needs of the community. Soon he had a following of about nine thousand monks and nuns in several monasteries.

Next came Basil the Great (330–379), who founded a monastery in Asia Minor, which copied the basic features of Pachomius, such as common life, liturgical prayer, and manual labor. Because of his deep influence within the Byzantine Empire and later in Russia, Basil is known as the "father of Eastern monasticism."

But it was an Italian monk, Benedict of Nursia (480–547), who is considered the patriarch of Western monasticism. He composed a rule, the Rule of Benedict, which eventually became the normative rule for the Western monastic movement. The monastery built by Benedict at Mt. Cassino in Italy, around 525, became one of the most significant factors in the development of Western civilization in the Middle Ages. The motherhouse, at Mt. Cassino, through great difficulties, kept bouncing back.

In 589, it was sacked by barbarian Lombards. In 884, it was destroyed by Saracens. In 1349, it was razed by an earthquake. In 1799, it was pillaged by French troops. In 1944, it was wrecked by bombs in WWII then rebuilt after the war.

Among their accomplishments, Monks preserved learning and culture after the collapse of the Western Roman Empire in 467.

> In addition to their careful preservation of the works of the classical world and of the church fathers, both of which are central to Western civilization, the monks performed another work of immeasurable importance in their capacity as copyists: their preservation of the Bible. Without their devotion to this crucial task, and the numerous copies they produced, it is not clear how the Bible would have survived the onslaught of the barbarians.
>
> —Thomas E. Woods, Jr.,
> *How the Catholic Church Built Western Civilization,*
> (Washington, DC: Regnery Publishing, Inc., 2005), 42

By the beginning of the fourteenth century, the Benedictine order had supplied the church with 24 popes, 200 cardinals, 7000 archbishops, 15,000 bishops, and 1500 canonized saints. At its height, the Benedictine order could boast 37,000 monasteries.[16]

Jesus came with a two-fold mission. His first mission was to fulfill, in his lifetime on earth, the Old Testament prophecies announcing his arrival. This was good news for all mankind, for all times. His second mission was to get this good news known by all people, in all times, until his return. Jesus established his church. One of its major purposes was to provide missionaries to fulfill his mission.

He handpicked twelve apostles. With the defection of Judas, eleven would be the beginning missionaries. We know them by name. We know by their results that they did a great job. By the year 70, except for John, ten were dead. That means that in thirty-seven years from Jesus' return to the Father, the apostles had reached India, North Africa, and all the lands along the Mediterranean—Greece, Italy, and Spain. This was an amazing start.

All Christians were, and are, called on to spread the good news. Those who were martyred brought in converts by their example, but there were some special missionaries who excelled, and we know them by name. They went after countries. Here are three examples:

St. Patrick of Ireland (387–461)

St. Patrick is one of the world's most popular saints. He was born in Scotland. As a boy of sixteen, he was captured during a raiding party and taken to Ireland to tend sheep. Ireland at this time was a land of druids and pagans. He learned the language and practices of the people who held him. His captivity lasted until he was twenty, when he escaped after having a dream from God in which he was told to leave Ireland by going to the coast. There he found some sailors who took him back to Britain, where he was reunited with his family.

He had another dream in which the people of Ireland were calling out to him, "We beg you, holy youth, to come and walk among us once more."[17] He began his studies for the priesthood and was ordained by St. Germanus, the bishop of Auxerre, whom he had studied under for years. Later, Patrick was ordained a bishop and was sent to bring the gospel to Ireland. He arrived in Ireland March 25, 433. One legend says that he met a chieftain of one of the tribes who tried to kill Patrick. Patrick converted Dichu (the chieftain) after he was unable to move his arm until he became friendly to Patrick. Patrick began preaching the Gospel throughout Ireland, converting many. He and his disciples preached and converted thousands and began building churches all over the country. Kings, their families, and entire kingdoms converted to Christianity when hearing Patrick's message. Patrick preached and converted in all Ireland for forty years. He died March 17, 461.

St. Augustine of Canterbury (year of birth unknown-died 605)

In the year 596, some forty monks set out from Rome to evangelize the Anglo-Saxons in England. Leading the group was Augustine, the prior of their monastery in Rome. Hardly had he and his men reached Gaul (France) when they heard stories about the ferocity of the Anglo-Saxons and of the treacherous waters of the English Channel. Augustine and his group returned to Rome and to the pope, St. Gregory the Great, who had sent them. They were assured by the pope that their fears were groundless.

Augustine again set out, and this time, the group crossed the English Channel and landed in the territory of Kent, ruled by King Ethelbert, a pagan married to a Christian. Ethelbert received them kindly, set up a residence for them in Canterbury and, within a year, on Pentecost Sunday 597, was baptized. After being consecrated a bishop in France, Augustine returned to Canterbury, where he founded his see. He constructed a church and monastery near where the present cathedral, begun in 1070, now stands. As the faith spread, additional sees were established at London and Rochester.

Laboring patiently, Augustine wisely heeded the principles (quite enlightened for the times) suggested by Pope Gregory the Great: purify rather than destroy pagan temples and customs; let pagan rites and festivals be transformed into Christian feasts; and retain local customs as far as possible. The limited success Augustine achieved in England before his death in 605, a short eight years after he arrived in England, would eventually bear fruit long after the conversion of England. Truly, Augustine of Canterbury can be called the "apostle of England."[18]

St. Boniface (680–754)

Boniface lived at a time of deep transformation in European history. The Western Roman Empire was disappearing, and new nations were emerging, fighting among themselves for supremacy. Boniface carried out his mission among the Germanic people under the protection of the powerful Franks. Here is his story.

Winfred was born into a noble English family in Devon, England, around 672. Later in his church career, he was given the name "Boniface" by the pope, who would send him on a mission to the Germanic peoples. Boniface means "well-doer." His parents intended secular pursuits for Winfred, but he had been inspired with higher ideals by missionary monks who visited his home when he was young, and he felt himself called to a religious state.

Boniface entered the Benedictine order and was ordained a priest at the age of thirty. Through his abbot, the fame of his learning reached high civil and ecclesiastic circles. He was also a great preacher. The thought of bringing the light of the Gospel to the old Saxons in Germany had taken possession of his mind. After many requests, Boniface at last obtained the permission of his abbot. In 716, he set out from England for the mission in

Frisia (Germany), intending to convert the Frisians by preaching to them in their own language (his own Anglo-Saxon language being similar to Frisian). His efforts were frustrated by the war then being carried out between Charles Martel of the Franks against Radbod, king of the Frisians. He returned temporarily to England.

Boniface went to Rome to obtain from the pope the apostolic mission and necessary faculties. The pope was Gregory II (715–731). On May 15, 719, the pope gave Boniface full authority to preach the Gospel to the Germans. But the pope instructed him to make his first missionary journey through the German territory only a tour of inspection. In many regions, Boniface found a flourishing church with churches and monasteries built all over the place. But he found other regions in bad condition. Previous missionaries had been murdered by Germanic tribes. Boniface tried to stir up a missionary spirit in the priests and to make people live up to the pure precepts of the Christian religions. There were some conversions, but he wasn't satisfied.

On his way to the court of Charles Martel to seek support, he heard the news about the death of the Frisian king Radbod, who had persecuted the church. Boniface went to Friesland. He spent three years with tireless energy, preaching fearlessly as he went. Multitudes who had fallen away during the persecution of Radbod were brought to repentance, and thousands accepted the faith. Many of the converts were brought together to lead a religious life under the Rule of St. Benedict.

In June 755, Boniface ordered new converts to assemble for confirmation at Dorkum on the River Borne. A group of Germanic tribesmen fell upon them and murdered Boniface and fifty-two companions. Soon afterward, the Christians who had scattered at the approach of the assailants returned and found the body of the martyr and beside him the bloodstained copy of St. Ambrose on the "Advantage of Death."[19] It is said that everything that has since developed politically, theologically, and intellectually in Germany stands on the foundation Boniface laid.

The City of Man

While the church was doing the things it was established to do, life was going on in the city of man. These were mostly battles for power. These fighting challenges impacted the church as it worked to fulfill its own goals. Let's take a look.

Now that the church had been accepted by the Roman Empire, the next problem to worry about was the barbarian invasions. By the late second century, a mixture of Germanic tribes was moving westward from central Europe. Roman generals were preoccupied with making and unmaking emperors and not paying attention guarding their frontiers. Tribesmen began pouring through gaps in the Roman defenses. The barbarians were rural and nomadic people with no written literature and little political organization, aside from loyalty to a chief.

These invasions hastened the collapse of Rome and presented the church with an unprecedented challenge and opportunity. The barbarian invasions were a very important event in Christianity. Up to this point, the spread of the Gospel had virtually been limited to people of Mediterranean culture. Now the church was in contact with a new culture and ethnic world. In the fifth century, Ireland was evangelized. This injected new life into the Christianity of the Celtics elsewhere.[20]

In 410, Rome was sacked. One of the most famous barbarians, Alaric the Goth, was the first barbarian to successfully capture the city of Rome. Although his troops spared most of the residents and architecture, he pretty much looted the city. St. Jerome expressed a profound shock and sadness:

> A terrible rumor has arrived from the West. Rome is besieged; the lives of the citizens have been redeemed by gold. Despoiled, they are again encircled, and are losing

their lives after they have lost their riches. My voice cannot continue. Sobs interrupt my dictations. The City is taken that took the whole world.

—J.N. Hilgarth, *Christianity and Paganism,* (Philadelphia, PA: University of Pennsylvania Press, rev. ed., 1985) 69

In 452, it was about to happen again. One of the most feared and notorious barbarians of all time, Attila the Hun, was planning a repeat performance of sacking Rome. Attila was believed to be of distant Mongol ancestry, with a reputation of ravaging much of the European continent during the fifth century. The western empire was in total political and military collapse. Pope Leo the Great was in power and trying to fill the void for temporal and spiritual needs. He successfully persuaded Attila to abandon his plan to sack the city of Rome and withdraw his forces beyond the Danube. Three years later, 455, Rome would once again have an invader. This time it was the ferocious Vandal barbarians who swept into central Italy. Once again, Leo came forward as an advocate for the people. He couldn't turn the Vandals away but did get concessions on going easier against the people.

By the middle of the fifth century, the effective reach of the old western empire, of Caesar's great conquests was contained behind the borders of Italy. Before the century was over, even the last remnants of the Western Roman Empire were crushed by the Ostrogoths.[21] However, the eastern empire would continue to exist for another thousand years.

It was in 476, when the Western Roman Empire finally came to an end. A Germanic general Odoacer overthrew the last of the Roman emperors, Augustulus Romulus. Out of the ruins of the Western Empire grew a number of new successor kingdoms, ruled over by barbarian warlords.

The universal church was still alive. This left the Western church free of civil authorities, and gradually, popes would become the most powerful men in the west. Crocker writes:

In the West, we enter the Dark Ages. The great unifying government of Roman law was shattered. There was now only one universal institution, the church, and it operated without the defense of the Roman legions, weaving between the authority of scores of Barbarian kings, and scores more subsidiary chieftains, in a western world that was now either officially Arian or pagan with Norse, Germanic, Celtic, or Slavonic Gods. It verges on the miraculous that from the wreckage of Rome, a Catholic network of monastic scholars and saints preserved the memory of the imperial city...its language, its literature, and its former grandeur. But more important, they preserved the wisdom of Christ's church, a wisdom that the world, in its ignorance, would have chosen to extinguish had it not been for the heroic witness of a new generation of brave, evangelizing saints. It is all the more amazing that even amidst this chaos and ruin, the Catholic Church calmly continued to proclaim its universality and the primacy of the Holy See of St. Peter even against the ambitious church patriarchs who lived in the safety of Constantinople.

—Crocker, *Triumph*, 90

The barbarians were warrior people whose customs and conduct struck the Romans as savages. As Christopher Dawson, one of the great historians of the twentieth century put it,

> The Church had to undertake the task of introducing the law of the Gospel and the ethics of the Sermon on the Mount among peoples who regarded homicide as the most honorable occupation and vengeance as synonymous with justice."[22]

The Franks were the most significant of this barbarian group. They had settled in Gaul, which is modern France. Unlike many of the other barbarian groups, the Franks had not been exposed to Arian adherents. From the church's missionary experience, they discovered that it was easier to convert primitive pagans than those who had already adopted another faith, like Arianism. The church could see some possibilities.

In 481, a man named Clovis became king of the Franks. This was the opportune moment for the church. It took action. A congratulatory letter was sent by an official to Clovis, reminding him of the benefits that would come his way if he would collaborate and cooperate with the church. Clovis was moved by much of what he had heard about the life of Jesus. In 496, Clovis was baptized. Important things happened because of that baptism. From that time on, there would be no longer just one Catholic monarch in the world, who was the emperor in the East. The West would now have its own Catholic king, the king of the Franks.

Barbarians had a strong identification with their kings. If you converted the king, his people would follow.

> But it wasn't enough to convert the barbarians. The Church had to continue to guide them, both to guarantee that the faith had truly taken hold and to ensure that the faith would begin to transform their government and their way of life."[23]

Clovis belonged to the Merovingian line of kings. Strong at first, their line of kings began to lose their vigor during the sixth and seventh centuries. Incompetent rulers were fighting, often vigorously, among themselves. Because of this, they became weaker. This was causing problems for the church. By the seventh century, the condition of the Frankish priesthood was becoming increasingly desperate with scandals of immorality. Eventually, Frankish church reform would be needed from the Irish and Anglo-Saxon missionaries, who had received their own Catholic faith from Europe.

After the collapse of the Western Roman Empire in 476, the only remaining "Roman" authority was the Eastern emperor in Constantinople, who had never succumbed to barbarian invaders.

At first, the papacy had a special relationship with those emperors, but later, the relationship became strained. First, the emperors couldn't give the protection against barbarians needed by the pope. The reason was that the emperors were fighting for their own lives against the Arabs and Persians. Emperors needed manpower and resources to keep themselves alive. Secondly, emperors would routinely interfere in the life of the church, which was clearly beyond the competency of the state. For example, there was the iconoclasm problem.

> The Church made a momentous decision to turn its desire for protection and cooperation away from the emperors in Constantinople and toward the still semi-barbarian Franks, who had converted to Catholicism without passing through the Arian phase. In the 8th century, the Church blessed the official transfer of power from the Merovingian dynasty to the Carolingian family. The Church thus facilitated the peaceful transfer of power from the decrepit Merovingians and into the hands of the Carolingians, with whom the churchmen would work so closely in the ensuing years to restore the values of civilized life. The Carolingians was the family of Charles Martel. Ultimately his grandson, Charles the Great, or Charlemagne, would become known as the father of Europe.
>
> Under the influence of the Church, the barbarian people would be transformed into civilization builders. Charlemagne (768–814), perhaps the greatest Frank of them all, exemplified that ideal. The Frankish realm, including the additions to it made by Charlemagne, extended from Spain in the east, through modern day France, northern Italy, Switzerland, and much of Germany.
>
> —Woods, Jr.
> *How the Catholic Church Built Western Civilization*, 15–16

As we close out the first eight hundred years of the church, St. Peter's ninety-fifth successor, Pope Leo III (795–816) was reigning. Of those ninety-five popes, two had earned the extra title "the Great": Leo the Great (440–461) and Gregory the Great (590–604). Why? What special accomplishments did each make? Let's look.

Leo the Great (440–461). Let's recall briefly Leo's heroic actions against Attila the Hun and the Vandals. In 452, Rome was in total political and military collapse. Leo was pope. When Attila the Hun and his forces came to destroy Rome, he met no army. Leo came out to meet him and successfully persuaded Attila and his savage Huns not to sack the city. In 455, the Vandals, known for their ferocity, approached Rome. Once again, Leo confronted them. While he was unable to keep the Vandals from looting the city, he did persuade them not to hurt the people and to leave ancient monuments undamaged. In saving the city of Rome from the full savagery of the Vandals, Pope St. Leo may have saved the entire church itself. If the see of Rome had been destroyed, the church would have lost its only source of orthodox and independent authority.

His tome of Leo, defining Jesus as one divine person with two natures—one human, the other Divine—clarified for all ages who Jesus is. Leo also defended the primacy of the see of Rome by refusing attempts by Eastern bishops at two church councils to claim that Constantinople was equal in authority to Rome.

Gregory the Great (590–604). Gregory was born into a Roman noble family that had a long tradition of civil and clerical service. He, himself, had been a prefect of Rome before becoming a monk. He soon earned a reputation for learning and administrative work. Pope Pelagius II (579–590) dispatched him as a papal emissary to Constantinople to warn the Eastern empire that another Germanic tribe, the Lombards, was threatening Rome. At this point, the emperor did not care. After six years,

Gregory was allowed to return to Rome, serving as a secretary to the pope.

When Pelagius II died, Gregory's popularity thrust him into the papacy. He accepted unwillingly, preferring to return to the monastery. As pope, here is what he faced—the Western Roman Empire and its protection was gone. The collapse of civil authority after the invasion of the Lombards meant that, as pope, Gregory would be forced to wear two hats. One, as chief civil administrator to physically protect the people of Rome and Italy; the second, to head the Catholic church for the whole world.

He appointed regional governors, gave orders to Roman generals, and negotiated peace with the Lombards.

> At one point, like Pope St. Leo and Attila, Gregory met the Lombard warlord Agilulf outside the gates of Rome and convinced him…apparently through promising a subsidy…to lift his siege.[24]

As pope, Gregory rigorously reformed the church. He removed and disciplined corrupt clergy, enforced celibacy, defended the church from heresies, revitalized the liturgy, and emphasized the absolute supremacy of the Roman pontiff by pointing out that even the bishop of Constantinople accepted Rome's primacy.

Gregory was a strong supporter of missionary work. He sent and supported the efforts of Augustine of Canterbury to convert England. He encouraged the church in southern France to buy British adolescent males from the local slave markets and train them as monks. He directed his missionaries not to worry unduly about perfection in their new charges but to make use of local customs and ways, turning them to the advantage of the church and gently leading the newly baptized to the light. This became a standard approach in the church. Crocker writes,

It is amazing that a man who achieved so much…including creation of the Gregorian chant…was bedridden for so much of his pontificate, and wracked by such pain that he prayed for death, which finally came in 604.[25]

Today, he is called Gregory the Great.

After eight hundred years, Pope Leo III (795–816), the ninety-sixth successor of Peter, was the leader of Jesus' church.

Notes

1. St. Augustine, *The Confessions of St. Augustine, Book VI*, Cardinal ed., trans. Edward B. Pusey, D.D. (New York, NY: Pocket Books, Inc., 1952) 88.
2. Crocker, *Triumph*, 83.
3. Richard P. McBrien, general ed., *HarperCollins Encyclopedia of Catholicism*, (San Francisco, CA: HarperSanFrancisco, 1995), 115.
4. William Jurgens, *Faith of the Early Fathers, Vol. 3*, (Collegeville, MD: The Liturgical Press, 1998), quoted in Crocker, *Triumph*, 88.
5. Alan Schreck, Ph.D., *What Did The First Four "Ecumenical" or Universal Councils of the Christian Church Teach About Jesus?*, http://www.thetruthdecoded.org.au/early-understandings-Jesus.php
6. Hughes, *The Church in Crisis*, 50.
7. Thomas D. McGonigle and James F. A. Quigley, *A History of the Christian Tradition, Volume 1* (Mahweh, NJ: The Paulist Press, 1988), 108.
8. Hughes, *The Church in Crisis*, 77.
9. Ibid., 81-82.
10. Ibid., 84.
11. Ibid.
12. Ibid., 88-89.
13. Ibid., 90.
14. Hughes, *The Church in Crisis*, 151.
15. *New World Encyclopedia*, s.v. "Second Council of Constantinople," http:// www.newworldencyclopedia.com/ (accessed) July 7, 2013.
16. Thomas E. Woods, Jr., *How the Catholic Church Built Western Civilization*, (Washington, DC: Regnery Publishing, Inc., 2005), 28
17. Saint Patrick, *Wikipedia*, http://www.orthodoxwiki.org/patrick_of_Ireland.
18. American Catholic.org, s.v. "Augustine of Canterbury" (accessed) July 6, 2013.

19. *Catholic Encyclopedia, http://www.newadvent.org.*, s.v. "St. Boniface," (accessed) July 21, 2013.
20. Jose Orlandis, *A Short History of the Catholic Church*, (Dublin, IR: Four Courts Press, 1993) 47, 49.
21. Crocker, *Triumph*, 90
22. Woods, Jr. *How the Catholic Church Built Western Civilization*, 11.
23. Ibid., 13.
24. Crocker, *Triumph*, 107.
25. Ibid., 108.

Jesus' Church

800–1200 AD

This time period begins with one of the great heroes of church history: Charlemagne (742–814). In the year 800, something very important in his career and for the fortunes of the church took place. Pope Leo III (795–816) was attacked by a mob during a public procession in Rome. He escaped and fled to France seeking protection from the king. After Charlemagne heard the pope's story, he sent him back to Italy, under guard, with the promise that he would personally return to Rome and settle things.

Charlemagne kept his word, going to Rome in November. At Mass on Christmas Day 800, Pope Leo III crowned Charlemagne as Holy Roman Emperor and protector of the Holy Father. The Holy Roman Empire of the west, after a gap of 324 years, was reinstated, establishing a sense of unity between the church and western Europe. Charlemagne, a great Christian leader, ruled alone for forty-two years (772–814). While he fought against the Muslims in Spain, and for thirty years against the Saxons, he was also known for his contributions to Western culture. Although he couldn't read, he undertook revival of the arts, architecture, and education throughout his kingdom.

Seeds of a Major Church Rebellion Planted Earlier

We have to go back in time to 330. Emperor Constantine, who had ended persecution against Christians in 313, had moved the empire's capital from Rome, Italy, to a strategically superior location on the Mediterranean called Byzantium, which was over a thousand miles east of Rome. It was referred to as New Rome. Constantine renamed it after himself, Constantinople. Today it is Istanbul. This move would unwittingly create a rivalry model that would have severe consequences for the church. It would be a gradual process.

Since Constantinople was considered the "new Rome," the emperor also wanted the spiritual capital of Rome moved to the new Rome. The church successfully resisted. The emperor wanted a patriarchate and wanted it to be equal to Rome's position, or number two, behind Rome. The papacy could not grant that status because it wouldn't be fair. While the church had many geographical divisions headed by bishops, it had recognized, at that time, only three patriarchates in this order of importance—Rome, Alexandria, and Antioch, which had rich spiritual backgrounds. However, the church was politically pressured into granting a patriarchate to Constantinople without a number two ranking.

But Constantinople was relentless in wanting to leap-frog in importance over Alexandria and Antioch. Remember how at the Council of Constantinople in 381, Eastern bishops had not invited the pope or any bishops from the West? While this council affirmed the Nicene Creed and added recognition of the Holy Spirit as divine, they also inserted a claim that Constantinople was second to Rome in importance. The pope denied that part of the council's results.

Again, at the Council of Chalcedon in 451, the bishops of Constantinople and Jerusalem were confirmed as patriarchs. The pope's legates, thinking all business had been concluded, left for home. The council, with a majority of Eastern bishops, once again, inserted Constantinople's claim to be number two. When the pope received the council's papers, he refused, once again, to approve that claim of the council.

There were now two rival groups in the church: the East and the West, based on empire political restructuring. The lineup in the East was Alexandria, Antioch, Jerusalem, and Constantinople, which was the capital of the Eastern Empire. The emperor of Constantinople usually worked hand-in-hand with his patriarch. The other sees in the east were weaker and influenced by the dominance of their emperor and his patriarch. The west was centralized in Rome and supported by the bishops in its area. This rivalry was contrary to the one unified Church Jesus wanted with Peter and his successors as leaders. From 330, when Constantinople was founded, there would be constant tensions between Constantinople and Rome about leadership authority. We'll now look at two patriarchs of Constantinople and their bold rebellion against papal authority—Photius (858–886) and Michael Cerularius (1043–1058).

Photius (858–886)

These tensions were about to take a critical turn. It involved a man named Photius, who, by his actions, was challenging the primacy of Rome. This was a serious problem. It would eventually require the fourth council of Constantinople in 869 to try to resolve it. Briefly, there were a series of events leading to that council and its aftermath. In 847, Ignatius became patriarch in Constantinople. In 858, a young emperor, Michael III, took over the empire. He was nineteen and would soon become known as Michael the Drunkard. He arranged the murder of his chief advisor who had guided him during his regency years and replaced him with his uncle, Bardas, who was capable but had very loose morals. Ignatius, the patriarch, would not allow Bardas to receive Holy Communion until he amended his immoral way of living. This action would lead to Ignatius's downfall. In November 858, it happened. Ignatius was arrested and deported, and the emperor announced that Ignatius had returned to his monastic life.

Photius, Ignatius's replacement was very learned and had been in the service of emperors, but he was a layman. Photius notified Rome of his election and consecration, seeking papal approval for his becoming patriarch.

Pope Nicholas the Great (855–867) would not approve Photius for that position until he had an onsite report about him in Constantinople. He sent two bishops as legates to find the facts. The legates delivered papal letters to Photius and the emperor and then, forgetting that they had been sent only as observers, they joined with Photius in a second council in which Ignatius was to be judged and deposed once again. This gave the impression that papal authority was on the side of Photius. Ignatius himself said to the legates, "I cannot be judged by you for you were not sent here to judge me."[1] This was in April 861. When the legates returned to Rome, Nicholas deposed them.

At a council of his own, the pope eliminated the whole proceedings of April 861. He dismissed Photius's plea that in the East, the law prohibiting laymen from being elected to sees was a "dead letter." Nicholas reminded Photius that what the pope decides in the exercise of the primacy is final. Months later, Ignatius appealed to the pope against his deposition, giving him the story of his actions with Bardas in regard to Holy Communion and its consequences. This would lead to another council in Rome.

In April 863, it happened. Pope Nicholas now had the whole story. At this council, there was a general deposition of Photius, the legates who erred in their job, and all people that Photius had ordained or consecrated in his nine years as patriarch. Ignatius was proclaimed the lawful patriarch and Photius was ordered to surrender his see to Rome. There was a long silence from Constantinople.

Two and a half years later, on September 28, 865, Michael III, the emperor, finally replied. He described the pope's letter as a mass of blasphemies. This letter reopened what had been settled in 863 when Photius was turned back into a layman. The pope, in a gesture of reconciliation, invited Photius and Ignatius to appear in Rome and put on their case. Now another long wait.

On November 13, 866, Pope Nicholas ended the silence with an angry reply by letter castigating the emperor for his previous letter about mass blasphemies. Nicholas warned that unless the emperor made amends by burning that letter publicly, the pope would do so "in the presence of all the bishops in the West."[2] It is not known whether the emperor received the letter as the legates carrying this reply were turned away at the Byzantine frontier. The legates then made their way to a band of legates sent to the court of Boris, king of the Bulgarians. Here is where we discover the hidden conflict between Rome and Constantinople—Bulgaria.

The Bulgarians had been a great menace to the European side of the empire for 150 years. During the Photius controversy, Emperor Michael offered to make peace with Bulgaria on condition that their king become a Christian. Boris, their king, agreed and was baptized. Shortly, a flood of missionaries set out to convert Bulgarians. This bothered the pope. Much of this territory had once been under the direct control of the pope as patriarch of Rome but was lost when emperors shifted territorial lines. Not lost to the pope were the continuing challenges from New Rome for authority.

A rift had developed between King Boris and Photius. Boris wanted a church under his control with his own patriarch. Photius did not have the authority to grant that request. Boris then turned to Rome, which also said no, but Rome offered him an archbishop. New Latin missionaries led by Formosus, a cardinal and future pope, met with King Boris and were happy to point out to him where the superiority lay between Constantinople and Rome. Boris agreed and then sent the Greek missionaries back to Photius. Photius sent an encyclical letter back to the bishops of the East, setting out points where Latins differed and condemning them. One point was the Filioque "heresy." Therefore, a council would be held shortly about these matters in Constantinople. Photius complained that people were getting tired of the tyranny "of him who is now, at Rome, in power."³

The council promised by the emperor met in the summer of 867 in Constantinople. Heavily attended by bishops of the East, it approved Photius's excommunication against Pope Nicholas. It called on the emperor of the West, the successors of Charlemagne, to carry out the sentence and expel the pope. It was not a denial of the Roman claim by divine appointment to be the head of all the churches. Pope Nicholas had been sick during the time of the Council and died November 13, 867, long before news of the sentence reached Rome.

On September 24, 867, Basil the Macedonian, came onto the stage of history. He had Emperor Michael III of Constantinople murdered and took his place as the new emperor. In a clean sweep of the old regime, Photius was dismissed in November 867, just about the same time Pope Nicholas died. Ignatius, still alive and willing to serve, was installed once again as patriarch of Constantinople. Basil, the new emperor, wrote to Rome about these changes, suggesting a new general council.

The Fourth General Council of Constantinople (869–870)

This was the eighth council of the church. Unlike the first seven, this one was not about theological matters. Emperor Basil's purpose for a council was to try and unite all rival parties of Ignatians and Photians and eliminate any reason for discontent.

The new pope was Adrian II (867–872). In preparation for the council, he called his own council in Rome on June 10, 869. The sole subject of their discussion would be the Byzantine Council of 867 that had excommunicated Pope Nicholas, his predecessor. The papers of that council were produced and burned. Likewise, the proceedings of earlier Photius councils in 859 and 861 were condemned. Photius himself was cast out of the church with a proviso that even if he were to repent, he would remain a layman. Legates were appointed to represent the pope and were given their instructions. The council was not to reopen past questions but simply to confirm the decisions expressed by the pope in the council of Rome in June 869. No bishop consecrated by Photius was to be given a seat.

The council began on October 5, 869. The main event of the council for the church was to condemn Photius and his associates for the crime of 867 when they tried to excommunicate and depose Pope Nicholas. In the mind of the pope, this council in Constantinople had been called for nothing else. The legates had their way. This was not to be a trial but the acceptance of decisions already reached in Rome. There was no sign of regret from Photius. A week after Photius was condemned, there was a solemn bonfire ordered by the pope of all Photius anti-papal writings and the proceedings of his council of 867.

The eighth council was over, but the legates' troubles were not. Present as spectators at the ceremonial closing were representatives from the king of Bulgaria. Boris had once again changed his mind because the pope had turned down his request to have Formosus as his archbishop. So the representatives had come to ask the emperor and Ignatius once more to take over the Bulgarian mission. The last act of the legates was to warn the newly restored Ignatius not to be involved with the Bulgarians. There would be severe penalties if he did. They even gave Ignatius a letter from the pope, who had anticipated this exact situation. Ignatius put the letter aside. The legates returned to Rome. The next news was that Ignatius had consecrated ten bishops for Bulgaria, ignoring the pope's command. On November 10, 870, Pope Adrian wrote a letter to the emperor regarding the attitude of Ignatius toward the Bulgarians, with threats about this. He also excommunicated the Bulgarian king.

Pope Adrian II died on December 14, 872. He was succeeded by Pope John VIII (872–882), whose mind was very clear about the problem. His first action was to renew the demands about Bulgaria by reminding Ignatius that he had been restored as patriarch of Constantinople because he had promised Pope Adrian that he would withdraw Greek missionaries from Bulgaria. The new pope warned the patriarch, Ignatius, that unless he made good on his promise, he would be deposed. The pope recognized that if a new convert nation was so closely related to the Byzantine Empire, it would be always in danger of schism and heresy. The pope had a sense of what was to come and explained so in a letter to Ignatius. There was no reply.

The patience of the pope toward Ignatius's endless delays on the Bulgarian problem was exhausted. In April 878, the pope sent two delegates to Constantinople to give Ignatius a final warning. Ignatius would have thirty days to act. If he didn't, the legates were given instructions and authority to excommunicate and depose him. When the legates arrived, they were in for several surprises. Ignatius had been dead for nearly a year. In fact, when Pope John VIII was drafting his letter, Ignatius had already been dead for six months. Such were the hazards of international relations that a letter could travel no faster than a horse could run. If you add fierce winters when everything stops, communications became very slow, but the legates were in for an even greater surprise. Ignatius's replacement was Photius! When Ignatius died, Photius had immediately taken his place.

The story gets more complicated. In addition to the Bulgarian problem, the legates had been given another task by the pope. They were to make an urgent plea to the Eastern emperor for military help to prevent the anticipated conquest of all Italy. The control of Sicily and places on the mainland was already lost. The remnants of the once strong house of Charlemagne were now woefully weak. The pope knew that Constantinople was his only hope. When Emperor Basil's delegation arrived in Rome in the spring of 879 to negotiate the peaceful recognition of Photius, they were in a strong bargaining position. The outcome of their visit would result in a follow-up council in Constantinople at which 385 bishops were in attendance. Photius, as the central figure, presided! The presence of the three papal legates gave a full outward sign of the pope's approval.

Pope John accepted the *fait accompli* of Photius who was to acknowledge his great crime of excommunicating the pope in 867 and express his sorrow. The pope agreed to wash clean all that the eighth council had enacted against Photius. Remnants of anti-Photians were now told by the pope that Photius was their lawful patriarch, and they were not to oppose him in the name of the council of 869. The Apostolic See can impose such sentences and remove them. Rome was not changing a declaration on faith and morals. Personalities were in conflict, not ideas or doctrine. Reconciliation continued under Photius. In 887, Emperor Basil's son, Leo VI, accused Photius of conspiracy. Exiled a second time, Photius died in retirement.[4]

But providentially, in 909, one hundred forty-five years before the death blow to church unity that will be delivered by Cerularius, a miracle seed was being planted in a small town in France called Cluny. The founding of this monastery at Cluny would become one of the most significant events in the history of the church and western civilization. What was the Cluny story?

Cluny (909)

In 909, Duke William I of Aquitaine, a wealthy man, donated a portion of his hunting preserve in the forests of Burgundy to build a monastery in a small French town called Cluny. The Cluny abbey would be free of all present and future financial obligations to him and his family. In this way, the monks could pursue spiritual good instead of material wealth. His main concern was prayer for himself. In his earlier years, in a fit of passion and rage, he had killed a man, and it bothered him. He wanted the monks to pray for him continuously, even after his death, as expiation for his sin.

> The genius of Cluny was its independence. The organizational structure of the monastery was revolutionary for its time. Wishing to ensure the monastery stayed free of ecclesiastical politics and lackluster practice of the faith, William of Aquitaine made Cluny beholden only to the pope and not the local bishop. The move assured that Cluny could become a center of authentic monastic renewal. The reform at Cluny would spread throughout the Church and would encompass even the papacy as three strong monks of Cluny would become noted papal reformers within the eleventh century…the same century of the Great schism.
>
> Weidenkopf and Schreck, Epic, 139

Each monastery was not autonomous but under the great abbot at Cluny. Therefore, each monastery was not subject to its local abbot, who might be there because of "connections." In turn, the great abbot at Cluny, who ruled over 3,000 priories, was loyal to the pope. These priors would periodically hold meetings at Cluny where they would discuss their problems and recommend measures that the abbot would make official policy. In this way, reform initiatives from all over western Europe were considered at Cluny and the entire weight of the Cluniac organization was thrown behind those considered worthy of such support. Cluny, in many ways, became the dynamo that powered the engine of reform directed toward rescuing the church and lay society as well.

Many bishops came from Cluniac monasteries, and from this sort of infiltration, gradual reform was brought about. The church could never flourish and fulfill its mission until it became absolutely independent of all temporal powers and interests—bishops belonged to the church, not to the prince; priests belonged to the church, not to the world, wives, or families; no ecclesiastical appointments should be made by laymen; priestly celibacy must be restored in all its vigor (this would prevent sons of clergy from inheriting church property); the church must be wholly spiritual; the church should gather around its spiritual head, the pope.

Cluny held to the tradition of one flock, one shepherd, and one church. In a Europe in which political authority had become permanently fragmented, they worked for a universal and centralized ecclesiastical establishment with the bishop of Rome to whom the Scriptures had given "the keys to the kingdom," as its supreme authority.[5] Monasteries were founded in great numbers. Religious enthusiasm ran high. Cluny became a home of learning and a training school for four popes and many, many bishops. Benedict XVI, the present pope emeritus, said:

> When the process of the formation of European identity was at its height, the Cluny experience spread over vast regions of the European continent, and made its important and precious contributions. It recalled the primacy of the good of the spirit; and from this it drew attention toward the things of God; it inspired and favored initiatives and institutions for the promotion of human values; it educated in a spirit of peace.
>
> —Pope Benedict (address to General Audience, 11/11/2009)

Meanwhile, east versus west tensions were reaching a breaking point. Peace with Photius was only on the surface. His cause did not die. It remained latent in the party he left that still hated the west and was ready to break out again at the first pretext. All it needed was the right man and the right circumstance to make it happen. That man was Michael Cerularius. In the *Pilgrim Church*, the author writes,

> As background to the case of Michael Cerularius, we must make mention of a growing 'nationalism' in both East and West. The Greek, or Byzantine, empire had regained some of its lost territories, with the result that it achieved a new sense of solidarity and identity. The West was now wedded to the Frankish kingdom; it had its protector. The net effect was that the mentality of both sides changed considerably. The East now felt itself politically equal to the West and, as always, culturally superior. The West looked on the East as heretical and decadent. It was from this mindset that the principal actors in the Cerularius affair would speak.
>
> —William J. Bausch, *Pilgrim Church,* rev. and exp. ed. by Carol Ann Cannon, M.A. and Robert Obach, Ph.D. (Mystic, CN: Twenty-Third Publications, 1989), 177

Michael Cerularius (1043–1058)

In 1052, Michael Cerularius, the patriarch of Constantinople, outlawed the celebration of the Latin rite form of Mass in Constantinople, angering a large Latin community in the city. When Pope St. Leo IX (1049–1054) heard about this, he sent a letter to the emperor and patriarch, and then decided to follow up on the letter by sending a delegation to Constantinople. Chosen to lead the group was Cardinal Humbert, learned but hot-tempered. Unsuccessful negotiations with Cerularius angered him. On Saturday, July 16, 1054, as prayers were about to begin in the cathedral of Hagia Sophia in Constantinople, Cardinal Humbert strode into the cathedral, walked up to the main altar, and placed on it a document that declared that Michael Cerularius, the patriarch of Constantinople, was excommunicated. The cardinal then marched out of the church and left the city. A week later, Michael Cerularius, with his patriarchal synod, solemnly excommunicated the cardinal and the pope.

The Great Schism (1054)

This dramatic incident marked the beginning of the schism that still separates Roman Catholics and the Eastern Orthodox to this day.

> The Eastern schism was not a movement arising in all the East; it was not a quarrel between two large bodies; it was the rebellion of Constantinople, one See, which by the emperor's favor had already acquired such influence that it was able, unhappily, to drag the other patriarchs into schism with it.
>
> —*Catholic Encyclopedia*, s.v. "Eastern Schism," http://www.newadvent.org/cathen/ 1335a.htm (accessed August 18, 2013)

The ecclesiastical communion between the Roman papacy and the Greek church was split. From that time forward, the restoration of unity was a permanent objective of Christendom. Political quarrels and personal antagonisms with faults on both sides were the original cause of the schism, not dogmatic differences.

Greek delegates to the Second Council of Lyons in 1274, and again at the Council of Florence in 1439, admitted that they should return to unity with Rome. But on each occasion on their return to the east their admissions were repudiated through national interests. "It wasn't until Constantinople fell to the Turks and the empire of Byzantium disappeared (1453) that the desire and hope of terminating the Eastern schism and rebuilding Christianity came to an end."[6] The excommunications existed until 1965 when Pope Paul VI and Athanagoras, patriarch of Constantinople, lifted them. But the schism is still a great wound to the church and Pope Benedict XVI carried on the work of Pope John Paul II in trying to reunite the east and west.

In the eighth, ninth, and tenth centuries, meddlesome secular rulers were displacing or installing bishops of their own choosing. Pope Gregory VII (1073–1085) brought things to a head in a clash against the Holy Roman Emperor Henry IV in Germany. This clash happened in a time period between the schism in 1054 and the first crusade in 1096.

At that time, Europe was a feudal society with lords and vassals. The lord would give a vassal land in exchange for loyalty and military support, if needed. Bishops were also given land as vassals with temporal authority. In Germany, Emperor Henry IV officiated at ceremonies where bishops received their land and secular authority, along with their symbols of ecclesiastical authority (crozier and ring). This brought up a crucial question: who has the right to install a bishop? Pope Gregory wanted to stop the practice as it challenged his authority to control his spiritual realm. He called an emergency meeting of top German nobles.

Henry was enraged. He denounced Gregory as an adulterer, a liar, illegitimately elected, and a menace to the peace of Europe. Henry basically deposed the pope. Again, this was a secular ruler meddling in affairs of the church. Pope Gregory, in return, excommunicated Henry and absolved all his subjects from loyalty to him. This opened doors for other rulers to take over his followers. This had never been done before. Various rulers tried to move in which created anxieties for Henry. Some German nobles called for a meeting in Augsburg to have Gregory judge Henry, who now began to panic, and wanted to make amends with the pope.

Gregory traveled to Augsburg, and on his way, came to a small town, Canossa, where he stayed at a castle. Meanwhile, Henry, dressed as a pauper with his family, traveled across the Alps in dead winter to beg forgiveness from Gregory. When Henry arrived at Canossa, he knelt barefoot in the snow, knocking at the castle door to beg for forgiveness. To make sure Henry was truly sorry, Gregory left him outside for three full days! Finally,

Gregory brought Henry into the castle, heard his confession, absolved him, and brought him back into communion with the church.

After several years, Henry resurrected lay investiture. Gregory excommunicated him again. Henry was furious. This time he didn't go begging for forgiveness. In 1083, Henry led his army to attack the pope in Rome. Gregory took refuge in Castel San D'Angelo and called for military protection from the Normans, who came and drove away Henry's army. However, the Normans sacked Rome for three days making Gregory unpopular with the people. In 1085, Pope Gregory VII died. The war against lay investiture continued through the reign of two more popes.

Finally, Pope Calixtus (1119–1124) became pope. The chief historical significance of his reign would be the settlement of the long and bitter investiture quarrel. After several false starts, he made things happen. In 1122, at a place called Worms, in Germany, a peace conference was held between the two parties at which the emperor agreed to give up the whole system of investiture so far as concerns the church. To affirm this, Pope Calixtus II called the first church council ever held in the West.

The First General Council of the Lateran (1123)

This was the ninth general church council, but the first one ever held in the West. It took place in Rome on March 18, 1123 at the Lateran Basilica. Over 300 bishops attended. Pope Calixtus II presided in person. At the First Lateran Council, both originals of agreements of the pope and emperor regarding lay investitures that occurred at the Treaty of Worms the previous year were read and ratified. "It put a stop to the arbitrary conferring of ecclesiastical benefices by laymen, and ratified the principle that spiritual authority can only emanate from the Church."[7]

The Second General Council of the Lateran (1139)

The second Lateran Council happened just sixteen years later, making it the tenth general church council. Here's why it was needed. When Pope Calixtus died in 1124, he was succeeded by Cardinal Lambert who had negotiated the Great Concordat at Worms. Taking the name Honorius II (1124–1130), he lived out his full pontificate in Rome, being the first pope to do so in the previous one hundred years. Rome was not a peaceful city at that time and dangerous for popes. Not having steady residential rulers had consequences—old wealthy family feuds were revived. Here's what happened. Honorius died in 1130. After his death, the Pierleone faction influenced the election of Petrus Leonis, one of the family. He took the name Anacletus II. The Frangipani faction elected Innocent II (1130–1143). The latter was the better of the two, but which one was the lawfully elected one? Neither had been elected exactly as the Law of 1059 prescribed in which

> Cardinals were to elect a candidate, who would take office after receiving the assent of the clergy and laity. The most senior cardinals, the cardinal bishops, were to meet first and discuss the candidates before summoning the cardinal priests and cardinal deacons for the actual vote. Imperial confirmation was dropped.
> —http://www.wikepedia.org/wiki/Papal-conclave

Innocent fled to France for support, which he received from King Louis V of France, the empire, England, and Spain. Both were acting as popes.

Anacletus, the antipope, died in 1138. Under St. Bernard of Clairvaux's influence, the would-be successor of Anacletus made his submission to Pope Innocent. With the death of the antipope, Innocent returned to Rome and called the Second Lateran

Council with the aim of strengthening Church unity. It met April 4–17 in 1139.

Five hundred bishops and one thousand abbots attended. The latter number reflects the growth and importance of monasteries within the church structure. The details of the council have perished, except for the thirty canons, dealing with church discipline that were enacted. There is a chronicler's story of the pope's fiery reception of his recent opponent.

> This bishop made his way to the papal throne, and laid down his mitre at the pope's feet, in token of submission. But the pope arose, and kicked the mitre down the church, calling out, "Away, henceforth you are no bishop of mine."[8]

Events Leading to a Third Lateran Council

Emperor Frederick I of Germany (called Barbarossa), had invaded Italy in 1158, working his way toward Rome. As cities everywhere in his path were submitting to the invasion, the emperor would appoint his own governors as rulers. Frederick was determined to make himself master of the church and reduce the papacy to an imperial dependency. This serious situation developed because of two weak popes who allowed Frederick to do what he pleased with the church.

Pope Adrian I (1154–1159), the 169th pope, was alarmed at Frederick's advances and began to mediate with the Normans for protection. Suddenly, on September 1, 1159, Pope Adrian died. The tragedy of the double election of thirty years before was about to be repeated! There were two candidates, both cardinals—Roland Baldinelli, who had been the right-hand man of Pope Adrian I, and his rival, Octavian, who came from one of the most powerful Roman families. He was also the emperor's man. Octavian got four votes, Baldinelli twenty-two.

On September 7, 1159, as successor of Pope Adrian, Baldinelli took the name Alexander III. However, a minority of cardinals, backed by Emperor Frederick II, elected Octavian, who assumed the name Pope Victor IV (1159–1164). He was an antipope. This double-pope situation would last for eighteen years with Victor IV based in Rome where the empire had control. The real Pope, Alexander III, was a wandering pope, mostly in France and sometimes in southern Italy near the friendly protection of the king of Sicily. When Victor died, he was followed by two successive antipopes, Paschal III (1164–1168) and Calixtus III (1168–1178).

In September 1174, Emperor Frederick embarked on his fifth Italian invasion campaign to settle the constant revolts in Lombardy and his quarrels with Pope Alexander III. It was a surprising and disastrous defeat for Frederick. His rule over Lombardy was decisively broken. The victory of the Lombard league forced the emperor to travel to Venice in 1177 to participate in an important peace treaty between the papacy and its allies and the emperor. After a preliminary agreement was made, a conference was scheduled for July 24, 1177, at which Frederick formally acknowledged Alexander as pope and abandoned his own surviving antipope, Calixtus III. When Calixtus made his submission to Alexander, the bad precedent of 1139, when Pope Innocent kicked the former antipope's mitre, was not followed. Alexander received him as a guest and gave him a job. Pope Alexander III (1159–1181), the 170th pope, is now considered to be one of the sixth or seventh greatest popes in the history of the church.

The Third General Council of the Lateran (1179)

This special council was the aftermath of these Venetian events. It opened on March 5, 1179. Three hundred bishops were in attendance. We know nothing of how the council conducted its business because its acts have not survived. However, the pope proposed twenty-seven canons. Firstly, he wanted to end the nightmare of double elections. He wanted to amend the law of 1059 about papal elections that left openings for these kinds of errors. There should be no uncertainty about the meaning of such a law, so he rewrote that law, which has lasted to the present day. Canon two dealt with the damage done by the three antipopes during their reigns. There were annulments of all ordinations performed by them and the individuals they ordained.

Church Reform

In the eighth, ninth, and tenth centuries, many ecclesiastical abuses began to negatively affect the church. Simony (the buying of church offices) was common. Celibacy was not faithfully followed. Some priests had mistresses and children. Homosexuality among the clergy was on the rise. The papacy began to reform itself under the strong leadership of three strong popes—St. Leo IX (1049–1054), St. Gregory VII (1073–1085), and Blessed Urban II (1088–1099). A doctor of the church, St. Peter Damien, wrote *The Book of Gomorrah*, which addressed the problems, urging the pope to take action. Pope Leo IX did. He took his reform program to France, Italy, and modern Germany, trying to restore the holiness of the church. He enforced the vow of celibacy by punishing priests who violated that vow, and he got rid of all bishops who bought their titles.

Growth of Intellectual Activity in the Church

The church would become the foundation of universities and learning that brought us to our present day. Here's how it progressed. In the ninth and tenth centuries, theology and philosophy were taught primarily in monasteries. In the eleventh and twelfth centuries, education moved from the monasteries to the establishment of cathedral schools. In the twelfth and following centuries, universities were founded and even funded by the churches. This would lead to scholasticism. What was scholasticism?

> Scholasticism was the attempt to use reason in trying to understand the truths of faith by correlating philosophical views with Biblical views. The developing scholasticism of the monastic and cathedral schools of the 12th century reached its full flowering in the great universities of the 13th century. Between 1140–1260, scholars tried to use philosophy provided by Aristotle to organize truths of faith and to show harmony between reason and faith. How can we use reason to understand the faith better?
>
> —McGonigle and Quigley,
> *A History of the Christian Tradition*, 152

St. Anselm (1033–1109) is considered the father of scholasticism. In his work, *Why Did God Become Man?* Anselm presented his theory of atonement by explaining how human beings are reconciled to God through Christ. Since sin was an infinite offense against God, the debt owed to God because of sin was also infinite. Only one who was both divine and human could pay such a debt. Therefore, it is the death of Christ, the God-man, on the cross as an infinite sacrifice, who pays the debt of sin and reconciles human beings to God.

Anselm had an interesting quote on faith and understanding, "I do not seek to understand so that I may believe; but, I believe in order that I may understand. For this, too, I believe that unless I first believe, I shall not understand."[9] When Charlemagne died in 814, his empire was divided among his three sons. Unfortunately, the peace and security established by him did not continue after his death. His sons and their descendants did not have Charlemagne's leadership and administrative skills, which eventually led to the collapse of the Carolingian Empire. Without Charlemagne's strong leadership, western Europe would be caught up in many violent battles. The ninth and tenth centuries particularly stand out because of the collapse of the empire and the rise of the Vikings.

Who were the Vikings? Aware of the internal divisions crumbling Charlemagne's empire, Vikings came from Scandinavian countries (Denmark, Norway, and Sweden). Around 830, they exploited this moment of weakness by beginning raids in Britain, Spain, France, and England. Lack of organized naval opposition throughout western Europe allowed Viking ships to travel freely, raiding or trading as opportunity permitted. They used their expertise of seamanship and battle to make bold and brutal raids on European towns and churches of neighboring kingdoms, burning, pillaging, and raping. One form of valuables taken in raids was people, whom they would then sell as slaves. Vikings sacked Paris on Easter Sunday 845.

This ravaging of Europe continued for about 200 years. Shortly after the year 1,000, the Viking king was baptized. They were no longer considered a threat to Europe.

The pope had three goals in proposing a Crusade.

The first major goal was to liberate Jerusalem and the Holy Land. On August 10, 1071, the Byzantine Empire (the East), suffered a devastating loss at Manzikert (in Turkey) at the hands of the ferocious Seljuk Turks. What had been long-settled areas in the heart of the Byzantine Empire were now gone. The emperor made a plea to the pope for help. The West saw this as a signal that the Byzantine Empire was no longer able to protect Eastern Christianity or Christian pilgrims to the holy places in the Holy Land. The pope agreed to the emperor's plea.

The second goal was to help the East halt the Seljuk Turk expansion.

The third goal was the hope that this military aid might reunite East and West. Their schism of 1054 was now in its forty-second year.

The First Crusade (1096–1099)

The First Crusade was launched by Pope Urban II in a speech at the Council of Clermont, France, on November 27, 1095. The pope pleaded for the leadership descendants of Charlemagne to liberate Jerusalem. The holy places were being desecrated, and pilgrims were being persecuted and denied access. The pope promised indulgences to those who would carry the cross to Jerusalem. Indulgences were assurances that those who carried the cross (a small cross sewn on their clothing) would merit remission of temporal punishment due to sin. The response was overwhelming. Motivated by love of Christ and the salvation of their souls, the crusaders embarked on their defensive war to recapture ancient Christian lands.

> Thousands took the cross. Bands of poorly armed pilgrims, most of them inexperienced and poor, set out for Constantinople under Peter the Hermit and Walter the Penniless, even before the army gathered. They began by massacring Jews in the Rhine Valley. Many perished on their way east, and the rest were destroyed when they crossed into Anatolia.
>
> The main army, mostly French and Norman knights under baronial leadership…Godfrey of Bouillon, Baldwin of Flanders, Raymond of Toulouse, and others…assembled at Constantinople and proceeded on a long, arduous march through Anatolia. They captured Antioch (June 3, 1098) and finally Jerusalem (July 15, 1099) in savage battles.
>
> —*Academic American Encyclopedia*
> (Danbury, CT: Grolier Electronic Publishing, Inc.), 2

Manpower cost had been great. Of sixty thousand fighting men, twelve thousand survived. Their pilgrimages complete, the majority of crusaders returned home. To protect the conquest of Jerusalem and the Holy Land, Crusader leaders formed four crusader states along the Syrian and Palestinian coast.

Constantly short of manpower, military orders were created. These were groups of fighting men who would make a permanent way of life in religious communities as "warrior monks." They formed the backbone of Christian defense by manning and running important fortifications throughout Palestine and Syria. The main military orders were the Hospitallers, Templars, Teutonic knights, and the Knights of the Holy Sepulchre. (The most important of all the military orders, the Hospitallers, still exists today. It had different name changes. It was known as Hospitallers until 1309, Knights of Rhodes from 1309 until 1522, and has been called the Knights of Malta since 1530.) Despite the rise of military orders, Christians were victims of a successful attack against Edessa, one of the four crusader states, in which 6,000 men, women, and children were massacred. After forty-eight years, this tragedy would become the catalyst for a Second Crusade.

The Second Crusade (1147–1149)

On hearing the shocking news of Edessa, Pope Eugene III (1145–1153) called for a Second Crusade. He needed someone to rally troops. St. Bernard Clairvaux (1090–1153) was the man. He was well-known during his lifetime and exercised an enormous influence in the affairs of the church. He preached the Crusade, motivating warriors to join the campaign. The Crusade was led by two of the most powerful kings of Europe— Conrad III (the Holy Roman emperor and king of the Germans) and Louis VII (the king of France). Its goal was to retake the city of Edessa, reestablishing the northernmost crusader state. Unfortunately, the kings did not coordinate their plans, and the Byzantines were not able to provide transport for their troops on time. The situation got desperate. Conrad III and his remaining troops went home. Louis VII stayed in the Holy Land trying to help solidify the Christian position.

The Third Crusade (1189–1192)

One fear among the Holy Land Christians was that the Sunnis and Shiites would someday unite their forces under one leader. There were two power bases near the Holy Land—in the north, the Sunnis in Baghdad and in the south, the Shiites in Egypt. Christian fear became a reality when Saladin, a Sunni leader from Iraq, conquered Egypt. He would soon control a united army with a purpose.

He preached against the crusades and wanted to regain Jerusalem. He launched a series of raids into their territory between 1170 and 1184. Saladin marched troops against the city of Tiberius. Christians begged King Guy Lusignan of Jerusalem for help. The king put together the biggest force ever seen at the time, 20,000 fighters, but in doing so he depleted the forces of different Christian garrisons, making them easy prey for attacks. Some nobles were against this plan, but Guy wouldn't listen.

In July 1187, Guy's forces went after Saladin's army in the heat of summer, through the desert, on the way to Tiberius. Saladin's troops held the high ground, surrounded the Christian troops and slaughtered them. Marching throughout the crusader states toward Jerusalem, Saladin's troops captured many towns and arrived at Jerusalem in October 1187. After eighty-eight years under Christian control, Jerusalem was recaptured by the Muslims on October 2, 1187.

News of the fall of Jerusalem and the majority of the crusader states sent shock waves throughout Europe. Pope Urban III (1185–1187) died of grief on October 20. The new pope was Gregory VIII (1187), who was elected October 25. After forty years, a third crusade was needed to try to repossess the Holy Land. Gregory's pontificate would last only one month and twenty-seven days. But he got it started.

This Crusade is sometimes called the Three Kings Crusade because the three major monarchs of Europe would participate—the Holy Roman emperor, Frederick Barbarossa of Germany;

Phillip II, king of France; and Richard the Lionhearted, king of England. There was a problem. France and England were at war with each other when Jerusalem fell. Pope Gregory VIII promulgated a seven-year truce throughout Christendom so that Christian warriors would be free to crusade. Once this treaty was signed, France and England made plans to go on crusade.

Barbarossa gathered a large army. Morale rose when they won a battle against the Turks. Unfortunately, the aged emperor drowned in a river near Tarsus on the way to Antioch. The loss of their revered leader overwhelmed the Germans, and most returned home.

King Richard led an effective campaign, capturing Cyprus, which he would use as a base of crusader operations. His forces met up with King Phillip at Acra, a town under siege. Both Richard and Phillip lifted the siege. They had been at war against each other before the Crusade, so there continued to be some infighting because Richard seemed to be getting most of the credit. Phillip, upset and jealous, returned to France, facing a lot of ridicule for his actions.

Now only Richard and his troops were left. While marching toward Jerusalem, he engaged in a battle with Saladin's army and was victorious but was unable to take Jerusalem. Saladin escaped and was able to reconsolidate his army.

In England's history, some high-profile religious leaders have been forced to make high-stake personal decisions on whether to support the church or the crown. St. Thomas Becket (1118–1170) was one of them.

England became a battleground between the church and the state in the period between the Second and Third Crusades (1149–1189). Henry was a strong-willed king who desired total control in his kingdom. He saw an opportunity to fulfill that desire when the archbishop of Canterbury died in 1162. Henry's plan was to replace him with a trusted friend and longtime advisor, Thomas Becket.

King Henry didn't like the idea that clergy charged with a crime were tried in a church court. Henry wanted the trial to take place in a royal court and tried to enforce his will by passing a law called *The Constitutions of Clarendon*. Becket, standing up for the independence of the church, refused to sign. Becket had to flee for his life to France and eventually ended in Rome to meet with the pope. In 1170, while Henry was away on a campaign in Normandy, Becket returned to England. When Henry found out, he "suggested" to some of his knights that they get rid of that "low-born" priest. Several came back, confronted Becket in his cathedral, and murdered him on December 29, 1170. Thomas Becket gave his life to maintain independence of the church.

Three years later, Becket was declared a saint. Henry, for his part in the murder, had to perform public acts of penance. He walked barefoot to Canterbury wearing a hair shirt and kissed the pillar where Becket was killed. He allowed himself to be publicly whipped by several bishops, an abbot, and eighty monks. Even the three knights who killed Becket repented, confessing to the pope. For their penance, they were instructed to join the templar order and go to the crusader states to fight. After three years in the Holy Land, all three knights died in the service of the church.

At the end of this time period (800–1200), the Catholic church was 1167 years old. Innocent III (1198–1216), the 176th successor of Peter as pope, was reigning in Rome.

Notes

1. Hughes, *The Church in Crisis*, 168.
2. Ibid., 169.
3. Ibid., 172.
4. Ibid., 181.
5. http://www.vlib.us/medieval/lectures/cluny.html
6. Orlandis, *A Short History of the Catholic Church*, 62.
7. *Catholic Encyclopedia*, s.v. "Lateran Council, First," http://www.newadvent.org/cathen/ 13535a.htm (accessed August 18, 2013).
8. Hughes, *Church in Crisis*, 198.
9. http://www.ewtn.com/library/mary/anselm.htm.

Jesus' Church

1200–1600 AD

The early half of the thirteenth century saw the beginning of a new church spiritual support group that still exists today. Friars, while not replacements of monks and the monastic life, would provide an important supplement to their works. This new group, founded on the idea of begging for their existence, allowed them to fully concentrate on their work. Franciscans, Dominicans, Carmelites, and Augustinians are all groups of friars who had their beginnings in that early thirteenth century.

How were monks and friars different? Both monks and friars sought to imitate Christ, but the monk followed the path of the contemplative Christ while the friars chose the apostolic life as described in the Gospels. Monks were concerned with their own conversion and spiritual rebirth. In their desire for silence and solitude, they built their monasteries on the edges of civilization. Their life was a routine of work and prayer with an emphasis on obedience, penance, and especially stability.

The friars sought their own conversion and sanctity in apostolic work by working for the conversion of others. Thus, they built their religious houses in towns and cities where they were mobile and free from encumbrances. Two outstanding founders were St. Francis of Assisi for the Franciscans and St. Dominic for the Dominicans. They had different missions in the church, but both orders embraced holy poverty as their means of existence.

St. Francis of Assisi (1181–1226) was born into a wealthy family in Assisi, Italy. One day, Francis said that he had stopped to pray at the church in San Damiano, when Christ came alive on a crucifix and asked him to "go and repair my church." Francis took it literally and started to repair the little church. Eventually, Francis understood this as a call for universal service. He renounced all his wealth for "sister poverty." Poor, like Jesus, he served the poor while preaching the simplicity of the Gospels. Holiness attracts, and before long, many men were drawn to Francis and joined his mission. In 1210, Pope Innocent III, formally approved the Franciscan community, which has provided some outstanding theologians, plus four popes.

St. Dominic (1170–1221), was born Dominic Guzman in Castile, Spain, and, during his career, became an assistant to a bishop. While traveling with his bishop, he came in contact with Albigensian heretics, who had organized themselves into a hierarchical counter-church and had many converts. *Epic* says,

> Dominic realized the success of the heresy was partially caused by the inability of the clergy to mount an effective verbal offensive against the errors. Linked to this problem was the fact the vast majority of people did not know their faith, primarily because there was no one qualified to teach them. Dominic founded the Order of Preachers (the Dominicans) in an effort to combat this problem. (Weidenkopf and Schreck, *Epic*, 152)

The Dominicans gave the church St. Thomas Aquinas, plus four popes.

St. Thomas Aquinas (1225–1274) was born in Roccasecca, a small town near Naples, Italy. At nineteen, he entered a recently established Dominican order. A humble and pious man, he would become known as the angelic doctor. He lived a busy life of preaching, teaching, and writing. As a Dominican, he studied under St. Albert the Great. This is when he came in contact with an organized presentation of the philosophy of Aristotle, who would be a great influence on his thinking. Aquinas wrote several commentaries on Aristotle, along with more than one hundred other books.

His two most famous books were *Summa contra Gentiles* (1259–1264) and *Summa Theologica* (1267–1273). *Summa contra gentiles* was a defense of Christianity. Aquinas's greatest work, *Summa Theologica*, was intended to be the sum of all life. He divided the Summa in three parts—the nature of God and the emanation of all creatures from God; the return of rational creatures to God; and Christ as the way by which rational creatures return to God.

> The *Summa Theologica* is a kind of literary cathedral in which each part of the mystery of the Christian faith is so presented and related to the other parts that the whole becomes a marvelous proclamation of the beauty of faith seen by the clear light of reason." (McGonigle and Quigley, *A History of the Christian Tradition*, 166)

Besides theological masterpieces, he wrote Eucharistic hymns like *Tantum Ergo*.

On December 6, 1273, Aquinas had a profound spiritual experience. As a result of it, he wrote, "I cannot go on…All that I have written seems to me like so much straw to what I have seen and what has been revealed to me."[1] He did not write or teach after this and died three months later on March 7, 1274. Less than fifty years later, Pope John XXII (1316–1334) officially canonized Aquinas as a saint. In 1567, he was declared a doctor of the church. Over the centuries, his teachings became increasingly influential. In 1879, Pope Leo XIII (1878–1903) mandated the study of Aquinas in all Catholic seminaries and universities.

Pope Innocent III (1198–1216) became head of the church in 1198. He had a brilliant mind, being cofounder with Pope Alexander III (1159–1181) of the canon law system. Innocent was saddled with some serious challenges to the church during his reign. He initiated the Fourth Crusade (120–1205), whose goal was to recapture the Holy Land. It got out of hand. The crusade was diverted by the Venetians to Constantinople, where terrible atrocities were committed by crusaders that, to this day, have created an immovable barrier to reconciliation between the Greek and Latin churches. The pope was unable to stop it. Now Innocent was confronted with another major problem. Great territories in southern France seemed ready to slip away from the Catholic Church because of the Albigensian heresy.

What was the Albigensian heresy? Albigensians believed that there were two Gods: a good God who created all good things that are spiritual, like angels and human souls and an evil God, Satan, who created the physical world. Their teaching was that a person's soul is good; a person's body is evil. Therefore, human salvation is a process of becoming aligned with the good God, by liberating the soul from the contamination of the flesh. To accomplish this, they rejected any sexual activity, refrained from eating eggs and meat, and practiced vigorous fasts. They rejected the Catholic hierarchy and its sacraments and established a counter church, complete with hierarchy and ritual worship. They developed their own ecclesiastical organization, dividing their territories into dioceses. Southern knights sacked churches, seizing property of abbots, bishops, and priests.

Pope Innocent III sent in the Dominicans. Their campaign was ineffective in ending the heresy. In 1208, Pope Innocent sent a papal legate to Count Raymond IV, a major ruler in southern France to meet, discuss, and negotiate on how to solve the heresy problem in his region. Raymond was non-cooperative. On the way home from Toulouse, the papal legate was murdered. There was a strong suspicion that Raymond had something to do with it. The pope had it. He considered the Albigensians dangerous to church unity. He ordered that there would no longer be any preaching or nonviolent means to end the heresy.

In 1208, Pope Innocent declared the second crusade of his reign, this time against the Albigensians and the secular rulers who supported them. This crusade was under the leadership of Simon de Montfort who made great gains in conquering territory held by the heretics. It was a bloody civil war that would last for eighteen years. In 1213, the pope tried to call off the crusade, but troop leaders wouldn't listen to him. The fighting would continue until 1229 when all territories were returned to France and the church, but the heresy wasn't completely wiped out. Preaching hadn't fixed it. Fighting hadn't fixed it.

Gregory IX (1227–1241) came up with a plan for ending the heresy—the medieval Inquisitors. In 1231, Pope Gregory IX formally instituted the legal rules and procedures under which medieval inquisitors would operate. The inquisitors, mostly Dominican, were given the responsibility for wiping out the Albigensian heresy in the south of France. Their purposes were two-fold: they wanted to bring lost souls back to the church, and they wanted to protect the peace and unity within the church.

Clergy, appointed by the pope, would go into a region and establish a tribunal to hear the cases of heretics and try to bring them back into communion with the church. These clergy were known as medieval inquisitors who had jurisdiction *only* over baptized Christians. They had a specific procedure when they entered a region—they would call the people and the clergy together and preach a sermon on the importance of orthodoxy, why they were in the region, and the dangers of heresy. They established a period of grace, which allowed people to make voluntary confessions to the tribunal. They then gave them absolution and penance, allowing them back in communion. After this period of grace expired, the tribunal encouraged people to make accusations of others. When the accused came in, he was asked to make a list of any enemies he might have. If the name of the accuser was on his list, accuser's evidence would be considered invalid. Torture was not authorized until 1252, twenty years after papal-appointed inquisitors were established. It was not mandatory. If one was obstinate in the heresy and would not come back to the church, the tribunal would turn him over to the secular court where punishment for obstinate heresy was death. From 1227 to 1277, a fifty-year period of time, 5000 Albigensian heretics were put to death by secular courts, about one hundred people a year. It took about one hundred years before this heresy finally ended.

In the latter part of this time period, 1517 AD, a Protestant revolution will jolt the church. Its causes were developing in the early 1300s. The process of electing a pope was taking too long. At conclaves, cardinals began to vote in nationality blocs, predominantly the French, who had more cardinals. These would cause delays and a perception of weakness in the papacy. Here's an example:

In 1292, Pope Nicholas IV (1288–1292) died. Two years later, a replacement still had not been made. Peter Murrone, an eighty-year-old holy hermit was deeply concerned. He wrote a letter to one of the cardinals in a conclave, expressing his disappointment on how long it was taking to elect a pope, pointing out that it is the cardinals' duty to put their differences aside and elect a new pope. The cardinal read the letter to the conclave, explained the holiness of Peter the hermit, and this cardinal said that he would vote for Peter Murrone to be the pope. A majority of cardinals elected Peter, and they then made a procession up the mountain to Peter's cell. They convinced him that his acceptance as pope would avoid a schism in the church. Peter accepted and took the name Pope Celestine V, living in Naples. Within five months, realizing that he didn't have the skills needed to handle the job, he resigned and established that a newly elected pope had the faculty to renounce his election. He was succeeded by Pope Boniface VIII (1294–1303).

Bad things were about to happen that would weaken the papacy. Boniface reigned when there were three major powers in

European Christendom—France, England, and the Holy Roman emperor, who were always jockeying to increase their power.

King Philip IV of France considered himself a good Catholic, showing it in a strange way. He began taxing the clergy in France, showing that his power was greater than the church. Pope Boniface was angry. In 1296, he immediately wrote a bull, *Clerecis Laicos,* to his clergy in France forbidding them to pay the tax, saying that the secular government cannot collect church revenue without papal approval. A papal legate delivered a copy to King Philip, who had the legate arrested for treason.

Boniface wrote a second Bull to King Philip, *Asculta Fili* (Listen, Son), threatening to ex-communicate the king unless the legate was released. Philip burned the Bull, and deposed Boniface as being an illegal pope. This raised the question: who rules the church, secular rulers or the pope?

Boniface issued a third Bull, *Unam Sanctum,* which basically stated that a pope is the highest authority on earth. King Philip now responded with force. In September 1303, the king dispatched William of Nogaret, his chief advisor, to take 300 knights and 1000 infantrymen and go to Rome. The pope was arrested and subjected to outrageous treatment until rescued several days later by townspeople. William and the troops then left. Pope Boniface died a month later from his injuries.

Pope Benedict XI (1303–1304) succeeded Boniface. He had a brief pontificate of eight months, but upon being elected pope, he released Philip IV of France from the excommunication that had been laid upon him by Boniface VIII. On June 7, 1304, Benedict excommunicated William of Nogaret, and all the Italians who had played a part in the seizure of Boniface VIII. Benedict died of poisoning by figs, which he loved to eat. His successor, Pope Clement V (1305–1314), would be the beginning of a major problem for the papacy, which would worsen and last for many years.

Raymond Bertrand de Got was a Frenchman who had held high church positions in France, but he wasn't a cardinal. There were rumors he had bound himself to King Philip IV of France by a formal agreement before his elevation as pope. Clement selected Lyon, France, for his coronation. One of his first acts was the creation of nine new French cardinals. King Philip IV wanted Clement V to do three things for him—put the dead Pope Boniface on trial, condemn the Templar Order of Knights, and move the residence of the pope from Rome to Avignon. Pope Clement agreed to do all three. However, Pope Clement's heart wasn't in the Boniface trial. He dragged his feet throughout the trial, and it never came to a conclusion.

The Templar order was a military-religious order founded in 1120 with their *Rule of Life* written by St. Bernard of Clairvaux. People had donated money and land to them so that they were very wealthy and influential throughout western Europe. King Philip didn't like the Templars because they were obstructing his attempt at consolidating power in France. Therefore, he trumped up false charges against them.

On October 13, 1307, Philip ordered the arrest of all Templars in France. Since the Templars were a religious order, only the pope could issue an edict. Pope Clement convened the Council of Vienne (1311–1312), which voted to suppress the Order of Templars. The council made no decision on the innocence or guilt of the charges but simply transferred all the wealth of the Templars to the Hospitallers and other orders in Spain.

The third demand of King Philip IV was that the residency of popes be moved to Avignon, which was a papal possession given to the papacy by King St. Louis IX. It was not a territory governed by the King of France. Pope Clement gave in. As a result, popes will live in Avignon for the next sixty-nine years (1309–1378). Clement and his successors conducted their pontificate as a mere tool of the French monarchy, which was a radical change in church policy. This angered Catholics in Germany, England,

and Italy who felt left out, causing a lack of respect for the papacy and the church.

Papacy returned to Rome in 1378. How did it happen? Great credit goes to St. Catherine of Siena, Italy, who was the twenty-fifth child of a wool dyer. A laywoman, she was associated with the Dominican order as a tertiary, but was known for her holiness. She frequently wrote letters to Pope Gregory XI (1371–1378) asking him to return to Rome. While they were developing a close relationship through their correspondence, she could see that the pope wasn't taking any action on her request.

In 1376, Catherine traveled to Avignon with her confessor as translator to meet the pope in person. After this meeting, Pope Gregory agreed to return. Confronted by French cardinals on his decision, the pope wavered. When Catherine heard of this, she reminded him of a vow he had once taken and had never disclosed to any human being. Greatly impressed by what he regarded as a supernatural sign, Gregory resolved to act upon it at once.[2]

The Great Western Schism (1378–1417)

The return of the papacy to Rome had been a brief honeymoon for the church before the Great Western schism would add another thirty-nine years of papal confusion that would bring further disrespect for the church, the faith, and the papacy. Three men were claiming to be the real pope!

Here's what happened. When Pope Gregory XI died, the College of Cardinals called a conclave to elect a new pope. One of the effects of the Avignon papacy was that the sixteen-member College of Cardinals was stacked with French cardinals—eleven French, four Italians, and one Spaniard. Afraid that the papacy would return to France, the Italian people wanted an Italian pope, and great crowds surrounded the conclave building in Rome. An Italian pope, Urban VI was elected. He ruled the cardinals with an iron fist, verbally and physically abusing them.

Even Catherine of Siena admonished Urban to calm down and be more charitable. Urban wouldn't listen.

All the conclave cardinals, except for the Italians, met secretly, declaring that Urban's election had been forced by threatening crowds. Therefore, they claimed Urban's election was invalid. This secret group elected Robert of Geneva in his place to be pope (actually an antipope taking the name Clement VII). Now there were two popes claiming to be the real thing. Catherine of Siena again got involved, writing a letter to all cardinals outlining why Urban VI was the true pope. They didn't listen.

Urban VI took action. He excommunicated Clement VII, throwing out the entire College of Cardinals and making the composition of cardinals more equitable by nationalities. Antipope Clement marched an army to Rome to depose Urban. Clement failed militarily and returned to Avignon.

Urban VI died in 1389 and was replaced by Boniface IX (1389–1404), who was now the legitimate successor of Urban. In turn, when Boniface died, he was succeeded by Innocent VII (1404–1406), which continued the legitimate line of succession. Finally, following Innocent, Gregory XII (1406–1415), would end the legitimate line of popes.

Meanwhile, the first antipope Clement VII died in 1393. This was an opportunity to end the schism, but instead, another antipope was elected as his successor, Benedict XIII (1393–1415).

In 1409, cardinals from both sides attended a council in Pisa called by both sides to end the schism. This council deposed both Benedict XIII, the antipope, who was successor to Clement VII as antipope, and Gregory XII (who was in the Urban/Boniface/Innocent/Gregory XII legitimate line.) The council elected Alexander V in 1409. The problem was that neither Gregory XII, the legitimate pope nor Benedict XIII, the antipope, believed that the Council at Pisa was legitimate and refused the council's decision to step down. Now there were three men claiming to be the real pope! A solution was badly needed.

The Council of Constance (1414–1418)

With the help of Emperor Sigismund, the Council of Constance was convened. Here's how they handled the multiple popes' problem. They first dealt with the third claimant, antipope Alexander V in 1409. He had died, so his successor, John XXIII (1410–1415), was deposed. Benedict, the antipope fled. The path was clear. Martin V was elected as the legitimate pope. The thirty-nine-year Western schism had finally ended. The church has suffered greatly from the Avignon papacy and the great Western Schism. Gregory XII, the legitimate pope, resigned.

Along with these papacy leadership problems, seeds were being planted by two key heretics for the Protestant revolution within one hundred years.

John Wyclif (1324–1384) and Jan Hus (1369–1415) were considered "Proto Protestants" or the earliest people who held the same ideas and teachings as the Protestants. Wyclif was an Oxford University professor who wrote a radical thousand-page book espousing some of the following ideas:

- That the pope could err and his office was not necessary for the governance of the church;
- the church did not have the right to own property;
- oral confession of sins was not necessary;
- transubstantiation did not occur;
- sacraments administered by a priest in a state of mortal sin were ineffective;
- the state was superior to the church;
- scripture was the sole authoritative source of divine revelation;
- veneration of the saints was wrong;

- prayer for the dead was superfluous;
- predestination overrode man's free will.

Wyclif was investigated by university authorities for his teaching and dismissed from his teaching position. Pope Gregory XI condemned his teachings as heretical in 1377.³

Jan Hus was a Czech priest, theologian, preacher, and rector of the University of Prague. He rightfully preached against the corruption of the church in Bohemia. Greatly influenced by the thinking of Wyclif on church reforms, Hus went too far in their application. He wrote a book on the church as Wyclif had done. In it, he challenged papal authority, saying that the church was built on the faith of Peter and not on any type of Petrine office. He was thus denying that Christ divinely ordained and structured the church in a particular way—on the rock of Peter and the bishops in union with him. He claimed that the pope did not have authority over the universal church but only the local church in Rome. Hus also denied Sacred tradition as an authoritative source of God's revelation, and adopted Wyclif's notion of sola scriptura (scripture is the only authoritative source of God's revelation). In 1410, Hus was excommunicated by the archbishop of Prague.

The Council of Constance also dealt with John Wyclif, who was now dead, and Jan Hus, who was still alive. Hus was asked to attend the council to present, explain, and defend his teachings. To do this, Hus was given an imperial safe conduct pass by the Holy Roman Emperor. This meant he could not be harassed or killed going to, during, and returning from the council meeting. On the twenty-sixth day after his arrival, Hus was arrested in violation of the imperial safe-conduct pass and carried before the pope and the cardinals. He was imprisoned. The emperor was told that he had no right to grant a safe conduct pass in the circumstances without the consent of the council and that the greater good of the church must overrule his promise.

During the council, Hus gave a spirited defense of his teachings. In 1415, he was declared a heretic and his teachings were condemned. He was ordered to repudiate his teachings and given many opportunities to do so. He refused, was turned over to secular authorities, and was burned at the stake. His death sparked a war in Bohemia, lasting fifteen years. In 1999, Pope John Paul II said he was saddened that the safe-conduct pass for Hus had not been honored. Wyclif's works were also formally condemned by this council. His remains were ordered by the council to be exhumed from consecrated grounds and burned.

The Black Death or Bubonic Plague (1347–1350)

The Bubonic Plague was probably the most horrific natural disaster in recorded history. Historians believe that it probably started in China in the early 1300s when fleas on the back of black rats found their way on homebound merchant ships to Italy. It was a devastating disease that quickly spread northward, ravaging Europe and England, causing great panic because there was no cure. Death could happen instantly, or it would take three days.

Clement VI (1342–1352) was pope in Avignon. In March 1348, four hundred people a day were dying in Avignon. He provided a cemetery for eleven thousand people at church expense. People began blaming Jews for the disaster. Clement responded quickly, proving he was a good leader by issuing a bull that would excommunicate anyone who harassed Jews on this matter. In 1350, Pope Clement VI sent people throughout Europe to gather data on the effects of the plague. Twenty-three million people, (thirty-one percent of Catholic Europe) died. Fifty percent of the population in England died in one year. One-third of the College of Cardinals perished because of the plague, greatly impacting the church. Many good clergy died ministering to the dying, leaving a crisis in the church—a lack of good priests, bishops, and religious.

The Renaissance Popes (1447–1524)

The renaissance was the artistic, literary, and scientific revival, which originated in Italy in the fourteenth century, and which, for the next two centuries, influenced the rest of Europe in a great variety of ways. Italy seemed uniquely suited for the rebirth of ancient Rome because it was the headquarters of the Roman Catholic Church. Ten Renaissance popes reigned from 1447 to the coming of Martin Luther in 1521. In these seventy-four years, this papal group did some great things, and they did some horrible things.

On the good side, In a time of increasing secularity, they upheld Catholic orthodoxy. They led an explosion of creativity and genius in architecture, statuary, and art that would renew and glorify Rome. Capitalizing on the recent invention of the printing press in 1436, they amassed great libraries copying the precious handwritten classical and religious works carefully preserved by monks over the centuries. The renaissance reached its height in the sixteenth century supported by Pope Julius II (1503–1513) with Michelangelo, DaVinci, and Raphael in Rome. In 1506, Julius approved replacement of ancient St. Peter's Church. People called him "the destroyer." It took 126 years and twenty-one papacies before the present St. Peter's church was completed.

On the bad side, All these renaissance activities cost money. Popes were using the sale of indulgences, which is a remission of punishment due to sin, to provide funds. In addition, many of these popes participated in serious ecclesiastical and moral abuses that were turning off people, such as simony (the buying and selling of church offices), pluralism (holding more than one diocese), nepotism (putting relatives in prominent Church positions), papal sexual scandals, and clergy not living their vow of celibacy.

The "poster boy" for the most immoral pope in papal history is Spanish-born Rodrigo Borgia, known as Pope Alexander VI (1492–1503). He had been made cardinal by his uncle, Pope

Callistus III (1455–1458). Alexander ignored the priestly vow of celibacy, having had seven illegitimate children from two different women when he was a cardinal and having a young mistress, Giulia Farnese, while he was pope. Giulia had a seventeen-year-old brother, Allesandro, a playboy, who needed a challenge. Alexander VI made him a bishop. At twenty-five, he was made a cardinal. More about him later.

All these negatives, in addition to the Avignon papacy and the great schism, were causing a loss of respect of Christians for the papacy and the church as a whole. Reform, not replacement, was desperately needed for the church. Princely greed for power and sexual misconduct by the popes and clergy were root causes of nonadherence to the Orthodox church teachings of fifteen hundred years. No renaissance pope ever changed those teachings. However, by non-obedience, they provided kindling wood for someone to strike a match. Martin Luther would be the man.

Martin Luther (1483–1546)

Martin Luther was born in Eisleben, Germany on November 10, 1483. His father Hans, a successful ex-miner, was determined that his son should become a lawyer. When Martin grew up, he was riding his horse back to the university during a thunderstorm, when a lightning bolt struck very near him. Petrified with fear, he cried out, "St. Anne! St. Anne! Save me! If you save me, I'll become a monk."[4] (St. Anne was the patron saint of miners).

When the storm passed, he went promptly to Erfurt and joined the Augustinian order, much to the anger of his father. Two years later, he was ordained a priest and studied theology for the first time. There were no seminaries in those days. In 1509, he began teaching theology at the University of Wittenberg, and in 1512, he received a doctor of theology.

During 1516–1518, Johann Tetzel, a Dominican friar and papal commissioner for indulgences, was sent to Germany by the

Roman Catholic Church to sell indulgences to raise money to rebuild St. Peter's Basilica in Rome. An indulgence is the remission, full or partial, of the temporal punishment due to sin whose guilt has already been forgiven.

What is temporal punishment? An example: Tommy, throwing a rock, breaks Mrs. Brown's window. Tommy says to Mrs. Brown, "I'm sorry." She forgives him. But that is not the end of the matter. Tommy must provide a new window to make Mrs. Brown whole. This ties in with the church's teaching on purgatory, where Jesus has secured forgiveness for our sins, but temporal punishment for consequences of one's individual sins must be settled here or in purgatory.

For Martin Luther, the abuse of "selling of indulgences" was a huge problem. Tetzel was twisting the teaching of the church against people who were ignorant of the faith by telling them that by giving money, they would be buying their way or their relative's way out of purgatory. Buying a soul out of purgatory was not a doctrine taught by the Catholic Church.

On October 31, 1517 (Halloween), Luther nailed on a church door in Wittenberg the ninety-five *Theses*. This was a traditional way of providing a community bulletin board for bringing up key issues for discussion. Luther argued that the sale of indulgences was a gross violation of the original intention of confession and penance; that Christians were falsely being told that they could obtain absolution through the purchase of indulgences. Luther sent a copy to Rome. Pope Leo X thought it was just a dispute between orders, Tetzel, the Dominican leader of the sale of indulgences, and Luther, an Augustinian monk. Leo did nothing. The posting of the ninety-five *Theses* is widely regarded as the catalyst for the Protestant reformation.

Gutenberg's recent invention of the printing press enabled Luther, a prolific writer, to quickly spread his writings throughout western Europe. Pope Leo now knew he had a problem. Luther was summoned to Rome for a trial. He refused to go. In October,

1518, Pope Leo sent the brilliant Cardinal Cajetan to Luther to resolve the problem. Cajetan was unsuccessful.

In 1520, Pope Leo X warned Luther with a papal bull, *Exsurge Domine*, that he risked excommunication unless he recanted forty-one sentences from his writings within sixty days. Luther publicly set fire to the bull at Wittenberg on December 10, 1520, and was excommunicated on January 3, 1521.

Luther had a deeper agenda than indulgences. He did not just want to reform behavior; he wanted to change the faith. He wasn't just a reformer; he was a revolutionist. There is an important distinction between reformation and revolution. Reformation takes that which exists and returns it to the original state, making it better. Revolution seeks to destroy that which exists and replace it with something completely different.[5]

What caused Luther's rebellion? Luther was obsessed with his own salvation. How could he know for certain that he was saved? He was conscientious in trying to do good things but didn't seem to register any spiritual progress. This bothered him. He went to confession every day. He beat himself with a whip. He was once found unconscious and bloody. Despite all his good works, he was worse. He began to wonder if this church teaching was a form of Pelagianism, a fifth-century heresy claiming that the realization of good lies within human nature without any need of supernatural grace.

The whole concept of a grace-filled life became difficult for Luther to accept. The Catholic teaching is that "sanctifying grace" inheres within the believer who can perform good works. There is a real state of intimacy between the individual and God, which is sanctifying grace.

Luther was saying that original sin was not just the darkening of the intellect and the weakening of the will. It was total depravity that continues throughout the life of the Christian believer. He still had sexual fantasies, a bad temper, and was following his own ambitions. Luther needed a solution to escape the depravity of original sin. He reasoned that faith alone was the only way to come to terms with the essential evil that dwells within us. To a Catholic, faith is acceptance of propositions because God revealed them. Luther didn't disdain that but reversed it. His emphasis was on the personal acceptance of Christ. We accept the truths of the propositions in the Creed because we trust the person telling us.[6]

Here are some examples of Luther's revolution against church teaching. He denied free will. He believed in the total depravity of man. Catholic teaching is that Adam and Eve's sin wounded humanity and deprived it of God's presence, but Jesus was sent to restore that relationship. He denied sanctifying grace. He described God's grace like snow that covers a dunghill, nice, pretty, and white on the outside but nothing more than manure on the inside. Catholic teaching is that God's grace is transformative in our lives. One can achieve that life of holiness and live in a state of sanctifying grace that was had before the fall. Because of the fall human nature is inclined to give in to the temptation to sin. It's called concupiscence. Grace helps avoid sin. Luther called the pope the anti-Christ.

> The abominable and horrid priesthood of papists came into the world from the devil…The pope is a true apostle of his master the hellish fiend according to whose will he lives and reigns.[7]

Luther taught *sola fide* (we are saved by faith alone) and sola scriptura. He denied the teaching authority of the church with its sacred tradition, and he advocated the complete destruction of the Mass:

> If I succeed in doing away with the Mass, then I shall believe I have completely conquered the pope. If the sacri-

legious and cursed custom of the Mass is overthrown, then the whole must fall.[8]

Luther advocated the complete destruction of the church.

> To speak plainly, my firm belief is that the reform of the church is impossible unless the ecclesiastical laws, the papal regulations, Scholastic Theology, philosophy and logic as they at present exist, are thoroughly uprooted.[9]

King Charles V, Holy Roman emperor, wrote this about Luther, "It is preposterous that a single monk should be right in his opinion and that the whole of Christianity should be in error a thousand years or more."[10]

All the above is a long way from the sale of indulgences, princely greed, and immoral living on the part of some popes and clergy. Effective correction of those terrible abuses will shortly come from the church itself at the Council of Trent. Luther created the Protestant movement in Germany. Church lands would be confiscated. Shortly, new leaders like John Calvin and Zwingli would emerge with their own agendas. Today, outside the Catholic Church, there are over thirty-three thousand separate Christian groups. Christian unity was not the fruit of Martin Luther's revolution.

While people in Europe were leaving the church, people in the New World were coming into the church in droves as a result of the alleged appearance of the mother of Jesus as Our Lady of Guadalupe. Here's that story.

Our Lady of Guadalupe (1531)

The story of Our Lady of Guadalupe really begins in 1519 when Hernando Cortez, a Spanish conquistador, arrived in Mexico with a mission to conquer the Aztec empire (a satanic society of fifteen million people who practiced ritual human sacrifices) and bring them into the Christian faith. There were two hundred fifty thousand Aztecs who lived on an island called Castle Rock, which would later be known as Mexico City. This was their capital. In 1487, when they dedicated a new temple in Mexico City, eighty thousand people were sacrificed over a four-day period. In the ten years after Cortez's defeat of the Aztec empire, there were not many conversions. Then something happened. At dawn on December 9, 1531, an Indian convert, Juan Diego, was passing at the foot of Tepeyac, when he saw a brilliant light. He heard strains of heavenly music and a feminine voice asking him to ascend Tepeyac Hill. Reaching the top, he saw a beautiful woman standing in the midst of a glorious light. Speaking in his Indian language, she announced that she was the immaculate Virgin Mary, mother of the true God. She asked him to go to the bishop of Mexico, Juan de Zumarrago, and tell him to build a shrine in her honor on this hill. On December 10, 1531, Juan went to Mexico City to meet with the bishop and present Mary's request. The bishop listened but told Juan that he needed proof that the message was from Mary before he could try to raise money to construct a shrine.

On December 11, Juan visited his sick uncle and was unable to meet with Mary. But on December 12, while going for a priest to attend his uncle, Mary appeared to him again. She instructed him to go to the top of Tepeyac Hill and gather the flowers he would find there. The hill is in a desert region with cactus and rocks, and usually, no flowers can be found there. But trusting in Mary, Juan went to the top of the hill and found beautiful Castillian roses that only grow in Spain. He put them in his *tilma* (cloak) and brought them to Mary. She arranged them on his *tilma*, telling him to take them to the bishop and that it would be the sign that would persuade him to carry out her wishes.

Juan hastened back to the bishop. As Juan opened his *tilma*, the flowers fell to the floor, but they were in for a big surprise. On the *tilma* was a miraculous image of Mary that is now known as Our Lady of Guadalupe. Bishop Zumarraga fell to his knees and realized that what Juan had told him was absolutely true and authorized the building of a shrine on Tepeyac Hill. The *tilma* was made from fibers of the maguey cactus, which has a life of twenty years. The image of Our Lady of Guadalupe is almost five hundred years old.

After Our Lady's alleged appearance, missionary evangelization skyrocketed! By 1548, when Juan Diego and the bishop died, there were nine million baptized native Indians in Mexico.

King Henry VIII

The English Problem

Three years later, another bombshell would hit the church. This time, instead of Germany, it would be England. The key player would be Henry VIII, king of England. First, some background.

The Tudor dynasty in England ran from 1485 to 1603 and had five sovereigns. The first sovereign was Henry VII, who emerged victorious after a great battle against a family competitor. Not feeling secure on the throne, Henry wanted to make an alliance with Spain. King Ferdinand and Isabella in Spain had a daughter, Catherine, better known as Catherine of Aragon. A marriage between Catherine and the king's oldest son, Arthur, would help unite England with Spain. The marriage was arranged.

Catherine (who became popular in England) and Arthur were only fifteen years old and thirteen years old when they married. By law, for a marriage to be valid, two conditions were necessary. First, there must be a public ceremony, and second, the marriage must be consummated, in privacy, with the sex act. If for any reason, it wasn't, the marriage would not be valid. Arthur was a kindly man but in bad health. Within months, he died of tuberculosis, making Catherine a widow. King Henry VII still wanted to continue the alliance. However, now there was an impediment.

There were three impediments to a valid marriage. One was sanguinity—blood closeness was prohibited. A brother couldn't marry his sister. Second, the imposition of force or fear could not be used. Third was affinity. You could not marry an in-law, even if the in-law's spouse was dead. Catherine was an in-law and an impediment if Henry VII wanted his son Henry to marry Catherine. Henry VII applied to the pope for a dispensation saying that the alliance of England and Spain was important for maintaining peace in Europe. Pope Julius II (1503–1513) responded favorably.

Henry VII died in 1509. Henry VIII became king. He married Catherine. He was eighteen; she was twenty-three. The early years went well. Then a serious problem developed. She could not produce a male heir, which was necessary for a dynasty to continue. Catherine did produce a daughter, Mary. After ten years, Henry started playing around with a string of mistresses. This did not end their relationship but eroded it. He then met Anne Boleyn whom he wanted badly as a mistress. Her response was she would be his queen but never his mistress. Infatuated, he wrote love letters and began to think this way: the reason Catherine and I can't have children is because we broke the law of affinity. No male children is God's punishment.

In 1527, Henry sent Cardinal Woolsey, his lord chancellor, to Rome to talk with the pope about an annulment. Pope Clement VII was in a very awkward position. King Henry VIII had been the "defender of the faith" for him against Luther, but Catherine had powerful relatives in Spain. The pope was struggling with the German problem, while Charles V, the Holy Roman emperor and a nephew of Catherine, was sacking Rome with imperial troops. The pope didn't have time to deal with Henry's request. However, he granted Cardinal Woolsey the authority to begin a marriage tribunal in England to hear the case with testimony from witnesses but only the pope would pronounce judgment on the validity of Henry's marriage to Catherine.

All 300 bishops in England showed up. All but one, John Fisher, bishop of Rochester, voted in Henry's interest. Both Henry and Catherine were present. When the in-law issue was brought up, Catherine walked over to Henry, knelt down before him, and basically said, "You know, as only you can know, I was a virgin on our wedding night. Arthur was too sickly. We never consummated our marriage. I am not related to you by affinity." Ultimately, the case was sent to Rome where it sat for a period of time. Woolsey lost favor as lord chancellor and was replaced by Thomas More.

While waiting, Thomas Cromwell, the prime minister, came up with an idea for King Henry. Henry should place himself at the head of the church in England and appoint clergy who would rule in his favor. Henry liked his idea. He appointed Thomas Cranmer as archbishop of Canterbury. In 1533, Cranmer opened his own marriage tribunal. He annulled Henry's marriage to Catherine. Now Henry was free to marry Anne Boleyn. The English people were upset because they loved Catherine. In 1533, Anne gave birth to her only child, Elizabeth.

In March of 1534, Pope Clement VII finally made his official decision ruling in favor of the validity of Henry's marriage to Catherine. Henry must separate from Anne. It was the final break with Rome. Upset with the pope's decision, Henry called parliament into session in 1534 and passed two specific acts taking England into schism with the church in Rome.

The Act of Secession reconfirmed as invalid Henry's marriage to Catherine as decided by Thomas Cranmer. It declared Elizabeth, Anne Boleyn's daughter, the sole and legitimate heir to the throne. It required all England to take the oath of secession, which included explicit denial of papal authority. John Fisher and Thomas More refused to take the oath. They were imprisoned.

The Act of Supremacy declared the king as the supreme head of the church in England, officially and formally breaking away the church of England from the pope in Rome. Refusal to take the oath of supremacy was a treasonable offense punishable by death. Carthusian monks in London refused to take the Oath of Supremacy and were hung, drawn, and quartered. St. John Fisher (1469–1535), bishop of Rochester, was beheaded. His head was mounted on a spike on London Bridge for two weeks as a warning to the people. St. Thomas More (1478–1535), husband, father, and lord chancellor, was executed July 6, 1535.

Henry wanted to get rid of papal authority but wanted to maintain all the rest of the Catholic system. He wanted Catholicism without the pope. He wanted to continue the Mass, celibacy of the clergy, auricular confession, and the seven sacraments, but he suppressed religious orders, lusting after their property. Between 1536 and 1538, a big land grab of church property took place. It was so immense that it shifted economic power away from the ecclesiastical to the rising middle class.

King Henry VIII had three legitimate children: Mary (daughter of Catherine); Elizabeth (daughter of Anne Boleyn), and Edward (son of Jane Seymour). Anne, who caused the church schism with England, would have her own problems. Unable to produce a male heir for Henry, he had charges of incest and adultery brought against her. On May 19, 1536, she was beheaded at the age of thirty.

Henry then married Jane Seymour. It was her nine-year-old son, Edward VI who was made king after Henry VIII died in 1547 under a Regency Council, headed by Thomas Cranmer, a secret Lutheran. Lutheran views became official ones. In 1553, young King Edward VI died of consumption.

The Regency Council wanted to eliminate Mary Tudor as a replacement. Mary went to the stable, mounted a horse, and galloped to London. She was joined by crowds. Her goal was to restore the Catholic Church in England. She married her cousin Philip, king of Spain, who urged her on. She had executions and persecutions (250 Protestants were burned at the stake). All this was confusing to the people. They had been converted to Lutheranism under Cranmer. Now the new leader wanted them to go back to a religion they had been taught was an abomination. Mary was unsuccessful. She died in 1558, having been queen for five years.

Elizabeth now became queen (1533–1603). She was the fifth and last of the Tudor sovereigns. Catholics thought she was illegitimate because she was the daughter of Anne Boleyn. She restored the reforming program begun under Edward VI and completed the process of making England a Protestant nation. Elizabeth died in 1603. In her forty-five-year rule, 2,432 people were executed. She is known as "Good Queen Bess" and Mary as "Bloody Mary." Winners write history.

When Luther struck in 1517, the church was not prepared for his revolution against basic church doctrine. A response from the church was desperately needed. It would have a two-fold task—the restatement of church belief in opposition to the new theology of Luther, and the end of papal and clerical abuses.

A special church council was badly needed, but this was more easily said than done. Remember Allesandro Farnese who was made a bishop at seventeen and a cardinal at twenty-five by ill-famed Pope Alexander VI? Allesandro had reformed from his playboy years and was now Pope Paul III (1534–1549). Paul wanted a church council, but he had a dilemma. There were two powerful Catholic sovereigns whom he had to satisfy—Charles V, who was king of Spain and emperor of Germany, and Francis I, who was king of France. Charles and Francis were enemies. Charles was interested in solving the reformation crisis in Germany by addressing abuses. Francis didn't want a solution because his military enemy was weakened by being kept occupied with his problem in Germany. The French king would keep his bishops home.

The Council of Trent (1545–1563)

Finally, on October 13, 1545, a persistent Pope Paul III would have his council. The northern Italian city of Trent was chosen, which seemed an ideal geographic location between Rome and Germany. Protestants were invited, but they refused to come. Thirty-four bishops from various parts of the Catholic world came to solve the abuses and doctrinal challenges. More would come later. Most people consider the Council of Trent (1545–1563), known the Counter-Reformation, as the most productive council in church history.

It began with a solemn Mass of the Holy Ghost. After Mass, Cardinal Reginald Pole of England, one of three papal legates of the pope, addressed the group, setting the tone of the council.

> It is we bishops who are responsible for all the evils burdening the flock of Christ. We cannot even name any other cause other than ourselves. If God punished us as he should, we would have long since been as Sodom and Gomorrah.
>
> —Rev. Marvin O'Connell,
> *Two Critical Moments in Catholic History* (audiotape)
> *Courses for Independent Learners,* International Catholic University (Notre Dame, IN, 1997)

He then ticked off the abuses of simony, nepotism, greed, luxuriousness, and lust, adding, "Why dwell on this shameful subject? Unless we place our own sinful responsibility upon our minds, it is useless to call on the Holy Spirit for help."[11]

This council lasted eighteen years. But two interruptions would cause three International separate meetings, lasting in total about four and one-half years. The first meeting was 1545–1547 and was temporarily suspended because of a plague in that area. The second phase was 1551–1552. A war broke out nearby and concerned about safety of the bishops, the council again was put on hold. The final segment was 1562–1563. Philip Hughes wrote:

> The council surveyed anew the greater part of the Christian belief and had re-affirmed it, always with a special explicitness about the points where Luther and the rest had gone astray. It had looked directly in the face of the dreadful disorders that had for centuries disfigured the practice of religion, and had laid the axe to the root of the tree. It no less boldly innovated in the remedies it provided.
>
> —Hughes, *The Church in Crisis*, 313

Let's look at some of the results.

The council reasserted the doctrine of "good works," saying that because of original sin, humans were damaged but not rendered incapable of doing good works. God's graces were in the sacraments.

- On justification, faith alone was not sufficient for justification. We have to actively participate in our redemption and live our faith through our works.

- On sacraments, the council undertook a doctrinal review providing definitive statements on each sacrament. One of the canons published by the council condemned those who say that there are more or less than seven sacraments instituted by Christ. Luther had eliminated five sacraments, keeping only Baptism and the Holy Eucharist.

- On indulgences, the council made it clear that in theory, money indulgences were perfectly appropriate. A good work could be almsgiving and would deserve, under the doctrine of indulgences, a kind of favor, which could be given to a person performing a good work. But since money indulgences open themselves so readily to corruption, and since they could be so readily manipulated, they were from that time on forbidden.

- On papal leadership, the council taught that the hierarchical structure of the church—popes, bishops, priests, and deacons—was divinely ordained by God. It was something permanently set up by Christ so that neither the church nor anyone else could ever change it.

The council abolished many practices previously deemed lawful and introduced much that was new. Of all the scandals of the fourteenth to the sixteenth centuries, the one that caused the most resentment was the papal license to ecclesiastics to hold more than one see, or abbey, or parish simultaneously. This allowed scandals. Trent eliminated the practice, ordering all existing pluralists to surrender all but the one they had. It forbade all licenses allowing clerics to reside away from their posts and detailed the limits of annual leave allowed them. Any concubinary prelate who defied the warning of the provincial council would lose his see.

The simplest remedy for all these scandals was to appoint to the office only good men, endowed with natural gifts and good training. The church had never faced the problem of training and educating the rank and file of the parochial clergy. Trent gave birth to seminaries. The council decreed that every bishop must set up a special college where picked boys shall live, be given a religious training, and be taught to live the clerical life.

The Council of Trent made it possible for Catholics to regain their confidence. The council had settled the most challenging doctrinal problems and established new rules to end abuses:

> To settle authoritatively all questions arising out of the interpretation of the decrees, Pope Pius IV (1555–1559) created a permanent commission of cardinals, the Congregation of the Council of Trent, a body which developed into a kind of permanent ministry of the interior of

the Catholic Church, and which functions to this day as one of the most important instruments of the government of the Church.

—Hughes, *The Church in Crisis*, 332

Ignatius Loyola (1491–1556) was a nobleman with a career in the military until a serious leg wound ended that career. While convalescing, he read about lives of the saints and was moved by their heroism. He made a one-year retreat during which he composed his famous *Ignatian Spiritual Exercises*, which became the core of a four-week retreat. The purpose of the retreat was to develop a consecration to Christ through a life of self-control and discipline. In 1534, Ignatius and six friends vowed to live in poverty, chastity, and special obedience to the pope, who was the representative on earth of Christ the king. They would defend the truths of the Catholic faith under the directions of the pope. This group was named the Society of Jesus, and its members were called Jesuits.

Five years before the Council of Trent began, Pope Paul III, who would call that council, granted approval to the Jesuits as a legitimate church order. Little did the pope realize that the Jesuits would become a principal agent for implementing the counter-reformation teachings of the Council of Trent (1545–1563).

By 1556, more than one thousand Jesuits were scattered throughout Europe, Asia, and the New World, providing spiritual direction and missionary work. They also had a great impact on education. Although they taught all classes of people, Jesuits were especially concerned about training those who would become leaders in the renewal of Catholic life. By 1623, Jesuits had established 400 colleges. By 1749, they had 800. St. Peter Canisius (1521–1597), a Jesuit, published a catechism in 1555 in which he used scriptural quotations to present the Catholic faith clearly and precisely.[12]

The Fourth Crusade (1201–1205)

Saladin died in 1193. With his death, the Islamic empire was weakening because of competing leadership claimants. Five years later, Pope Innocent III (1198–1216) became pope and wanted another Crusade to regain the Holy Land. In addition, he wanted to reconcile Rome and Byzantine Christianity. In those times, it wasn't easy to gather an army because Crusader idealism was suffering from self-interest.

Frenchmen again dominated the Crusader army. Marquis Boniface de Montferrat was given command of the Crusade. They planned to leave Venice by sea and first attack Egypt, dividing the Muslim world, before heading to Jerusalem. They made a contract with the doge of Venice to build a fleet of ships to transport troops to Egypt. Grossly overestimating the number of troops that would come, crusader leaders were unable to meet the terms of the deal. Greatly upset, the Venetians demanded that they conquer a Christian city named Zara. Although strictly forbidden by the pope, the majority of crusaders followed through.

After their victory, a man named Alexius Angelus approached their leaders and offered them a deal. He said that his father, Emperor Isaac II of Constantinople, had been illegally removed and blinded by his father's brother, Alexius III. The deal was that if the crusaders would overthrow his uncle, he and his father would be restored as co-emperors of Constantinople. Alexius promised to reunite the Byzantine church with Rome, join the crusade with 10,000 men, permanently maintain 500 troops in the Holy Land, and pay the crusaders a large sum of money. Once again, the pope begged and threatened the crusaders not to deviate from the goal of the Holy Land. Once again, they did not listen.

After the crusaders attacked, Alexius III fled the city. Alexius Angelus became Alexius IV. The crusaders thought their job was finished and wanted to head for the Holy Land. But the nobles leading the Crusade wanted payment from Alexius IV. He only came up with half the money and took precious jewels from icons to make up the difference.

The people were outraged. Alexius IV was killed by a trusted lieutenant, who took over the throne for himself. The crusaders were upset and sacked the city for three days with much of the city's precious art being sent to the west. The relationship between east and west was severely damaged. Despite the protests of the pope against the sack of Constantinople, the east still considers Pope Innocent III responsible for the sack of the city. The year was 1204. When Pope John Paul II visited Athens in 1996, orthodox monks along the motorcade held signs with the year 1204.

There would be four more crusades with the same objective: reconquer the Holy Land. None succeeded. The only crusade that worked was the first, when Jerusalem itself stayed in Christian hands for eighty-eight years. The crusades were an example of a high-minded ideal betrayed by human nature.

St. Joan of Arc (1412–1431)

A secular warrior becomes a saint. On January 6, 1412, Joan of Arc was born in the obscure village of Domremy, France. She came into a world at a time and place of turmoil. The Hundred Years War between France and England was in full force (1336–1453).

In 1415, King Henry V of England laid claim to the throne of France. He sailed to France and began to conquer their lands, winning a decisive battle at Agincourt, even though outnumbered, capturing many northern French towns. Things looked very bleak for France. It seemed that the smaller island nation of England would swallow the larger nation of France.

In the summer of 1425, Joan of Arc, now thirteen, began receiving messages from St. Michael, St. Margaret, and St. Catherine, which continued for three years. Joan said Michael also told her to go and inspire French troops to fight better, with more courage and valor. She said that Michael had told her that God had chosen her for the task of personally leading these soldiers into battle. While she was always reluctant to speak of her "voices," by May 1428, she no longer doubted that she had been chosen to go help the king. In 1429, Joan met with Charles VII and convinced him of her special holy and unique calling by revealing to him something about his past that only he and God would know. Charles agreed to let Joan lead the troops.

The French town of Orleans had been under siege by the English for seven months. Orleans was important. It was the last obstacle for the English to begin their assault on the French heartland. Joan of Arc, at seventeen, with 4,000 troops, lifted the siege in nine days. Several more swift victories led to Charles VII being crowned king in 1429 with Joan at his side.

In May 1430, Joan was captured by the Burgundians at the Siege of Compiegne and sold to the English. It was customary for a captive's family to ransom a prisoner of war, but Charles VII and France did nothing to save her. The English used French bishop Pierre Cauchon to try her for heresy. The bishop sided with the English because he hoped that they would help him become an archbishop. Even though this was an ecclesiastical court, the bishop denied Joan's appeals to the pope.

Her trial began in 1431. After three months of fifteen interrogation sessions, Joan signed a statement that was read to her on May 30, 1431. (She couldn't read.) A few days later, she recanted her confession saying it had been forced, they had confused her, and she didn't believe what she had signed. At nineteen, she was burned at the stake. On July 7, 1456, Pope Calixtus III (1455–1458) began a rehabilitation process concerning Joan and ultimately found that her trial was a complete and utter fraud. The sentence passed on her was declared null and void. Joan was later canonized a saint by Pope Benedict XV in 1920.

The Spanish Inquisition (1478–1820)

For more than 770 years, Spain had been fighting wars with Islam to reconquer its country. In 1469, Isabella I of Castille married Ferdinand II of Aragon, and through this marriage, the kingdom of Spain was formed. The monarchs focused on finishing the *reconquista* or the retaking of the Iberian peninsula from the Moors. It finally happened in 1492 when the last Moor stronghold in Granada was captured.

The king and queen saw Roman Catholicism, the religion of the majority of the Spanish people, as the cohesive force that could hold the emerging country together. They considered two groups in Spain as threats to that desired unity. Some Jews (*Marranos*) and some Muslims (*Moriscos*) still living in Spain converted to the Catholic faith for various reasons. These converts created a new social group called *Conversos*. The question was did *Conversos* only do so publicly, while continuing to practice their original religion privately?

Most *Conversos* were Jewish. Spain was the most diverse and tolerant place in medieval Europe. England expelled all of its Jews in 1290. France did the same in 1306. Yet in Spain, Jews thrived at every level of society. The expansion of this *Converso* power led to a backlash, especially among the aristocrats and middle-class Old Christians. Rumors were circulated such as *Conversos* were part of an elaborate Jewish plot to take over the Spanish nobility and the Catholic Church and that they were secret Jews, not sincere Christians. Constant repetition of these accusations convinced Ferdinand and Isabella that they should investigate these "secret Jews."

In 1480, the Spanish Inquisition began. It would last for three hundred fifty years. The king would have complete authority over the inquisitors and the inquisition. Its major purpose was to monitor the orthodoxy and conduct of Jewish and Muslim converts. Practicing Christians, Muslims, and Jews were excluded from the Inquisition.

In the early stages, there were many abuses and much confusion. On April 18, 1482, Pope Sixtus IV (1471–1484) wrote a letter to all bishops of Spain, asking that they take a direct role in all future tribunals. When Ferdinand heard of the letter, he was outraged and wrote to Pope Sixtus, openly suggesting that the pope had been bribed by "*Converso* gold," and advising the pope to back-off. This ended the papacy's role in the inquisition.

In 1483, Ferdinand appointed a Dominican, Tomas Torquemada, as inquisitor-general for most of Spain. Problems multiplied. Tomas's methods strayed significantly from church standards. The first fifteen years under Torquemada were the deadliest. Two thousand *Conversos* were burned at the stake.

As the inquisition picked up momentum, those involved became increasingly convinced that Spain's Jews were actively converting *Conversos* back to their old faith. Influenced by that, in 1482 Ferdinand and Isabella began to expel Jews from specific areas where troubles seemed the greatest. Finally on March 31, 1492, the monarchs issued an edict expelling all Jews from Spain. At that time, the Jewish population in Spain numbered eighty thousand. About half accepted baptism immediately and kept their properties and livelihoods.

> In 1530, the Inquisition turned its attention away from the *Conversos* toward the new Protestant Reformation. The people of Spain and their monarchs were determined that Protestantism would not infiltrate their country as it had in Germany and France.
>
> The ideas of the Protestant reformers made little headway in Spain because the Inquisition broadened the scope of its religious oversight to include anything that threatened Spanish unity and identity by moving people away from the traditional doctrines and practices of the Roman Catholic Church.
>
> —McGonigle and Quigley,
> *A History of Catholic Tradition*, 20

Thomas F. Madden wrote that European Protestants

> had a potent new weapon: the printing press...the famous "Black Legend" was formed...accusing the Spanish Empire of human depravity and horrible atrocities... Although modern scholars have long ago discarded the Black Legend, it still remains very alive today.[13]

- 1453-The fall of Constantinople. The fall of Constantinople marked the end of the final remnant of the Roman Empire, which had lasted for nearly 1500 years. St. Sophia, the largest church in all Christendom, built in the sixth century, became a mosque. This was a massive blow to Christendom. After the conquest, Mehmed made Constantinople the Ottoman's new capital.

- 1529-The Siege of Vienna. The siege of Vienna in 1529 was the first attempt by the Ottoman Empire, led by Suleiman the Magnificent, to capture the city of Vienna, Austria. His failure to capture Vienna turned the tide against almost a century of unchecked conquest through eastern and central Europe.

- 1565-Malta. The siege of Malta took place in 1565 when the Ottoman Empire invaded the island, which was then held by the Knights of Malta. "The Knights won the siege, one of the bloodiest and most fiercely contested in history, and one which became one of the most celebrated events in sixteenth century Europe...The siege was a climax of an escalating contest between a Christian alliance and the Ottoman Empire for control of the Mediterranean."[14]

- October 7, 1571-The Battle of Lepanto. In the sixteenth century, Ottoman Turks continued their unchallenged dominance throughout the Mediterranean, attacking and pillaging Christian strongholds, capturing Christians and using them as chained oarsmen for their ships. Vienna and the eastern borders continued to be threatened by military power and incursions, and the Papal States themselves would soon be at risk. Pope St. Pius V (1566–1572), deeply concerned, wrote letters to all the monarchs of Europe, asking their assistance in creating a defense against those threats. Spain was the only major power in Europe that responded.

The Turks had assembled a great fleet at the Gulf of Lepanto, next to Greece, ready for action. The Holy League, which was an alliance between the Papal States, Spain, Genoa, Venice, and the Knights of Malta, was formed to challenge the threat of the Turkish fleet. The Holy League would build a fleet to attack the Turkish fleet before they could carry out their intended attacks on the heartland of Christendom. Pope Pius V put at the head of this fleet Don Juan of Austria, the twenty-four-year-old illegitimate son of the Holy Roman Emperor Charles V. He was a young but an able commander.

The Turkish, fleet consisted of three hundred war galleys with one hundred thousand men, which included seamen, fierce fighting men, and fourteen thousand Christian galley slaves used as rowers. The Christians built two hundred war galleys with lesser manpower, but more fire-power.

Every Christian was given a rosary before the fleet sailed to meet the Turks. In addition, each ship had an image of Our Lady of Guadalupe on it. The Turkish fleet aligned itself in the form of a crescent, and Don Juan aligned his ships in three columns which formed a cross going through the crescent. The reason for Don Juan's cross formation was his secret weapon: side mounted cannons. Most galleys only had front-mounted cannons located in the bow of the ship. Another strategy employed by Don Juan was using musketeers on deck to fire volleys when they got close to an enemy ship.

The battle lasted five hours. The Christians captured or destroyed two hundred galleys, while losing twelve galleys. Thirty thousand Turks died, against seven thousand five hundred Catholics. Also, twelve thousand of the thirteen thousand galley slaves of the Turks, who had been chained as rowers for the Turks, were set free.

Pope Pius V had not received any news about the battle, but at a meeting with his treasurer in Spain, at the very moment of the victory, he got up, walked to the window, and said, "This is not a moment for business. Make haste to thank God, because our fleet this moment won a victory over the Turks."[15]

In 1572, Pope Pius V ordered an annual commemoration of this victory to be held on October 7 with the title, "Our Lady of Victory." In 1573, the new pope, Gregory XIII (1572–1585), changed the name of the commemoration to "Our Lady of the Rosary," which continues to the present day.

The victory of the holy league prevented the Mediterranean from becoming an uncontested highway for Ottoman forces, protected Italy from a major Ottoman invasion, and prevented the Ottoman from advancing further into the southern flank of Europe. Also it was a great psychological boost for Christians who had come to believe that these forces were invincible.

At the end of this time period (1200–1600), Clement VIII (1592–1605), the 230th successor of Peter, was reigning as pope in Rome.

Notes

1. McGonigle and Quigley, *A History of the Christian Tradition*, 163.
2. http://ewtn.com/library/MARY/CATSIENA.htm.
3. Steve Weidenkopf & Dr. Alan Schreck, *Epic, A Journey through Church History*, (West Chester, PA: Ascension Press, 2008), 161.
4. Rev. Marvin O'Connell, *Two Critical Moments in Catholic History*, (audiotape) *Courses for Independent Learners*, International Catholic University (Notre Dame, IN, 1997).
5. Weidenkopf & Schreck, *Epic*, 165.
6. O'Connell, *Two Critical Moments in Catholic History*.
7. Martin Luther, "On the Abuse of the Mass" (1520).
8. Martin Luther in a Writing to King Henry VIII of England *http://www.anglicanhistory.org/ lutherania/against-henry.html)*.
9. Martin Luther to Jodocus Trutfetter, May 9, 1518, Erfurt.
10. Crocker, *Triumph*, 235.
11. O'Connell, *Two Critical Moments in Catholic History*.
12. McGonigle and Quigley, *A History of Catholic Tradition*, 23.
13. Thomas F. Madden, "The Truth about the Spanish Inquisition," *Crisis Magazine*, September, 2003.
14. https://www.fittours.com/viewpackage.htm?pid=285.
15. http://www.mindmeister.com/es/41672867/the-holy-league-and-the-battle-of-lepanto.

Jesus' Church

1600–2000 AD

When Christopher Columbus discovered the New World in 1492, little did he realize that this New World included North, Central, and South America, providing great opportunities for colonization and missionary work.

The City of God

During the sixteenth century, missionary work had been more or less turned over to the two Catholic nations who had pioneered the age of exploration, Portugal and Spain. The objectives of these two maritime powers were conquest, settlement of the lands, and evangelization of the peoples they encountered. To settle any disputes about ownership of the newly conquered lands, they turned to Rome.

In 1493, Pope Alexander VI (1492–1503) divided the New World lands between Spain and Portugal by establishing a north-south line of demarcation about three hundred miles west of the Cape Verde Islands. Undiscovered non-Christian lands to the west of the line were to be Spanish possessions, and those to the east belonged to the Portuguese, making them unhappy. In the spring of 1494, representatives of Spain and Portugal met in the Spanish town of Tordesillas and negotiated a solution to their dispute. The new line was now about 1,270 miles west of the Cape Verde Islands. As a result, Portugal got Brazil. That's why people in Brazil speak Portuguese, while the rest of Central and South America speak Spanish.

The interference of the state in the affairs of the church in Latin America during the seventeenth and eighteenth centuries was a major obstacle to effective evangelization.

> In an attempt to regain control over the Church's missionary efforts and to reform abuses, Pope Gregory XV (1621–1623) established the Congregation for the Propagation of the Faith in 1622. The pope hoped to limit the power of secular governments over the missions so that Christianity would not be seen as another aspect of colonialism. The congregation was also concerned for the development of an indigenous clergy so that the Church would not be a foreign institution in its pastoral leadership.
>
> —McGonigle and Quigley,
> *A History of the Christian Tradition*, 43

In the sixteenth century, the enslavement of conquered Native American people had become a problem, which caused Pope Paul III in 1537 to issue a special decree forbidding enslavement of native Americans. The Spanish in Columbia then contracted with the Portuguese to bring Africans to the New World to work as slaves. In 1639, Pope Urban VIII (1623–1644) issued a decree prohibiting the capture and removal by Catholics of blacks from their native countries. Enslavement of Indians was forbidden in 1758, but slavery of black Africans continued until the end of the nineteenth century.

In what is now the United States, Spain began colonization and evangelization efforts in the middle of the sixteenth century establishing the first permanent colony in St. Augustine, Florida, in 1565. Their efforts to preach the Gospel reached out to the natives of Texas, New Mexico, Arizona, and California. Upper California was ignored until Russia, in 1741, showed interest in it. Then the Spanish staked their claim, establishing twenty-one missions from San Diego in the south to San Francisco in the north.

French colonization and missionary efforts were in North America (modern-day Quebec and the upper reaches of New York State). In 1608, Samuel Champlain (1567–1635) founded the city of Quebec as the first French colony in Canada. French missionaries, especially Jesuits, labored to implant the church by preaching to the native peoples of the region. Missionary work was severely hampered by the hostility between the various tribes. There were martyrs.

English colonization began with the first settlement at Jamestown, Virginia, in 1607. The English were concerned that the Anglican church be the foundation of the Protestant church in the New World. The first group of Puritans, the pilgrims, landed at Plymouth, Massachusetts, in 1620. By 1641, at least twenty thousand pilgrims had immigrated to New England. Puritans were strong in their theological positions. Many opposed this religious rigidity and moved to Rhode Island, where Roger Williams founded a colony at Providence on Narragansett Bay as a place of religious freedom. His church later became Baptist. Where were the Catholics?

In 1632, King Charles I granted land in the new world to Cecil Calvert, Lord Baltimore, as a place of refuge for the harassed Catholics of England. The first colonists began to come in 1634. The number of Catholics was small and shortly outnumbered by the Protestants who had also come. The state eventually became Anglican. Catholics would have to wait until the creation of the thirteen colonies before truly experiencing religious freedom.

Jesuits had labored for many years in China.

> They made every effort to learn Chinese and to accommodate the Gospel to the legitimate customs of the culture. When Spanish Franciscans and Dominicans arrived in the 1630s, they pursued traditional methods of evangelization and accused the Jesuits of making unwarranted adapta-

tions of the faith to make conversions. Fearful of the progressive approach of the Jesuits, Rome issued a decree in 1708 which condemned their method of evangelization and forbade the veneration of ancestors and Confucius.

—McGonigle and Quigley,
A History of the Christian Tradition, 45

Pope Pius IX (1846–1878) and the First Vatican Council (1869–1870)

There were some great popes after the Council of Trent. Pope Pius IX was one of them. Giovanni Mastai-Ferretti was born in Sinigaglia, a port town of Italy on the Adriatic on May 13, 1792. At twenty-two, in opposition to his father's wishes, he asked to be admitted to the pope's noble guard. Being subject to epileptic fits, he was refused admission. Later, his malady ceased, and he was ordained a priest in 1819. On June 14, 1846, he was elected pope and took the name Pius IX. This former sickly pope would have the longest papal reign in the 2,000-year history of the church (thirty-two years), second only to Peter.

When Pius began his reign, there was a strong political and social movement underway to unite all the different states of the Italian peninsula into a single state of Italy, with Rome as its capital. Two major groups had something to lose by unification—the Austrian empire and the church.

The Austrian empire directly controlled the predominantly Italian-speaking northeast part of present-day Italy. They had powerful military forces to maintain their position.

The church was deeply concerned. For almost eleven hundred years, they had been governing the Papal States, land given to them by King Pepin (Pepin's donation) back in the eighth century. Pepin had officially conferred on Pope Stephen III (768–772) a strip of territory extending diagonally across Italy from the Tyrrhenian Sea to the Adriatic. One hundred thirty-eight popes spanned the time from Stephen III to Pius IX. As popes, they were responsible for the spiritual needs of the whole human race. In their role as pope-kings, they were also responsible for the temporal needs of the people in the Papal States.

The Holy See was opposed to unification, being unable to broker a confederation, which would include the Papal States. Pius feared that giving up power in the region could mean persecution of Italian Catholics.

Pius IX, considered a liberal, was in favor of political reforms. His first great political act was the granting of a general amnesty to political exiles and prisoners on July 16, 1846. People greeted this act with enthusiasm. However, when Pius solemnly proclaimed that, as the father of Christendom, he could never declare war against Catholic Austria, his popularity took a nosedive. He was denounced as a traitor to his country. When his prime minister Rossi was stabbed to death, Pius IX fled in disguise to Gaeta for refuge. Rome was taken over and ruled by traitors who abolished the temporal power of the pope on February 9, 1849, under the name of a democratic republic.

The pope appealed to major countries for help. Only France responded, sending troops to restore order in his territory. On April 12, 1850, Pius IX returned to Rome, no longer a liberal. The pope had to rely on French and Austrian troops for the maintenance of order in Rome.

The defeat of Austria in 1859 and the subsequent withdrawal of Austrian troops, who had been their protectors, left the Papal States open for dissolution. Victor Emmanuel completed the takeover of papal possessions by seizing Rome and making it the capital of a united Italy. Ironically, the church would later view this defeat as a blessing. The territorial loss freed all future popes from secular responsibility, permitting the papal office to fully focus on the spiritual needs of the whole world.

Pope Pius IX's reign faced another major problem, which would prove more disastrous to the church than just losing land. It was the consequences of the age of enlightenment. France would break away completely from the church, causing great disruption in the church and the world. Europe was moving from its Christian roots, moving from a God-centered society to a man-made society.

> For over a thousand years, the existence of God and the importance of religion had been unquestioned in the Western world. But, beginning in the 16th century, the Protestant Reformation and the scientific revolution began to erode the position of authority held by religion. A new willingness to confront religious authority and a new respect for reason and its accomplishments began to counter established ways of thinking. As a result, modern philosophy began to separate from theology, and new philosophers began constructing a universal, human rationality independent of faith. For the first time in human history, it had become possible to not simply ponder faith and its forms of expression, but to challenge it as fundamental truth—and to even question the existence of God.
>
> —Professor Tyler Roberts, *Skeptics and Believers: Religious Debate in the Western Intelligence Tradition*, http://www.goodreads.com/author/show/ 445684tyler-t-roberts

Enlightenment thinkers hoped to extend this progress by applying reason to all problems of human life. "These thinkers accepted religion only as a provider of moral guidelines, dismissing as groundless, affirmations based on revelation, rejecting subservience to any authority other than reason."[1]

There are limits to human reason. One of these later thinkers was Emmanuel Kant (1724–1804), distinguished philosopher, who believed that science should be understood as applying to the world of data rather than "the other world." In showing the limits of reason, Kant said he did "make room for faith." This faith comes from God's revelation to man. If we lose a sense of authentic truth and authentic faith, before long, we'd lose our understanding of our authentic story and why our civilization exists and what our civilization is supposed to do.

> Ever on guard, given his insights, graces, and limitations, Pius IX, published in 1864 an encyclical, *Quanta Cura*, with its attached *Syllabus of Errors*. The latter was a list of propositions that the pope maintained a good Catholic could not affirm. The *Syllabus* was, in fact, a list of references to various other papal announcements that treated the topics mentioned. Basically, the *Syllabus* rejected many of the tenets of liberalism; for example, rationalism, indifferentism, socialism, and the idea that the pope should reconcile the Church with the tenets of liberalism. Thus, the pope had drawn a line in the sand, putting the Catholic Church against the so-called modern world.
>
> —McGonigle and Quigley,
> *A History of the Christian Tradition*, 115

While Pius IX was unfortunate in temporal happenings, he showed himself a vigorous leader in spiritual matters. An example:

Throughout his life, Pius IX had a deep devotion to Mary. As early as 1849, while he was exiled in Gaeta, he wrote letters to bishops of the church, soliciting their views regarding the Immaculate Conception of Mary. At a gathering of two hundred bishops on December 8, 1854, Pius IX declared the dogma of the Immaculate Conception.

> The Most Blessed Virgin Mary was, from the moment of her conception, by a singular grace and privilege of almighty God and by the merits of Jesus Christ, savior of the human race, preserved immune of all stains of Original Sin.[2]

One scriptural support cited is Luke 1:28 when the angel Gabriel said to Mary, "Hail, full of grace." This was said BEFORE Mary gave her assent to do God's will. This meant she had been in a state of sanctifying grace from the first moment of her conception, free of sin.

Catholics believe,

> When Pius IX defined this Catholic doctrine in 1854, he gave not a new truth to be added to Christian teaching, but merely defined that this doctrine was part of Christian teaching from the very beginning, and that it is to be believed by all as part of Christian revelation.[3]

Four years later, an unusual event happened in Lourdes, France, that affirmed the pope's declaration. Here's that story.

The apparitions of Our Lady of Lourdes began February 11, 1858, when St. Bernadette Soubirous, a fourteen-year-old peasant girl from Lourdes, was gathering firewood with her sister, Toinette, and a friend. They were in Massabielle, about a mile from Lourdes. Bernadette saw a light in a nearby cave and a young beautiful lady, who was lovelier than anyone she had ever seen. Of the three girls, only Bernadette saw it. There would be seventeen more similar appearances until the final one on July 16 that same year. Bernadette wanted to keep this a secret from her mother. However, her sister told her mother what happened. After parental cross-examination, Bernadette and her sister were punished and were ordered never to go there again. Bernadette returned on February 24. The lady gave her a message to pray and do penance for the conversion of sinners.

The next day, Bernadette said that the apparition asked her to dig in the ground and drink from the spring she found there. As the word spread, this water was given to medical patients of all kinds, and reports of miraculous cures were heard. Some cures were short term and several were hoaxes. Church and government officials became concerned. The government took action, fencing off the grotto and issuing stiff penalties to anybody entering the forbidden area.

Bernadette was very familiar with the local area. Under the cover of darkness, on March 5, she managed to visit the barricaded grotto. The lady was there and announced to Bernadette, "I am the Immaculate Conception."[4] Most Catholics believe this affirmed the declaration of Pope Pius IX.

On July 16, Bernadette went for the last time to the grotto. The church, faced with nationwide questions, created an investigation commission on November 17, 1858. On January 18, 1860, the local bishop finally declared that the Virgin Mary did appear to Bernadette Soubirous.

A basilica was built upon the rock at Massabielle. Over a million people visit the site annually. Although the church never encouraged it, Lourdes's water has become a focus of devotion to the Virgin Mary. Since the apparitions, many people claim to have being healed by drinking or bathing in the water. This water is provided free of charge. "Approximately 7000 people sought to have their cases confirmed as a miracle, of which only 68 have been declared as scientifically inexplicable by both the Bureau and the Catholic Church."[5] Because the apparitions are private (not public) revelations, Catholics are not required to believe them.

The Age of Enlightenment was one of the major challenges in the church. Pope Pius IX did something that hadn't been done by any pope in the previous three hundred years, going all the way back to the Council of Trent (1545–1563). He convoked the twentieth ecumenical council in the history of the Catholic Church. Unlike the five earlier general councils held in Rome, which met in the Lateran Basilica and are known as the Lateran Councils, this new one met in the Vatican Basilica, hence its name of First Vatican Council. It opened on December 8, 1869, and adjourned on October 20, 1870. This was the first general council where American bishops (forty) were involved.

The council wanted to deal with the contemporary problems of the rising influence of rationalism, liberalism, and materialism. In addition, its purpose was to define the Catholic doctrine concerning the church. The council produced two major documents: *Dei Filius* and *Pastor Aeternus*.

Dei Filius concerns faith, reason, and revelation. There *is* God-given, objective truth; the church can know and teach this truth. The existence of God can be known by human reason alone; faith is not necessary to know that God exists. Faith and reason are complimentary, not at odds with one another, because they both have the same source - God.

Pastor Aeternus concerns the role of the pope and the gift of infallibility. The pope is supreme head of the whole church of God and cannot err when as shepherd and teacher of all Christians he defines a doctrine to be held by the whole church. This document lists the ways in which the Holy Father can exercise this gift of infallibility so all Catholics will know when he is specifically speaking infallibly. He must teach as the successor of Peter, not as the bishop of Rome; the subject must be on a matter of faith and morals. The teaching must be stated as binding on all the faithful, and the pope must declare the teaching to be definitive.

> Nowhere in the Church, from the beginning of the Catholic revival, had the renewed activity of the papacy been anything but welcome to the majority of Catholics. Their whole-hearted acceptance of the decrees of 1870 was natural and inevitable. It was an acceptance that was in the nature of things, and that meant no more change than that they now believed explicitly what, like their fathers for centuries, they always implicitly had taken for granted.
>
> —Hughes, *Church in Crisis*, 365

As mentioned previously, the pope wanted a doctrinal statement on the church concerning the roles of the pope, the bishops, deacons, and laity. The council had to be suspended prematurely. Here's why.

When the papal lands were taken away from the church, French troops came to protect the pope and the Vatican. However, during the council, the Franco-Prussian War broke out. The French needed all the troops they could muster, which included the troops protecting the pope. In the interest of safety for all council clergy, the pope sent them home. The council would not be officially ended until the calling of the Second Vatican Council in the 1960s when one of the first official actions of the council was to close the First Vatican Council.

Pope Leo XIII (1878–1903)

When the aged Pius IX died in 1878, Gioacchino Pecce became Pope Leo XIII. His main objective as pope was to reach out to the modern world. He was concerned that because so many European societies moved away from their Catholic roots, there were some Catholics who wanted the church to just focus on itself. The pope felt that as much as the world had changed, we, the church, must understand the changes and find ways to bring the Gospel to the modern world. This was the pope's number one objective.

In 1891, Pope Leo XIII issued one of the great encyclicals in the history of the Catholic Church, known as *Rerum Novarum*, which was a strong appeal to the working class. Leo was bringing Christ into the factories and slums. This was the time of industrialization, when there could be injustices against workers.

This encyclical indicates the rightful place labor unions have in society, the right of workers to join together to ensure their rights are safeguarded. Man precedes the state; therefore, the state does not have complete control over the individual nor *should* the state have complete control over the individual. The first foundational cell of society is the family; man and family precede the state. Workers have the right to earn a livable wage; companies should pay their workers a livable wage. *Rerum Novarum* was hailed by Catholics and non-Catholics alike. "Leo defended workers' rights as a matter of strict justice. It was the first time in history such a thing had been done by any authority of the standing of the Holy See."[6] With the church under fire in many countries, Leo's talent and policy was conciliation. When in 1885, Germany and Spain accepted Leo's arbitration in a dispute over the Caroline Islands. It was a sign of the pope's new prestige.

As a leader of ideas, Leo was truly great. When Italian anti-clericals began to blame the pope for all the ills of Italy, Leo XIII opened the enormously rich Vatican archives to historians so they could set the record straight. A year after his election as pope, Leo published an encyclical urging Catholics to look at the teachings of St. Thomas Aquinas for guidance in philosophy.

In 1896, Leo came out with an interesting bull entitled *Apostolicae Curae* in which he declared that holy orders in the church of England were "absolutely null and utterly void" as far are Catholics were concerned.[7] Though Pope Leo XIII died on July 20, 1903, his influence lives on.

Pope Pius X (1903–1914) and Fatima (1917)

On June 2, 1835, in the little Italian town of Riese, near Venice, a future pope was born. Son of a cobbler, his name was Giuseppe Melchiore Sarto, who would one day become the 257th pope of the Catholic Church. Pope Pius X would be pope from 1903 to 1914. He was possessed of so many of the saintly virtues—piety, charity, deep humility, pastoral zeal, and simplicity. He remained a country priest at heart throughout his life and faced the problems and evils of a strife-torn world with the fervor of a crusader.

Pius, like Leo XIII, opposed modernism, which claimed that Catholic dogma should be modernized and blended with nineteenth-century philosophy. He saw modernism as an import of secular errors affecting three areas of Catholic belief—theology, philosophy, and dogma.

> Modernists found it impossible to accept that God had revealed absolute truths to the Church once and for all, and that the Church had transmitted these truths down the ages in an unchanging, and unchangeable form.[8]

Pius predicted that a great war would break out in 1914, but when it came, it nearly broke his heart. He died on August 20, 1914. On May 29, 1954, amid the traditional pealing of the bells in the great churches of Rome, Giuseppe Sarto, the humble parish priest of the world, was canonized as a saint. He was the first priest canonized since St. Pius V (1516–1572).

While Europe was involved in this mutually destructive warfare, a miraculous event was happening in Fatima, a tiny village in Portugal. On May 13, 1917, in the first of six apparitions, the Blessed Virgin Mary appeared to three young peasant children: Francisco, Jacinta, and Lucia; ages ten, nine, and seven respectively. The children were tending their family's sheep when "a lady all in white, more brilliant than the sun…indescribably beautiful,"[9] appeared to them, standing above a bush. She told them to pray the rosary everyday to bring peace to the world.

The heart of Our Lady's message to the world is contained in what has come to be called the "secret" which she confided to the three children at their July 13 meeting. The secret actually consists of three parts:

1. *A vision of hell.* This vision showed what it is like for souls to be in hell. It showed the importance of praying the rosary and living a life in imitation of Christ in virtue and Christian morality.

2. *The consecration of Russia to the Immaculate Heart of Mary.* Mary revealed that the war was going to end, but she warned that if people did not stop offending God, a worse war would break out in the pontificate of Pius XI. She said:

> When you see a night illumined by an unknown light, know that this is the great sign given you by God that he is about to punish the world for its crimes, by means of war, famine, and persecutions of the Church and the Holy Father...To prevent this, I shall come to ask for the consecration of Russia to my Immaculate Heart. If my requests are heeded, Russia will be converted, and there will be peace; if not, she will spread her errors throughout the world, causing wars and persecutions of the Church. The good will be martyred, the Holy Father will have much to suffer, various nations will be annihilated. Lucia Santos, *Fatima in Lucia's own Words*, (Still River, MA: Ravengate Press, 1976), 104

Mary's request was not heeded. As fulfillment to this prophecy, the nighttime skies over much of Europe were seen to glow inexplicably in 1937. One daily newspaper said that this Aurora Borealis glowed in the widest area since 1709.[10]

In 1939, WWII broke out, followed by the spread of communism from Russia to various countries throughout the world. Only after John Paul II consecrated Russia to the Immaculate Heart of Mary in 1984 did communism die out in Eastern Europe, including in Yugoslavia where the Medjugorje apparitions are still happening.

—Medjugorje-online.com/apparitions/fatima.php

3. *The third secret given the children was for the future.* This third secret, written on paper and placed in an envelope

by Lucia, was to be opened in 1960 by the pope. When that date arrived, the letter was opened by the pope, but he chose not to release it. This led to all kinds of speculation as to why not. "Shortly after this controversy, Sister Lucia said in a rare interview with Spanish Television that the Third Secret was for the guidance of the pope, who was never obliged to release it."[11]

The third secret was not revealed until 2000, coinciding with the beatification of Francisco and Jacinta, both of whom had died within a year of Mary's appearances. The third secret did not contain any striking or cataclysmic prediction but affirmed the immense suffering endured by witnesses of the faith in the twentieth century.

The final appearance of Mary would be October 13, 1917. Over seventy thousand people showed up because Mary had promised a great miracle, and they hoped to see Mary. While they didn't see Mary, they witnessed the miracle of the sun. This great sign would show the divine approval of Fatima's message. It was the most widely witnessed miracle in all of history. Rain was pouring down, and everything was muddy.

> At the pre-determined hour, the rain stopped, and the thick mass of clouds broke. The sun looked like a disc of dull silver, and started dancing wildly. A majority of the people saw the sun trembling and dancing, and it descended low enough to burn the earth with its rays. Many thought the end of the world had come, as the sun seemed to fall on them. The event lasted about ten minutes. People reported color changes in objects on earth, caused by the rays of the sun.
>
> —www.fatimaconference.org/sixthapparitionoctober131917.htm

The people were stunned because their clothes, soaking wet moments before, were now completely dry.

Mary had appeared in Fatima to give a warning to Europe to return to their Christian roots. It didn't. Among the consequences were WWII, which was a more devastating war, along with the rise of communism and socialism. The Catholic Church approved the apparitions, and today, Fatima is one of the most visited Marian shrines in the whole world.

Pope Pius XII was succeeded by Pope John XXIII, who had had a long career in diplomatic service during which he developed an interest in Eastern churches and in Islam. The problem he faced was that the Christian roots of Europe had been destroyed as a result of following the enlightened and modernist principles, which led to fascism and communism. At seventy-seven years of age, Pope John XXIII shocked the world by calling the twenty-first council of the church, saying that it was time to open the windows of the church and let in some fresh air.

> Pope John saw his pontificate as an opportunity to go in Christ-like pursuit of his lost sheep, "to all men of goodwill." He felt that by calling a Second Vatican Council, he could make a Christmas-like gift to God's people; a refurbished Catholic Church to God's people...that is, to all people: a refurbished Catholic Church that no longer set up barricades against the modern world, but threw open the doors of welcome. The dawning of the 1960s seemed to make everyone...popes, prime ministers, and pop stars...assume that the "winds of change" were blowing.
>
> —Crocker, *Triumph*, 414

On October 11, 1962, Vatican Council II opened in Rome at St. Peter's Basilica at the Vatican. About two thousand three hundred bishops were present plus many invited observers from the Eastern and Protestant churches. Pope John hoped that this council would be a new Pentecost with the Holy Spirit coming into the life of the church in a new way to fill the bishops, priests, and laity with the graces necessary to go into the world to preach the Gospel. "It would be a renewal. In Italian, the word used to capture this papal hope was *aggiornamento*.

On June 3, 1963, Pope John XXIII, the man who combined the best qualities of parish priest and papal delegate, died in the seventh month of the council. The work of the council halted because ecumenical councils are automatically dissolved upon the death of the pope who convened it. Pope Paul VI was elected on June 21, less than three weeks later, and immediately announced that the council would continue. Pope Paul listed four goals for the council:

1. to more fully define the nature of the church and the role of the bishop;
2. to renew the church in all aspects of its life;
3. to restore unity among all Christians, including seeking pardon for Catholic contributions to separation; and
4. to start a dialogue with the modern world.

The task of the council was to restate, in a friendly, welcoming language, the ancient truths of faith. The council produced sixteen written documents; four of them were considered to be key.

1. *Sacrosanctum Concilium* (constitution on the sacred liturgy). This document describes the important role and function of liturgy in the life of the church. How we worship illustrates what we believe. It calls for more active participation in the liturgy but not to take it over. It specifically states that Latin should be preserved as the main language but did allow the wider use of the vernacular.
2. *Lumen Gentium* (dogmatic constitution on the church). This document provides a definition of the Catholic Church:

Christ, the One mediator, established and continually sustains here on earth His Holy Catholic Church, the community of Faith, Hope, and Charity, as an entity with visible delineation through which He communicates Truth and Grace to all.

The fullness of the means to salvation subsists within the Catholic Church, which is governed by the successor of Peter and by the bishops in communion with him. However, many elements of sanctification and Truth are found outside its visible confines.

—Pope Paul VI, *Dogmatic Constitution on the Church, Lumen Gentium*, promulgated November 21, 1964

3. *Dei Verbum* (dogmatic constitution on divine revelation). This document discusses the meaning of "revelation" and how it operates within the church. It covers the roles of the Old and New Testaments.

    "The New Testament is hidden in the Old and the Old Testament is manifest in the new…Ignorance of Scripture is ignorance of Christ." St. Jerome, Commentary on Isaiah (Nn. 1.2: CCL 73, 1–3), http://www.crossroadsinitiative.com/library_article/257/ignorance_of_scripture_is_ignorance_of_christ_st._jerome.html

    This Magisterium is not superior to the word of God, but is its servant. It teaches only what has been handed down to it. At the divine command and with the Holy Spirit, it listens to this devotedly, guards it with dedication and expounds it faithfully. All that it proposes for belief as being divinely revealed is drawn from this single deposit of faith. (Pope Paul VI, *Dogmatic Constitution on Divine Revelation, Dei Verbum, no. 10*, promulgated November 18, 1965)

4. *Gaudium et Spes* (pastoral constitution of the church in the modern world). This document discusses the church's role

in the modern world—how she sees herself and what her purpose is in the modern world, a world that has separated itself from its Christian roots. In the 1960s (and today) there's a notion of challenging traditional values of people no longer holding on to the values that the church had given to Western society, moving away from how to live as a Christian. "The modern world shows itself at once powerful and weak, capable of the noblest deeds or the foulest. Before it lies the path of freedom or to slavery."[12] Life should be ordered to selflessness, not selfishness. The church can help the world choose the path to freedom.

Was this council successful? The answer is "yes" and "no." On the positive side, in Poland, Africa, and Asia, where decrees were implemented, good things happened. However, Crocker writes:

> Unfortunately, the actual documents of the Council often proved less important than did the fact that they had been hi-jacked by invokers of the 'spirit' of Vatican II to enact sweeping 'reform' that the documents themselves did not call for. Thus, out went the Latin Mass in favor of a vernacular liturgy…in one stroke eliminating the historic and universal language of the church that echoed from Rome to Mexico to India every Sunday. In came guitars and more lay participation, including in some dioceses, such elicit and unwelcome innovations as hand-holding… The modern world was not condemned, as in the past, but accepted as the world in which the church and every Catholic was on pilgrimage.
>
> —Crocker, *Triumph*, 415–416

Other disastrous results followed. The number of seminarians collapsed. Thousands of priests and religious abandoned their vows to participate more fully in the world. Laypeople followed, becoming more like their non-Catholic brothers and sisters, divorcing, using contraceptives, and eventually aborting at similar rates. "Openness to the world" brought with it a spirit of non-discipline. Vatican II documents were broadly interpreted to justify experimentation, beliefs, and practices that were unjustifiable.

Social scientist Robert Nisbet said,

> I think it would be difficult to find a single decade in the history of Western culture when so much barbarism—so much calculated onslaught against culture and convention in any form, and so much sheer degradation of both culture and the individual—passed into print, into music, into art and onto the American stage as the decade of the 1960s.
>
> —Robert Nisbet, quoted in Kevin Price Phillips, *Post-Conservative America: People, Politics and Ideology,* (New York, NY: Random House, 1982), 18

Pope Paul VI died August 6, 1978. He was succeeded by Pope John Paul I, the "smiling pope," whose simplicity and sense of humor quickly won the admiration of the world, which was then shocked and saddened by his sudden death on September 28, 1978—thirty-three days after his election. The next day, I talked to a friend about it. He said, "It means one thing. He's not the right man for these times." How prophetic! History has shown that Pope John Paul II was the right man for these times.

Karol Wojtyla was born on May 18, 1920, in Wadowice, Poland. His university studies were interrupted by the German and Russian invasion in September 1939. When the Russians conquered all of Poland, Karol continued to work as a laborer while finishing his studies in an underground seminary in Cracow. He was ordained on November 1, 1946, and sent to Rome for further studies. Eventually, he would become a cardinal in Poland. "The world and the church were in a precarious place. Communists had firmly grasped the territories of Eastern Europe and were engaged in a military, economic, political, and culture cold war with Western civilization."[13]

> The difficult situation in which the church found herself in Poland is well-known. Although about 90% of the Poles were practicing their faith, the government was in the hands of the local Communist party, backed up by the presence of Soviet troops. In these circumstances, Cardinal Wojtyla showed himself a courageous and adroit leader. His election to the papacy astounded the world. He was not only the first non-Italian pope since 1523, but the first Pole or Slav ever chosen. Multilingual, he was the first pope to have spent his entire priestly life under Communist rule.
>
> —Brusher, *Popes through the Ages*, 528

In looking back at church history, Pope John Paul II wanted to reconcile the times in the past when some church members were not as faithful to the teachings of the Gospels as they should have been. This had contributed to disruptions and separations from the church. In an effort to rectify past sins and reach the youth of the world, he made eighty-five trips, which was equivalent to flying around the world twenty-eight times.

> His initial ecumenical moves were toward Eastern Orthodoxy and Anglicans, but his greatest achievement came on October 31, 1999, when Catholics and Lutherans signed at Augsburg, Germany, an accord ending the dispute over the doctrine of justification, which sparked the Protestant Reformation 482 years earlier. During this same period, he also contributed to the restoration of the democracy and religious freedom throughout the Eastern European Communist countries, especially in his native Poland, and made numerous journeys, including those to Africa, Asia, and the Americas.
>
> —http://www.helpfellowship.org/ Pope_John_Paul_II.htm

Despite health problems in the 1990s, John Paul did not slow down his travels. In September 1993, he traveled to the Baltic Republics, which was the first papal visit to countries of the former Soviet Union. In May 1997, he journeyed to Lebanon to give his support to the Christian minority and to heal religious divisions. In January 1998, he made a five-day visit to Cuba, denouncing US trade sanctions against that country, while pressing Castro to ease restrictions on religious rights.[14]

"His institution of World Youth Day was a brilliant strategy to bring the Gospel to the youth and foster in them a love for Christ and the Church."[15] In 1984, over three hundred thousand young people from around the world gathered in St. Peter's Square. It was from this event that the Holy Father developed the masterful strategy of World Youth Days going to specific cities in different countries, inviting the youth to be faithful living witnesses as Christ's disciples. Pope John Paul II would have nine World Youth Days, which drew millions at each stop. His multiple apostolic visits increased the visibility of the papacy and provided an international platform for preaching the Gospel.

Pope John Paul II has written fourteen encyclicals, forty-five apostolic letters, and five books. The encyclical *Evangelium Vitae,* written in 1995, defends life, speaking out against abortion, euthanasia, and the death penalty. On October 11, 1992, he approved the new catechism of the Catholic Church, which has been translated into every language.

On May 13, 1981, Pope John Paul II was shot at close range and severely wounded in an assassination attempt as he entered St. Peter's Square in the Vatican, but he made a full recovery. His attempted assassin was Mehemet Ali Agca. At a later time, the pope visited Agca in prison and forgave him for what he did.

A boyhood friend of mine was Edgar LeBlanc. His wife was in Rome the day the pope was shot. She had a front-row location with two women friends to see the pope as he went by on his pope mobile. As the pope neared her location, someone behind her was trying to desperately push her aside, but she wouldn't budge. It was Agca. He was trying to get a clear shot at the pope. Some local newspapers claimed she helped save the pope's life. His impact on the church and the world was enormous during his twenty-seven-year reign, with many people clamoring for him to be called "John Paul II the Great."

Pope Benedict XVI (2005–). After the death of the popular and long-serving Pope John Paul II, Cardinal Ratzinger was elected pope on April 19, 2005, and took the name Benedict XVI. At seventy-eight, he became the oldest person to have been elected pope since Pope Clement XII (1730–1740.) Ratzinger had served longer as a cardinal (over twenty-seven years) than any pope since Benedict XIII (1724–1730).

After World War II, Ratzinger studied theology and became an expert advisor at Vatican II. Prior to his elevation as pope, Cardinal Ratzinger had led the Congregation for the Doctrine of the Faith, a key Vatican office, in which he was seen as a tough enforcer of Pope John Paul's strongly conservative views. From 2002 until his election as pope, he was dean of the College of Cardinals. He became a major figure on the Vatican stage for a quarter of a century as one of the most respected, influential, and controversial members of the College of Cardinals. In April 2005, before his election as pope, *Time Magazine* identified him as one of the one hundred most powerful people in the world. Benedict is also multilingual. In addition to his native German, he speaks French and Italian fluently. He also has a very good command of Latin while speaking English and Spanish adequately.

Like his predecessor, Pope Benedict is theologically conservative, and his teachings and prolific writings defend traditional Catholic doctrine and values. He has advocated a return to fundamental values to counter increased secularization of many developed countries. He views relativism's denial of objective truth and the denial of moral truths in particular, as the central problem of the twenty-first century. As pope, he has continued to defend the teachings of Second Vatican Council by his writings and travels.

Among his many writings are three encyclicals. In one, *Spe Salve 49* (Saved by Hope), he gives us the understanding and motivation the church should have as it moves forward into the twenty-first century. Pope Benedict writes:

> Life is like a voyage on the sea of history, often dark and stormy, a voyage in which we watch for the stars that indicate the route. The true stars of our life are the people who have lived good lives. They are lights of hope. Certainly, Jesus Christ is the True Light, the sun that has risen above all the shadows of history. But to reach him, we also need light close by…people who shine with His light and so guide us along the way.
>
> —Pope Benedict XVI, *Spe Salvi*, promulgated November, 30, 2007

Pope Benedict has traveled extensively as an octogenarian to different parts of the world, bringing the Gospel. During his pontificate, he has made twenty-five trips out of Italy, three of which continued the highly successful World Youth Day tradition, initiated by Pope John Paul II. The church had been placed on a firm foundation by John Paul II. His members now prayed and hoped that during the time of Benedict and into the future, the Western world would come back to embracing her Christian roots, especially that Europe would recognize the role the church played in her history and return to it.

On February 28, 2013, Pope Benedict XVI dropped a bombshell that stunned the world! At what was scheduled to be a routine meeting to discuss three potential saints, Pope Benedict, eighty-five years old, announced his retirement. He would be the first pope in six hundred years to do so. In his retirement text he said,

After having repeatedly examined my conscience before God, I have come to the certainty that my strengths, due to an advanced age, are no longer suited to an adequate exercise of the Petrine ministry.[16]

Jorge Mario Bergoglio of Argentina was a surprise choice to be the new leader taking the name Francis I and becoming the first non-European pontiff in nearly thirteen hundred years. Although a conservative theologically, Francis is known for his concern for the poor and is expected to bring a radical change of style to the church leadership.

Contemporaneously with the above events, the following were occurring in the secular world.

The City of Man

The Galileo Controversy (1633)

Prior to the sixteenth century, most educated people accepted the theories of the Greek astronomer Ptolemy (second century), who held that the earth was stationary and the sun revolved around it. Christians accepted it because it seemed to be supported by common sense. Thomas Kuhn gives us some examples:

> The earth does not appear to move and we can all witness the sun rise in the morning and set at night. Also, if the earth moves at high speeds around the sun, then birds and clouds and other objects not attached to the ground, should be left behind. Human beings on the ground would be flung about.
>
> —Thomas Kuhn, *The Copernican Revolution: Planetary Astronomy in the Development of Western Thought*, (Cumbreland, RI: Harvard University Press, 1957) 43–44

In 1514, Nicolaus Copernicus (1473–1543), a Polish astronomer, unveiled a revolutionary new theory for understanding the world. He claimed in a book he wrote that the sun, not the earth, is the center of the universe. While Copernicus was unable to provide any physical proof, the power of his theory was that the sun at its center produced much more accurate predictions of planetary orbits. His theory was published during the Reformation and was condemned by Luther as being antibiblical.

Galilei Galileo (1564–1642), an Italian astronomer highly respected by the Catholic Church, had developed a more powerful telescope than others of his time. Using it, he made important new observations that were consistent with the Copernican theory. Galileo took his observations to the Jesuits, who were among the leading astronomers of the day, and they agreed that his sightings had strengthened the case for the earth going around the sun.

In 1613, convinced that Copernicus was right, Galileo published his *Letter on Sunspots* in which he openly advocated the Copernican theory, which was subsequently attacked by the scientific community. In 1616, because of teaching his theory as absolute truth, he was called before an inquisition. The head of the inquisition was Cardinal Bellarmine, one of the most respected theologians of the time. One of the touchy things was that some scriptures were more accommodating to the immovable earth theory, describing the earth as motionless and the sun as moving. Some examples are:

> On this day, when the Lord delivered up the Amorites to the Israelites, Joshua prayed to the Lord, and said in the presence of Israel, "Stand still, O sun of Gideon, O moon in the valley of Aijalon!" And the sun stood still, and the moon stayed, while the nation took vengeance on its foes. (Jo 10:12–13, NAB)

And "You fixed the earth on its foundation never to be moved" (Ps 104.5, NAB). Also, "The sun rises and the sun goes down; then it presses on to the place where it rises" (Eccl 1:5, NAB).

Bellarmine argued,

> If we have been reading Scripture one way, and the natural evidence shows that we were wrong, then, we need to revise our interpretation of Scripture and acknowledge our mistake. But, first let us make sure that there is conclusive scientific proof before we start changing Scriptural interpretations that have been taught for a very long time.
>
> —D'Souza, *What's so Great about Christianity*, 107

Bellarmine proposed a solution. Since evidence for the "sun" theory was inconclusive, and because of the sensitivity of the religious issues involved, Galileo was not to teach or promote heliocentrism. Galileo, a practicing Catholic, wanting to keep his good standing with the church, agreed with the cardinal's proposal. Bellarmine issued an injunction, recorded details of their meeting, and placed these notes in a church file.

For several years, Galileo kept his word. Cardinal Bellarmine died in 1621. Pope Gregory XV died in 1623. Galileo then received exciting news. Gregory's successor would be Pope Urban VIII (1623–1644), who was a scientific progressive. As a cardinal, he had fought hard to keep Copernicus's book off the index of forbidden books. He also was a fan of Galileo.

Galileo now felt confident he could preach heliocentrism. In 1632, he published *Dialogue Concerning the Two Chief World Systems* in which he claimed to have demonstrated the truth of heliocentrism. His proof was wrong. His main argument was that the rapid motion of the earth created ocean tides. Questionable at the time, we now know the moon is responsible for tides.

In his book, he also embarrassed the pope by having a dialogue between two main characters; one representing him, the other the pope. The pope's character had the name Simplicio, which in Italian means simpleton. The dialogue consisted mainly in foolish claims by Simplicio about the earth as center, with brilliant belittling responses from Galileo's character.

Galileo's writings were not confined to scientific issues. He advanced his own ideas about interpreting scripture, arguing that the Bible was largely allegorical and required constant reinterpretation to understand its true meaning. When Galileo was reported to the inquisition by his opponents, it was not only because of his scientific views but also on the grounds that he was trying to undermine the teachings of the church.

In 1633, Galileo was ordered to stand trial on suspicion of heresy. Returning to Rome, he was treated with respect. Someone had found Bellarmine's notes from the first Inquisition that read:

> It was decided at the Holy Congregation on 25 February, 1616, that the Holy Office will give you an injunction to abandon this doctrine, not to teach it to others, not to defend it, and not to treat of it; and, if you do not acquiesce in this injunction, you should be imprisoned.
>
> —Maurice A. Finocchiaro, *The Galileo Affair*, (Berkeley, CA: University of California Press, 1989), 288

Galileo had not told anybody about this previous meeting not to teach heliocentrism. He was now viewed as deceiving the church and not living up to his agreements. Galileo denied that his book promoted heliocentrism. Inquisitors concluded it did and demanded he recant. He did, and was sentenced to house arrest. His first five months were in a palace, after which he was permitted to return to his villa in Florence under house arrest. His penance was to read seven psalms a day for three years. In 1642, he died of natural causes.

On November 1, 1992, the *New York Times* reported the following:

> Moving formally to rectify a wrong, Pope John Paul II acknowledged in a speech today, before the Pontifical Academy of Sciences, that the Roman Catholic Church had erred in condemning Galileo 359 years ago for asserting that the Earth revolves around the sun. John Paul said that the theologians who condemned Galileo did not recognize the formal distinction between the Bible and its interpretation. "This led them unduly to trespass into the realm of faith a question which in fact pertained to scientific investigation."

D'Souza writes, "There is no other example in history of the Catholic Church condemning a scientific theory."[17]

We saw earlier in the sixteenth century how Luther in Germany and King Henry VIII in England had delivered severe blows to the unity of the Catholic Church. Now, in the eighteenth century, a big disunity problem was about to erupt in France.

The French Revolution (1789–1799)

Modernism and The Enlightenment had planted the seeds of intellectual confusion by changing the understanding of philosophy. The French Revolution would be the climax of The Enlightenment which brought about what the enlightened thinkers wanted: a society separate from the church; a society that didn't even recognize the roots of Europe linked to the church.

King Louis XVI (1774–1792) was king of France during this time. He was a devout Catholic, a good king with a good heart but a weak leader. He was married to Marie Antoinette, also a devout Catholic. Louis began to clash with the wealthy and increasingly powerful nobility with everything coming to a head in 1789 during a financial crisis that erupted throughout the country. The main reason was France's monetary support to aid America during its war of independence from Great Britain.

The continual decline eventually caused the revolution, which happened July 14, 1789.

In the fall of 1789, the royal family was captured and held in captivity by the revolutionary elements and eventually overthrown officially in 1792. During the captivity of the king, the revolutionaries began the total dismantling of the faith and the church in France. In 1792, in an effort to separate the church in France from the Catholic Church in Rome, a new law was enacted—the Civil Constitution of the Clergy. The government would assume control of the church. Bishops would be elected by the people, not appointed by the pope. All clergy had to take an oath of fidelity to the new government. In France, only six of the one hundred thirty-four bishops took the oath of fidelity, holding on to their loyalty to the pope. About forty-five percent of the priests did take the oath. More than two hundred priests and religious martyrs were killed in one day.

France broke away completely from the church, causing a great disruption in the church and in the world. In 1792, a reign of terror began in France with the guillotine established as a weapon of persuasion. King Louis XVI and Marie Antoinette were executed. The process of de-Christianizing France had begun. Half of the clergy were gone, either executed or fled. There were no new ordinations. It is estimated that twenty thousand people were killed by the guillotine. Sixteen Carmelite nuns offered their lives as a holocaust to end the terror. Ten days after the last nun died, the reign of terror officially ended.

Napoleon Bonaparte (1769–1821)

Napoleon came to power in France in 1796. He brought the church back into being because he saw that the people needed the church and that there was a strong link between the French people and the church. But his intention was to control the church. Napoleon marched an army down to Rome, conquering Italy and the city of Rome. He took Pope Pius VI prisoner, who later died in French captivity in 1799. In 1801, he signed a concordat with the church, stating that the Catholic Church was a privileged but not a state religion, allowing the church to again exist in Rome, but priests and bishops had to take an oath of allegiance to the state. In 1804, Napoleon became emperor, and in 1809 annexed the Papal States against the wishes of the pope, resulting in Pius VII excommunicating him. Napoleon's troops captured Pius VII, who was kept in exile for six years, until Napoleon's reign ended in 1813.

In 1815, at the Council of Vienna, the Papal States confiscated by Napoleon were returned to the church. However, in 1871, the former Papal States were permanently taken away from the popes and absorbed into the modern nation of Italy. Throughout the French Revolution, the reign of terror, and the reign of Napoleon, we see a devoted Catholic country separate itself from its Catholic roots that helped build French culture. Also, persecution of the church continued in different countries.

Kulturkampf (1871–1879)

Germany did not become a united country until the nineteenth century. It had been a collection of over three hundred principalities and regions. In the north, Protestant Prussia was the dominant state, while in southern Germany, Catholic Bavaria and Austria were the dominant states. This was about to change.

Otto von Bismarck, minister president and foreign minister of Prussia, was made imperial chancellor of the German empire and wanted to unite all the principalities politically and socially. He wanted the Catholic Church states to be subject to him as part of his unity plans. He wanted to achieve this by forcing the Catholic states to become Protestant. In 1872, the Jesuits, who were loyal to the pope, and other religious orders were expelled from Germany being seen as loyal to a foreign power (the pope).

Priests and bishops were imprisoned. Church-run schools were taken over by the state and became state-run schools. Church lands were seized and monasteries closed.

This culture war existed over a fifteen-year period until a peaceful resolution was made with an agreement reached by Bismarck and Pope Leo XIII. Pope Leo XIII conceded that the church would allow for the state approval of clerical appointments, that public education would be controlled by the state, and that the state law would reign supreme throughout Germany. The state agreed to allow Catholics the public exercise of their faith without any fear of governmental control or intrusion. The papal reigns of two holy and saintly popes, Pope Leo XIII, and his successor, St. Pius X, would address modernism and put the church on a firm foundation before she is attacked again.

WWI (1914–1922) and Pope Benedict XV

With World War I, an ugly reality involving many nations, the cardinals realized that the next pope should be a diplomat. Cardinal Giacomo della Chiesa, who had a strong background in papal diplomatic service, became pope, taking the name Benedict XV. A major problem faced him immediately—World War I. Sadly, it was an unstoppable train of events.

> The cold-blooded murder of one man, Archduke Franz Ferdinand of the Austro-Hungarian Empire, ushered in this satanic age of war. Austria declares war upon Serbia for the assassination of one of her most beloved sons, but Serbia does not fight alone. An international pact draws Russia to Serbia's defense, which motivates Germany to take action on behalf of her Austrian ally. Germany's ruthless offensive against France, however storms through Belgium, an innocent bystander, and England quickly lunges to her defense. Through a well-woven web of treaties, all Europe is ensnared in war. Pride blinds them to

the horrors suffered by their men, and they continue to stubbornly order their men into slaughter.

—Weidenkopf and Schreck, *Epic*, 97

Benedict, as the sign of Catholic unity, faced enormous obstacles. Two thirds of Europe's Catholics were involved: 124 million on the side of the allies; 64 million on the side of the Central powers.[18]

He immediately pursued three objectives:

1. perfect neutrality (the church would not take sides);
2. the church would extend charity to all victims of war regardless of nationality; and,
3. the church would call for peace at every opportunity.

Pope Pius XII would use these same guidelines in WWII.

In 1917, Benedict called a *Plea for Peace*, a discussion on how all the nations could come to peace. Woodrow Wilson took many of Benedict's ideas and put them into his fourteen points. One of Benedict's ideas that was not accepted was no reparations from the losers. If the world had listened to Benedict concerning reparations after the war, perhaps Hitler may not have come to power and World War II may have been avoided. This war was a horrible, unnecessary, disaster. To avenge the murder of one man, "more than 8 million people died in WWI; 21 million were wounded."[19]

There was much international respect for Pope Benedict's actions during and after the war. The Turks even erected a statue in his honor because of his peace efforts during the war. He died January 22, 1922. His whole life and pontificate shapes our lives even today.

Russia: The Bolshevik Revolution (1917)

Revolutionaries, atheists at heart, took over Russia and began to attack religion and persecute the Catholic Church. In January 1918, a decree was issued against religion calling for the complete separation of church and state and calling for the Catholic Church to be deprived of all its lands and possessions, which were confiscated by the government.

In 1922 alone, eight thousand priests and monks were executed throughout Russia simply for being Catholic. In 1925, it's estimated that around two hundred thousand Catholics and every bishop in Russia vanished; all were killed. In the 1940s, the Soviets continued their persecutions but this time in the surrounding countries and those they occupied, especially the country of Ukraine, a country that has a deep relationship with the Catholic Church. Soviets tried to force them to join the Orthodox church, but the Ukrainians remained loyal to the Catholic Church, avoiding a schism.

Mexico (1920s to 1930s)

Under the Mexican revolutionary socialist regime in the 1920s and 1930s, a country once aligned with the church was now actively persecuting the church. Between 1931 and 1936, 480 churches were closed. Church-run schools, orphanages, and hospitals were shut down by the revolutionary government. Bishops were stripped of their citizenship and were expelled from the country (1927). Clergy were arrested and forced to act in secret, ministering to Catholics in the area.

One popular priest, Miguel Pro, was arrested along with two of his brothers on the trumped-up charge of plotting to assassinate the president. He was tried and sentenced to die by a firing squad. The regime, hoping to use the media as a means of prompting people to leave the church, invited journalists and photographers to record his execution. Before Father Pro was executed by the firing squad, he stretched out his arms in the form of a cross. His last words were "Viva Christo Rey" (Long live Christ the King.)[20]

The dying image of Father Pro's death caused people to be drawn to the faith. Recognizing their mistake, the regime banned the use of photos and stories because of the strong image that was presented, causing people to gravitate toward the church. An estimated two hundred fifty thousand to three hundred thousand people were killed during the revolutionary socialist regime in Mexico during the 1930s and 1940s. Mexico still suffers from the effects of this revolution. In 1991, the anti-Catholic articles in the Mexican revolution were finally repealed.

Spanish Civil War (1936–1939)

The radical liberalism of the "enlightenment" preached secularism versus the sacred and had no boundaries. In Spain, during liberal regimes (1854–1856 and 1873–1874) the church was persecuted with the killing of priests and religious and the confiscation of church properties. The problem was that there were "two Spains." There was the Catholic Spain with its saints, missionaries, art, literature, and church organization, which desired stability, known as the Nationalists. Then there was the liberal Spain with its intellectual and political movements, anti-Catholicism, and its desire for change, known as Loyalists and Republicans.

Discontent and violence caused constant changes in government control. Things came to a head in 1936, when extreme rebels took control. In July of that year, General Francisco Franco led a successful uprising, and soon, Spain was in the midst of a civil war. The Spanish civil war pitted the Loyalists (socialists, liberals, and communists) against the Nationalists.

> While Russians sent money and an international brigade from many countries who fought on the side of the Loyalists, the Italians and Germans supported Franco's

nationalists. There were atrocities on both sides. Almost 7,000 priests, sisters, brothers were killed by mutilation, fire, and crucifixion. Twelve bishops were martyred. 20,000 churches were destroyed. Nationalists under Franco fought hard and long, finally defeating the Loyalists. During the Franco dictatorship, the Catholic Church's position in the nation was officially recognized and restored.

—McGonigle and Quigley,
A History of the Christian Tradition, 167–168

Fascism in Italy and Mussolini (1922–1943) and Pope Pius XI (1922–1939)

Ever since the Papal States were taken from the pope when Italy was unified in 1871, there was the question of what was to be done with the pope in the Vatican. "Is the Vatican independent of Italy?" Or "Is the Vatican a part of Italy?" In 1922, King Victor Emmanuel III named Benito Mussolini as prime minister of Italy. That same year, Pope Pius XI was elected pope. He was a very shrewd diplomat who wanted to safeguard the independence of the church and the rights of all Catholics among the different European nations.

Mussolini, atheist and anticlerical, had an interesting approach to the church. He knew he couldn't go out of his way to actively persecute the church in Italy because he knew his history and what happened to those who persecuted the church. Mussolini entered into negotiations with Pope Pius XI to resolve "the Roman question." The question was resolved with the Lateran Treaty in 1929, which created a sovereign nation, the Vatican City State, where the Holy Father would be in charge and make his home. This continues to the present day.

Under the Lateran Treaty, the rights of the church in Italy were guaranteed. It declared that Catholicism would be the sole and official religion in the country. The church would be allowed to teach Catholic education in the public schools. The church would divorce itself from any active role in Italian politics. A financial agreement was accepted as settlement of all the claims of the Holy See. The pope was pledged to perpetual neutrality in international relations. The pope officially recognized the Italian nation. This helped to maintain the independency of the papacy and not have it subject to secular rulers.

In 1984, an agreement was signed, revising the concordat. Among other things, it ended the church's position as the state-supported religion of Italy. In 2008, it was announced that the Vatican would no longer immediately adopt all Italian laws, citing conflict over right-to-life issues.

Nazism in Germany, Adolf Hitler (1933–1945), and Pius XII (1939–1958)

During the 1920s, Germany was struggling financially because of the reparations forced on their country by the Treaty of Versailles June 28, 1918, ending WWI. Angry at the harsh reparations and longing for leadership that would restore their national pride, they entrusted their future to the National Socialists, who appointed Adolf Hitler as chancellor on January 29, 1933.

In the years 1925–1927, Hitler wrote a two-volume work called *Mein Kampf,* which set out the central tenets of National Socialists. The religion of Christianity eventually would be replaced by the religion of National Socialists. Hitler would be absolute ruler (fuhrer) and the prophet of a new religion. The Nordic race was supreme, and the Aryans as the master race were entitled to rule all others. Germans had a right to dominate the world and especially the subhuman races (i.e. the Jews and Negroes). The state had a right to use any means to achieve its goals, and Germany needed living space and thus was justified in territorial expansion.[21]

Pope Pius XI could see that the National Socialists' ideology would result in persecution of the church. He and cardinal secretary of state Pacelli (the future Pope Pius XII) tried to deal diplomatically with the National Socialist leaders. At the urging of Germany, the Vatican entered into a concordat, or treaty, with the Nazis in 1933 to guarantee the rights of the church. Unfortunately, this move gave Hitler prestige and undercut Catholic opposition to his government. Hitler never had any intention of upholding his promises of security and began violating the agreement within five days.

Because of breaking pledges of the concordat, on Palm Sunday, March 21, 1937, a papal encyclical, *Mit Brenneder Sorge* (With Burning Concern), was read to Catholic Churches throughout Germany. It taught that the radical ideas of Hitler and totalitarianism stood in opposition to the Catholic Church. The letter let the world know that German Catholics clearly opposed the doctrine of the Nazis.

In September 1939, Hitler invaded Poland. He rounded up seven hundred priests who were shot and killed. Three million poles were sent to concentration camps. Dachau was designated as camp for priests. Of three thousand priests from all Europe, one thousand perished. "By the end of the war, over 12 million allied military and more than 5 million of the Axis military had been killed. More than 6 million Jews (more than one half of German Jews, one-third of world Jews) were murdered in gas chambers and concentration camps as part of Hitler's "final solution."[22] All of this heartbreak happened because of one man's satanic dreams.

Eugenio Pacelli was born in Rome on March 2, 1876, into a family devoted to papal service. As Apostolic Nuncio in Berlin, Germany, during the rise of Hitler and National Socialism, Pacelli was well-informed about the situation in Germany and was an outspoken critic. Thus, he possessed the diplomatic experience needed in these troubled times. Eventually, in 1939, Pacelli was elected pope and took the name Pope Pius XII.

THE CATHOLIC STORY

The Nazis saw Pius XII as an enemy. Hitler hated the church because their moral force would be an obstacle to his conquest goals. Part of his plan was to destroy the Catholic Church. Three million Catholic Poles would be sent to concentration camps, many of them priests. Three thousand priests were rounded up from all over Europe, many from Poland. About one thousand priests perished during their captivity.

Maximillian Kolbe, a Polish Franciscan, was captured and sent to the camp at Auschwitz. While there, a prisoner escaped. To discourage escapes, Germans would pick out ten prisoners and have them executed. One of the ten selected was a Polish soldier/husband/father who became very distraught at being executed and never seeing his family again. Kolbe went to the commandant and asked that he take the place of that soldier. His request was granted. He and nine others were sent to a starvation bunker where they were starved for two weeks. Many died. Eventually Kolbe and the remaining few were executed by injections of carbolic acid. Kolbe's body was cremated, and his ashes scattered on August 14, 1941. Eventually, he would be declared a saint by the Catholic Church.

Pius XII embraced the principles of Pope Benedict XV during WWI. The Vatican policy would be strict neutrality because the church had children on both sides of the conflict. However, he would dispense charity to the victims of the war, no matter which side they were on. Pius tried to ensure the safety of Jews by trying to prevent them from being rounded up and executed by the Nazis. He also approved the issuance of false baptismal certificates for Jews throughout the church in hopes that the Nazis would not round them up and send them to concentration camps.

Two modern-day accusations are leveled against Pius XII for his wartime activities related to the Jews. It started in 1963 with the writing of a seven-hour play, *The Deputy*, by a German named Rolf Hochhuth. It was based on Pius and his wartime activities.

The play characterizes Pius as a money-grubbing hypocrite, very passive, and disinterested in what was going on in the world at that time. The whole message of the play is that Pius should have been more vocal in speaking out against Nazism and about what the Nazis were doing with the Jews.

Pius XII did speak publicly about Nazi treatment to the Jews. He authorized Vatican Radio to issue broadcasts about the Catholic Church and Jews in Poland so the world would know in the early stages when the Nazis invaded Poland. Vatican Radio condemned Nazi atrocities. In one specific broadcast, it said, "He who makes a distinction between Jews and other men is unfaithful to God and in conflict with God's command."[23]

The *New York Times*, after hearing Pius's 1941 Christmas address, wrote in an editorial:

> The voice of Pius XII is a lonely voice in the silence and darkness enveloping Europe…He is about the only ruler left on the continent of Europe who dares to raise his voice at all. The pope puts himself squarely against Hitlerism.[24]

The *New York Times*, after hearing his 1942 Christmas address, wrote, "The pope has repudiated the National Socialist new European order…he is virtually accusing the German people of injustice toward the Jews."[25]

Pope Pius was trying to keep a balance as to when and how to speak. He was aware of what happened in Holland. In 1942, the Dutch bishops as a whole spoke out against the deportation of the Jews and, as a result, the Nazis increased their efforts to deport Jews. It is estimated that eighty percent (highest percentage of any nation) of the entire Jewish population of Holland was deported or sent to the camps.

Albrecht von Kessel, an official at the German embassy to the Holy See during the war, wrote in 1962,

THE CATHOLIC STORY

> We were convinced that a fiery protest by Pius XII against the persecution of the Jews…would certainly not have saved a single Jew. Hitler, like a trapped beast, would react to any menace that he felt directed at him, with cruel violence.[26]

Pope Pius knew that Hitler had a plan to invade the Vatican, remove him from power (even kill him), and set up an antipope in Germany. Even with this knowledge, Pius instructed bishops to allow Jews to live secretly in monasteries and convents. He hid five hundred at his summer residence at Castel Gandolfo.

> The vindication of Pius XII has been established principally by Jewish writers and from Israeli archives. It is now established that the Pope supervised a rescue network which saved 860,000 Jewish lives…more than all the international agencies put together.[27]

After the war, Pius XII was widely praised for his wartime efforts. The chief rabbi of Rome, Israel Zolli, converted to Catholicism in part because of the actions of Pius XII and took the baptized Christian name "Eugenio," the first name of the pope.

In 1958, when Pius died, Golda Meir, prime minister of Israel, had this to say,

> During the ten years of Nazi terror, when our people went through the horrors of martyrdom, the pope raised his voice to condemn the persecution, and to commiserate with the victims.[28]

Albert Einstein stated,

> Only the Church stood squarely across the path of Hitler's campaign for suppressing truth…I never had any special interest in the Church before, but now I feel great affec-

tion and admiration…and am forced thus to confess that what I once despised, I now praise unreservedly.[29]

In addition to the problems of the war, Pope Pius XII was remarkably productive and successful in his pastoral and ecclesiastical activities. There were few religious and moral topics he did not touch upon in his forty encyclicals. In his encyclical *Divino Afflante Spiritu*, Pius officially urged and approved the use of modern critical approaches to the study of the Bible.[30]

His personal devotion to the Blessed Virgin Mary and his conviction that she was the main bulwark against atheistic communism led him to define the document of the bodily assumption of Mary into heaven (November 1, 1950). He also promoted devotion to Fatima.

Pius XII died in 1958, having clearly laid the foundation for an extraordinary happening in the next pontificate. That happening was Vatican II, which was covered above in the City of God section.

Jesus established his church with Peter as leader, promising that "the gates of hell" would never prevail against it. We've highlighted two thousand years of church history, showing major challenges from outside and inside, trying to destroy the church. All have failed. Jesus' church is still here. Peter's 265th successor, Pope Francis I, is its present head. Jesus keeps his promises.

Notes

1. *Encyclopedia of Catholicism,* 469.
2. *Catechism of the Catholic Church,* #491.
3. Leslie Rumble and Charles M. Carty, *Radio Replies #1, 769.*
4. Elizabeth Ficocelli, *Lourdes Font of Faith. Hope, and Charity,* (Mahweh, NJ: Paulist Press), 34.
5. Raj Persaud, "Where Scientists are looking for God" Http://www.telegraph.co.uk/connected/ main.jhtml.
6. Michael Walsh, *The Popes,* (New York, NY: St. Martin's Press, 1980), 204.
7. Ibid., 206.
8. Ibid., 208.
9. http://www.fatima.lakewood.com/fatima_story.htlm
10. *Chicago Daily Tribune,* January 26, 1938, page 2.
11. http://www.ewtn.com/expert/answers/FatimaSecret.htm.
12. Pope Paul VI, *Pastoral Constitution on the Church in the Modern World, Gaudium et Spes,* promulgated December 7, 1965.
13. Weidenkopf & Schreck, *Epic,* 109.
14. Http://www.helpfellowship.org/Pope_John_Paul_II.htm.
15. Weidenkopf and Schreck, *Epic,* 110.
16. http://religionnewws.com/2013/11/read-pope-benedict-xvis-resignation-speech/
17. D'Souza, *What's So Great About Christianity,* 110.
18. McGonigle and Quigley, *A History of the Christian Tradition,*155.
19. Ibid.
20. Crocker, *Triumph,* 397.
21. McGonigle and Quigley, *A History of the Christian Tradition,* 170.
22. Ibid., 171.
23. Vatican Radio, 2/27/1943.
24. Editorial, *New York Times,* December 25, 1941. Editorial, *New York Times,* December 25, 1941.

25. Editorial, *New York Times*, December 25, 1942.
26. http:/www.jewishvirtuallibrary.org/jsource/anti-Semitism/piusdef.html.
27. Ibid.
28. http://www.michaeljournal.org/piusXII.htm.
29. *Time*, December 23, 1940.
30. Richard P. McBrien, *Lives of the Popes: The Pontiffs from St. Peter to John Paul II*, (San Francisco, CA: Harper San Francisco, 1997) 366.

Conclusions

What Is the Truth That Will Set Us Free?

The nine preceding chapters gathered the necessary data to help us clearly identify the truth that will set us free from life's fears and uncertainties. We need a completely trusted "voice" that will provide guidance and aids for us during our life's journey, a voice which will guarantee a peace and certainty in this life and, more importantly, in the world to come.

There are over thirty-three thousand separate Christian groups. The one true church, clearly identified throughout this book, is the Roman Catholic Church. Does that mean that all mankind outside the visible church cannot be saved? Absolutely not. By the same token, all members within the visible true church are not automatically saved just because of their membership within the true church. Why is the Catholic Church the one true church? There are two major reasons:

First, the church Jesus established in 33 AD with Peter as its head, is one and the same as the Catholic Church today, currently led by Peter's 265th successor, Pope Francis I. Here's where Jesus created his church.

> "And I say also unto thee, thou art Peter and upon this rock I will build my church; and the gates of hell shall not prevail against it. And I will give unto thee the keys of the kingdom of heaven; and whatsoever thou shalt bind on earth shall be bound in heaven; and whatsoever thou

shalt loose on earth shall be loosed in heaven." (Mt 16: 18–19, KJV)

The gates of hell have not prevailed against his church! It survived the first three hundred years of persecutions by Roman emperors, who tried to stamp it out, heresies from without and within, the East-West split in 1054 AD, Islamic invasions, the Martin Luther revolt and its consequences, the King Henry VIII loss of England, and scandalous behavior from some of its own clergy, even at its top levels.

Jesus also gave Peter an authority that no man in the history of the world ever possessed. Peter, with his Apostles, were given the power to "bind and loose" in matters of faith and morals, and their decisions would be approved in heaven. This unprecedented authority was to safeguard the apostolic deposit of faith from that first century beginning when Jesus and the Apostles were active. That authority has been exercised in twenty-one church councils and on other rare special occasions. Jesus also promised that he and the Holy Spirit would be with his church until the end of time.

Jesus Christ wanted his church to be one in faith, worship, and government. Jesus prayed for this unity: "That they may all be one, as you, Father, are in me and I in you, that they also may be in us, that the world may believe that you sent me" (Jn 17:21, NAB).

He spoke of only one church, one fold, and one shepherd. "I have other sheep that do not belong to this fold. These also I must lead, and they will hear my voice, and there will be one flock, one shepherd" (Jn 10:16, NAB).

Paul says, "But if I should be delayed, you should know how to behave in the household of God, which is the church of the living God, the pillar and foundation of truth" (1 Tm 3:15, NAB).

The second major reason for being Catholic is that Jesus gifted his church with "the full means of salvation" through the seven sacraments.

Most of us eat three meals a day to take care of our physical needs. The average person lives seventy-eight years. After death, that well-nourished body will begin the process of disintegration. The spiritual soul will live forever either in heaven or hell. In which place it will live eternal life depends on how it lived its life journey. If we find enough time to feed our bodies three times a day, how much time do we spend providing for our spiritual needs for an eternally happy future?

Our physical needs are satisfied with food. Our spiritual soul needs graces, which are "muscle food" for our souls. Graces come from the seven sacraments that were gifted by Jesus to provide the full means of salvation through his church, covering all stages of our life journey, giving meaning to a person's life. It is Jesus alone who mediates the sacraments to allow graces to flow to mankind. He does it through the sacrament of holy orders to priests. In confession, it is not the priest who forgives sins but Jesus. Only priests and higher clergy ordained with holy orders can turn bread and wine into the body and blood of Jesus, but it is Jesus who actually performs the transubstantiation.

Roman Catholics, Eastern Catholics, as well as Eastern Orthodox churches, all recognize the seven sacraments of baptism, confirmation, holy Eucharist, penance, anointing of the sick, holy orders, and marriage. Remember that sacraments give us much needed graces to guide us on our life journey. Two sacraments the Eucharist and penance (or reconciliation) are our support system regularly throughout our life journey. Let's take a closer look at each.

Eucharist

The Eucharist is the summit of all sacraments and is the source of unity for all Catholics in the world. It is celebrated in the Mass. I've been to Mass in different countries, and while I didn't know their language, I knew exactly what was going on. I also knew what the person sitting next to me believed. Eucharist means thanksgiving. It's thanksgiving for how Jesus atoned for the sins of mankind, original sin and individual sins, by his death on the cross. Heaven, which had been lost because of original sin, was reopened. The good news promise in Genesis 3:15 had been fulfilled. Jesus was the promised "seed."

Reconciliation

When we sin, we lose our peace with God and jeopardize our salvation. When our sins are forgiven, that peace is restored. Jesus established this sacrament with his Apostles after his resurrection, giving them the power to forgive sins:

> Jesus said to them again, "Peace be with you. As the Father who sent me, even so I send you." And when he had said this, he breathed on them, and said to them "Receive the Holy Spirit. If you forgive the sins of any, they are forgiven. If you retain the sins of any, they are retained." (Jn 20:21–23, NAB)

This is the power through which God utilizes the priest to hear and determine if indeed the penitent is sorry and provide the grace of forgiveness that God offers. Those who find it difficult to confess find a way around it by developing the theory that you can confess your sins directly to God and receive forgiveness without confession. It sounds nice and non-threatening, but it is not how God set up the sacrament. How would one who confesses directly to God know if his sins have been truly forgiven or have "been retained?"

Jesus had powerful credentials supporting his claims. In addition to his birth being pre-announced, Jesus did things no human in the history of the world has ever done. He raised three people from the dead. He showed his control over nature by calming the winds and the waves. He performed numerous miracle healings every day. Jesus rose from the dead. Ten of the apostles, eye-witnesses to the daily miracles and his resurrection, died horrible deaths in strange countries, preaching the life, death, and resurrection of Jesus. Why die for a lie?

Jesus had a worldview of humanity. At his ascension, he commanded his Apostles to go to all the nations of the world, baptizing them in the name of the Father, and of the Son, and of the Holy Spirit. He wanted all mankind to come into his church and know the good news of his salvation story. This was a fulfillment of Abraham's prophecies that God's message would reach all nations of the world. Jesus promised his church would never die and that he and the Holy Spirit would be with his church until the "end of the age."

We all have to die, and we all have to live the rest of our lives. During this remaining life journey, we are constantly exposed to temptations. Whether we believe or not believe in God determines how we respond to these temptations. This can create anxieties and uncertainties. We need to know the truth. Jesus is the way, the truth, and the life. Jesus controls the passageways of death. Jesus provided his Catholic Church with a leadership structure of Peter and his Apostles for guidance. Jesus' church, with its leadership structure of Peter as the leader and the Apostles, is still intact today with their successors, the pope, and the bishops. This provides believers with complete certainty that the church Jesus established two thousand years ago and the Catholic Church today are one and the same.

Jesus provided his church, through his seven sacraments, the full means of salvation—getting us to heaven at the end of our earthly journey and providing us during our journey a complete confidence that we are on the right path. Despite some poor decisions and scandals during the church's two-thousand-year history, these life-giving sacraments remained intact. These holy sacraments are what make his church holy and the fountain of life. The truth that will set us free is a complete commitment to

Jesus' teachings, sacraments, devotional guides, and spiritual aids found in Jesus' church, the Catholic Church. God is real.

I'll close with pertinent comments by Pope Benedict XVI, who writes:

> Anyone who excludes God from his horizons falsifies the notion of reality, in consequence, can only end up in blind alleys or with recipes for destruction…The first basic point to affirm, then, is the following: only those who recognize God know reality and are able to respond to it adequately and in a truly human manner…Yet here a further question immediately arises: who knows God? How can we know him?

> For a Christian, the nucleus of the reply is simple: only God knows God, only his son who is God from God, true God, knows him. And he "who is nearest to the Father's heart has made him known" (John 1:18). Thus, the unique and irreplaceable importance of Christ for us, and for humanity. If we do not know God in and with Christ, all of reality is transformed into an indecipherable enigma; there is no way, and without a way, there is neither life nor truth…God is the foundational reality, not a God who is merely imagined or hypothetical, but God with a human face; he is God-with-us, the God who loves even to the cross. Pope Benedict XVI, *Magnificat* (9/2011)

References

This is not a complete listing of all the works consulted in the writing of this book but is intended as a convenience for the reader.

Ali, Daniel & Spencer Robert. *Inside Islam*. West Chester: Ascension Press, 2003.

Agius, George (monsignor). *Tradition and the Church*. Rockford, Ill: Tan Books and Publishers Inc., 2005.

Augustine of Canterbury. American Catholic.org (accessed July 6, 2013).

Aquinas, Thomas. *The Summa Theologica and Summa Contra Gentiles*. Timothy McDermott, ed. Westminster, MD: Christian Classics, 1993.

Barclay, William. *Daily Bible Study Series*. Book 5. Edinburgh, UK: St. Andrew Press, 1955; Philadelphia, PA: Westminster Press, 1975.

Bausch, William J. *Pilgrim Church*. rev. and exp. ed. by Carol Ann Cannon, M.A. and Robert Obach, Ph.D., Mystic, CN: Twenty-Third Publications, 1989.

Benedict XVI (pope). General audience 11/11/2009.

———. *Magnificat* 9/20/11

Brusher, Joseph S.J. *Popes Through the Ages*. New York, NY: D. Van Nostrand & Company, 1959.

Burke, John J. *Characteristics of the Early Church*. Baltimore, MD: McCormick Press, 2008.

Catechism of the Catholic Church. Liguori, MO: Liguori Publications, 1994.

Crocker, H.W. III. *Triumph.* Roseville, CA: Prima Publishing, 2001.

D'Souza, Dinesh. *What's So Great About Christianity.* Washington, D.C.: Regnery Publishing, Inc., 2007.

Hawkings, Stephen. *A Brief History of Time.* Bantam Trade paperback ed., New York, NY: Bantam Books, 1998.

Hilgarth, J.N. *Christianity and Paganism.* Philadelphia, PA: University of Pennsylvania Press, rev. ed., 1985.

Hughes, Philip. *The Church in Crisis, A Popular History of the Catholic Church.* Garden City, NY: Hanover House, 1960.

Irenaeus. *Adversus Heresus*, IV 2, 2.

John Paul II (pope). *The Splendor of Truth.* Electronic copyright 1999 EWTN, http://www. EWTN.com.

——— *Crossing the Threshold of Hope.* New York, NY: Alfred A. Knopf, 1994.

Jurgens, William. *Faith of the Early Fathers, Vol. 3.* Collegeville, MN: The Liturgical Press, 1998.

Kierkegaard, Soren. "Journals IVA 164 (1843)."

Kreeft, Peter. *The Luke E. Hart Series Basic Elements of the Catholic Faith*, Part Three, Section Four of "Catholic Christianity" New Haven, CT: The Knights of Columbus, 2001.

Kuhn, Thomas. *The Copernican Revolution: Planetary Astronomy in the Development of Western Thought.* Cumbreland, RI: Harvard University Press, 1957.

Madden, Thomas. "The Truth about the Spanish Inquisition," *Crisis Magazine*, September, 2003.

McBrien, Richard P. *Lives of the Popes: The Pontiffs from St. Peter to John Paul II.* San Francisco, CA: Harper San Francisco, 1997.

———, general ed., *HarperCollins Encyclopedia of Catholicism.* San Francisco, CA: HarperSanFrancisco, 1995.

McGonigle, Thomas D. & James F. A. Quigley. *A History of the Christian Tradition,* Mahweh, NJ: The Paulist Press, 1988.

Mohammad. *The Qur'an,* trans. M.H. Shakir. Elmhurst, NY: Tahrike Tarsile Qur'an, Inc., 1999.

Nisbet, Robert quoted in Kevin Price Phillips. *Post-Conservative America: People, Politics and Ideology.* New York, NY: Random House, 1982.

O'Donnell, Rev. Marvin. *Two Critical Moments in Church History,* audiovisual, AMCN 31463–31474 Group. Notre Dame, IN: International Catholic University, Lecture Series, 1997.

Orlandis, Jose. *A Short History of the Catholic Church.* Dublin, IR: Four Courts Press, 1993.

Parker, Barry. *Vindication of the Big Bang.* New York, NY: Plenum Press, 1993.

Paul VI (pope). *Dogmatic Constitution on the Church, Lumen Gentium.* Promulgated November 21, 1964.

Premm, Rev. Matthias. *Dogmatic Theology of the Laity.* Staten Island, NY: Alba House, 1967; Rockford, IL: Tan Books and Publishers, Inc., 1977.

Roberts, Tyler. *Skeptics and Believers: Religious Debate in the Western Intelligence Tradition,* http://www.goodreads.com/author/show/ 445684tyler-t-roberts.

Rumble, Leslie and Charles M. Carty. *Radio Replies.* St. Paul, MN: Radio Replies Press Society, 1938.

Santos, Lucia. *Fatima in Lucia's Own Words.* Still River, MA: Ravengate Press, 1976.

Schreck, Alan, Ph.D. *What Did The First Four "Ecumenical" or Universal Councils of the Christian Church Teach About Jesus?,* http://www.thetruthdecoded.org.au/ early-understandings-Jesus.php.

Sheed, F.J. *Theology for Beginners,* Ann Arbor, MI: Servant Books, 1958.

Sheen, Fulton (bishop). *Ye Shall Know the Truth.* Audiocassette. Montvale, NJ: Catholic Historical Society in cooperation with Keep the Faith Inc., 1980.

Toropov, Brandon and Father Luke Buckles. *Complete Idiot's Guide to World Religions,* 2d ed. 2000; repr. Indianapolis, IN: Alpha Books, a Pearson Education Company, 2002.

Walsh, Michael. *The Popes.* New York, NY: St. Martin's Press, 1980.

Weidenkopf, Steve & Dr. Alan Schreck. *Epic: A Journey through Church History.*

West Chester, PA: Ascension Press, 2008.

Woods, Jr., Thomas E. *How the Catholic Church Built Western Civilization,* Washington, DC: Regnery Publishing, Inc., 2005.

Index

A

Abraham, 12, 16-18, 43-45, 51-52, 54, 57, 59, 62-66, 74-76, 87, 263
Adam and Eve, 49, 57, 194
afterlife, 22-23, 36, 41, 46-47, 55
Albigensian heresy, 180-181
Alexander the Great, 72, 88
Ambrose, 106-107, 109, 113, 138
Anglican Church, 17-18, 217
Anselm, 168, 175
Anthropic Principle, 34
Antiochus Epiphanes IV, 73
Aquinas, 116, 178-179, 226
Arius, 101-103
Assyria, 70
Athanasius, 102-103, 105
Attila the Hun, 140, 144
Augustine, 96, 106, 113-118, 136-137, 145, 147, 216
Aurelius, 94-95

B

Babylon, 70-71, 93
Baptism, 12, 80, 89, 103, 115-116, 142, 203, 210, 261
Baptists, 17
Basil the Great, 133
Becket, Thomas, 173-174
Benedict of Nursia, 134
Benedictine, 134, 137
Bernadette, 222-223
Big Bang, 23, 28-30, 36, 42, 44
Bishop Sheen, 39
Boleyn, Ann, 198-201
Boniface, 137-139, 148, 182-184, 186, 206
Boris, 153, 155
Bubonic Plague, 189
Bulgarians, 153, 155

C

Canaan, 51, 61, 64-65
Catherine of Siena, 185-186
Cerularius, 151, 157, 159-160
Chalcedon, 102, 118, 123, 126-128, 132, 150
Champlain, 217
Charlemagne, 132, 143, 149, 154, 156, 168-170
China, 189, 217
Christopher Columbus, 215
Clovis, 142
Cluny, 157-159, 175
concupiscence, 50, 58, 79-80, 194

Confirmation, 12, 82-83, 138, 164, 261
Constance, 187-188
Constans, 104, 129-130
Constantine, 97, 99-105, 107, 130-132, 149-150
Constantine II, 103-104
Constantine IV, 130
Constantinople, 102-103, 107-108, 118, 121, 123, 125-131, 141-145, 147, 150-157, 160-161, 170, 180, 206-207, 211
Council of Carthage, 110, 116
covenants, 58-59, 73
Cranmer, 199-201
Crusades, 172-173, 207
Cyril, 119-121, 124

D

Daniel, 46
Darwin, 37
David, 44, 51, 54, 59, 68-71, 74-76
Decius, 94-95
Dei Filius, 224
Dei Verbum, 232
Diocletian, 96-97, 100, 109
Discoros, 122
Domitian, 93
Donatism, 115

E

Eastern Orthodox, 17, 19, 129, 132, 161, 261
Edict of Milan, 97, 100, 105
Egyptians, 62-64
Encyclopedia Judaica, 47, 56

Ephesus, 88, 91, 118, 120, 122-123, 127
Ephraim, 61
Esau, 60
Eucharist, 74, 81-83, 90-91, 109, 203, 261-262
Eusebius, 90, 102, 121-122, 124
Eutyches, 121-122, 124
evolution, 36-37
Ezra, 16, 72

F

Fatima, 226-230, 256-257
Ferdinand, 197, 209-210
Ferdinand, Archduke Franz, 246
Filioque, 153
First Crusade, 162, 170
First General Council of the Lateran, 163
Flavian, 121-124
Francis of Assisi, 177-178
Franco, 225, 249-250
French Revolution, 243, 245

G

Gabriel, 221
Gad, 64
Galerius, 97
Galileo, 239-243
Gideon, 66-67, 240
Gnostics, 98
Golden Calf, 64
Good Friday, 52, 76
Gospels, 118, 177-178, 235
Gratian, 106
Great Schism, 158, 161, 191
Great Western Schism, 185, 187

Guadalupe, 195-197, 212

H

Hagar, 59
Haggai, 71
Hawkings, Stephen, 29, 42
Heaven, 13, 48-50, 55, 58, 71, 77-79, 83, 86, 101, 256, 259-263
Hell, 55, 97, 110, 227, 256, 259-261
Hitler, Adolf, 247, 251-253, 255
Hubble, Edward, 28-29
Hus, Jan, 187-189

I

Ignatius Loyola, 205
Ignatius of Antioch, 94
Immaculate Conception, 221, 223
Irenaeus, 98-99
Isaac, 12, 44, 59-60, 62-63, 206
Isaiah, 44-45, 75-76, 232
Ishmael, 59
Israel, 45, 48, 60-61, 63, 66-67, 69-70, 72, 74, 76, 86, 240, 255

J

Jacob, 12, 44-45, 59-63
Jericho, 65
Jeroboam, 69
Jerusalem, 68-74, 82, 87-90, 103, 117, 150-151, 169-170, 172-173, 206-207
Jesuits, 205, 217-218, 240, 245
Joan of Arc, 207-208
Joseph, 18, 44, 59-61, 71, 111
Joshua, 16, 44, 51, 54, 59, 64-66, 84, 240
Jovian, 105
Judaism, 17-19, 43-48, 75, 87, 94
Judeo-Christianity, 45
Judges, 16, 65-67

K

Kant, Immanuel, 24, 39, 220
Kierkegaard, Soren, 28, 42
King Henry VIII, 17, 197-198, 200, 214, 243, 260
King Saul, 65
Knox, John, 17
Kolbe, Maximillian, 253
Kulturkampf, 245

L

Leah, 60
Lepanto, 211-212, 214
Levites, 64
Lord Baltimore, 217
Lourdes, 222-223, 257
Lumen Gentium, 231-232
Lutheran, 17, 200

M

Maccabees, 16, 73
Maimonides, 45
Malachi, 18, 44, 75
Manasseh, 61, 64
Manichaeism, 114
Marcian, 123
Marcionites, 98
Martel, 138, 143
Martin Luther, 17, 190-192, 195, 214, 260

Mary, 12, 50, 58, 71, 118, 121, 127, 132, 175, 196, 198, 200-201, 214, 221, 223, 227-230, 256
Matrimony, 84
Messiah, 44-46, 49, 51-52, 54, 70, 73, 75-76
Mexico, 195-197, 233, 248-249
Midianites, 66-67
Mit Brenneder Sorge, 252
Modernism, 227, 243, 246
Monophysitism, 121, 127-128
Mormonism, 18
Moses, 12, 16, 44, 46, 51, 54, 59, 62-64, 70, 72, 74, 76, 84
Mussolini, 250

N

Napoleon Bonaparte, 244
Nathan, 68, 74, 76
Nehemiah, 16, 72
Nero, 90, 93
Nestorius, 118-121
New Testament, 15-16, 45, 47-49, 52, 77-78, 88, 92, 110, 232
Nicaea, 101-102, 107, 118, 120, 124, 126-127, 131-133
Nicene Creed, 101-102, 104, 107-109, 127, 150
Noah, 54, 58-59, 74

O

Old Testament, 15-16, 18, 43-45, 48-50, 52-53, 57, 73, 75, 84, 86, 98, 106, 117, 135, 232
One year Bible, 15-16

Original Sin, 49-51, 53, 80, 115-116, 193-194, 203, 221, 262

P

Papal States, 212, 218-219, 245, 250
Pascal, Blaise, 25
Pelagianism, 115-116, 193
Pharisees, 47, 84
Philistines, 68
Photius, 151-157, 159
Pilgrims, 169-170, 217
plagues, 62
Pompey, 73
Pope Adrian II, 154-155
Pope Alexander VI, 190-191, 201, 215
Pope Benedict XI, 183
Pope Benedict XV, 208, 246, 253
Pope Benedict XVI, 159, 161, 237-238, 264
Pope Boniface IX, 186
Pope Boniface VIII, 182-183
Pope Calixtus II, 163
Pope Callistus III, 191
Pope Celestine, 118-119, 182
Pope Celestine V, 182
Pope Clement V, 183-184
Pope Clement VII, 17, 186, 198-199
Pope Clement VIII, 213
Pope Francis I, 86, 201, 239, 256, 259
Pope Gregory IX, 181
Pope Gregory the Great, 118, 136-137, 144, 146

Pope Gregory VII, 99,
    162-163, 167
Pope Gregory XI, 185, 188
Pope Gregory XII, 186-187
Pope Gregory XIII, 213
Pope Gregory XV, 216, 241
Pope Honorius, 129-131, 164
Pope Innocent III, 174,
    178-180, 206-207
Pope Innocent VII, 186
Pope John Paul I, 234
Pope John Paul II, 22-23,
    161, 189, 207, 228,
    234-238, 243, 258
Pope John VIII, 155-156
Pope John XXIII, 187, 230-231
Pope Julius II, 190, 198
Pope Leo III, 131, 144, 146, 149
Pope Leo the Great,
    121, 140, 144
Pope Leo X, 192-193
Pope Leo XIII, 179,
    225-227, 246
Pope Martin, 129, 187
Pope Miltiades, 97
Pope Nicholas IV, 182
Pope Nicholas the Great, 152
Pope Paul III, 201-202, 205, 216
Pope Paul VI, 161, 231-
    232, 234, 257
Pope Pius IV, 204
Pope Pius IX, 218-219,
    221-223, 225
Pope Pius V, 212-213, 227
Pope Pius X, 226, 246
Pope Pius XI, 228, 250-251
Pope Pius XII, 230, 247, 251-256

Pope Sixtus IV, 210
Pope Stephen III, 218
Pope Sylvester, 101
Pope Urban VI, 185-186
Pope Urban VIII, 216, 241
Pope Vigilius, 127-128
Premm, Matthias Rev., 31
Presbyterian, 17
Pro, Father, 248-249
prophets, 44, 46, 54, 70-71,
    73, 75-76, 78
Protestants, 19, 187, 200,
    202, 211, 217
Purgatory, 55, 192
Puritans, 217

R

Rachel, 60
Radio Replies, 36-37, 257
Rebecca, 59-60
Reconciliation, 80, 153,
    157, 180, 261-262
Rehoboam, 69
Renaissance popes, 190
Rerum Novarum, 225-226
Reuben, 64
Robber's Council, 124
Rumble and Carty, 36
Russia, 134, 216, 228, 246, 248

S

Sacrament of the Sick, 85
Sacraments, 12, 79, 83-84,
    115, 180, 187, 200, 203,
    260-261, 263-264
Sadducees, 47
Saladin, 172-173, 206

Samuel, 16, 67-68, 217
Saul, 65, 67-69, 87-88
Savior, 45, 49-52, 54, 73, 221
Scholasticism, 168
Second Council of Constantinople, 118, 127-129, 147
Second Council of Nicaea, 118, 131
Second Crusade, 171, 181
Second General Council of the Lateran, 164
Septimus, 94
Shiites, 172
Shiloh, 65
Sola Scriptura, 188, 194
Solomon, 68-71
Spanish Civil War, 249
St. Dominic, 177-178
St. Ignatius, 99
St. Patrick of Ireland, 135
St. Paul, 37, 53, 78
Stephen, 87
Sun Sentinel, 38, 42
Sunnis, 172

T

Templar Order, 174, 184
Tetzel, 191-192
Theodosius, 106-107, 109, 118, 121-123
Theodosius II, 118, 121, 123
Theology for Beginners, 37, 42
Theotokos, 119, 121, 127
Third Council of Constantinople, 118, 130
Third Crusade, 172

Third General Council, 166
Torah, 45-48
Torquemada, Tomas, 210
Townes, Charles, 30, 42
Trajan, 93-94
Trent, 195, 202, 204-205, 218, 223
Tudor, Mary, 197, 200-201

V

Valarian, 96
Vatican Council II, 230
Vikings, 169

W

WWI and Pope Benedict XV, 246
WWII, 134, 228, 230, 247
Wyclif, John, 187-189

Z

Zerubbabel, 71, 74